LINCOLN-DOUGLAS DEBATE: VALUES IN CONFLICT

by Jeffrey Wiese

Consulting Editors
Diana Prentice Carlin
and
Dana V. Hensley

Clark
Publishing
Since 1948

Post Office Box 19240 • Topeka, Kansas 66619-0240
Phone (913) 862-0218 • In the U.S. 1-800-845-1916
Fax (913) 862-8224

About the Author

Jeffrey Wiese is a native of Oklahoma who competed on the national Lincoln-Debate circuit, winning more than 90% of his rounds. He has lectured extensively throughout the country and is a popular speaker at Lincoln-Douglas workshops.

ISBN 0-931054-27-3

Acknowledgments

I believe the success of any man or woman is solely symbolic of the contributions made by others to that success. The writing of this textbook is certainly no exception.

My deepest thanks to Richard Young, Diana Carlin, Dana Hensley, Ann Ozegovic, Caryn Goldberg, and Trey Parker for their advice and assistance in getting this book ready for publication.

I would also like to acknowledge Janna Young, Chris Ruhl, Britt McCabe, and Tony Allison for their support and assistance as friends, advisors, and mentors of my debate career.

Finally, I would like to acknowledge the Drake University Sociology Department for their assistance in the research and theory contained within this book.

Dedication

To Grant and Margaret Biehler
Both of whom taught me the meaning of values.

Table of Contents

Unit I
An Introduction to Lincoln-Douglas Debate

Unit II
Developing a Lincoln-Douglas Case

Unit III
Refutation and Rebuttal in Lincoln-Douglas

Unit IV
The Mechanics of Lincoln-Douglas Debate

Unit V
Advanced Lincoln-Douglas Debate Strategies

Foreword

Welcome to Lincoln-Douglas debate! While the "game" of Lincoln-Douglas may be foreign and a bit scary, you will soon find all of the excitement and challenge that accompanies one of the most noble of all high school competitions. Intimidation is normal at first, but do not let it discourage you. Once you break the ice, you will find an event that can take you places to which you had previously only dreamed!

This book is designed to help you become familiar with the event of Lincoln-Douglas debate. As you progress through the text, you will become more and more involved in the event, and you will begin to see the excitement that accompanies its rounds. What you may not see, however, are the benefits Lincoln-Douglas will give after your days of competition. While you will undoubtedly take away memories of your competitive days, you will also leave with many practical skills.

Initially, debate will teach research. In this day and age, the ability to draw upon other people's research and ideas is critical. The individual who can effectively sort through the multitude of written information on file in libraries will have an advantage over most of the competition. Lincoln-Douglas will teach research skills in a way that will last a lifetime.

In addition to finding information, society now demands that its leaders be able to present that information to others. Lincoln-Douglas will provide the skills to stand up confidently in front of people and make a persuasive presentation. Throughout the countless number of rounds experienced, you will become well-versed in the techniques of effective communication.

By the nature of its content, Lincoln-Douglas will also teach the ins and outs of many academic disciplines. You will become trained in philosophy, political science, social science, and history. Through the many topics with which you will struggle, you will learn the process of solving ethical dilemmas, which will be a lifetime skill.

Lincoln-Douglas will also teach how to organize thoughts and ideas in a coherent form. Learning organization skills allows you to be more efficient and persuasive, and will be a determining factor in your success in college and the larger world.

Finally, Lincoln-Douglas will allow you to learn from others. Through your experience as a debater, you will acquire the skill of taking notes while listening to a speaker. Not only will you be able to record what is being said, but you will also be able to critically assess what is being said as the speaker talks.

All of these skills combine to make the successful Lincoln-Douglas *debater* a successful *person*. While you learn all of these great skills, you will also be afforded the opportunity to have fun with a head-to-head competitive activity that tests skill, courage, and dedication.

Unit I
AN INTRODUCTION
TO LINCOLN-DOUGLAS DEBATE

Unit I is designed to introduce the novice as well as the experienced debater to the nature, theories, history and principles of Lincoln-Douglas debate. For some individuals, Unit I may seem elementary; for others, it may seem challenging. The unit is designed, however, so that every debater can profit from the discussion. For the beginning debater, the essential components of Lincoln-Douglas are exemplified; and for the advanced debater, the fundamental components of more complex Lincoln-Douglas elements are presented as a refresher. Regardless of skill, all debaters should be informed as to the history and nature of Lincoln-Douglas, since these two components more than anything else will determine the future of the event.

Chapter 1 is devoted to explaining the general nature of Lincoln-Douglas debate. The fundamental principles that compose Lincoln-Douglas—the resolution, the affirmative and the negative, the value and the case—are all introduced in a way that shows how each works to shape the event of Lincoln-Douglas debate. Chapter 2 provides the debater with a brief history of the event as well as the implication this history has for the present state of Lincoln-Douglas.

Chapter 3 begins the discussion of the mechanics of Lincoln-Douglas with an overview of the "value" concept. Chapter 4 furthers this discussion by tying the value to the event of Lincoln-Douglas, and illustrating how values are evaluated as to their respective worths. Chapter 5 continues the discussion of comparing values by introducing the concept of the criteria.

Chapter 6 begins the discussion of how to research a Lincoln-Douglas resolution. Finally, Chapters 7 and 8 explore the division in "philosophy" Lincoln-Douglas has experienced over recent years. These two chapters illustrate the polarity of "how Lincoln-Douglas debate should be performed," and in doing so, provide the debater with an idea of how important the development of speaking style is to the event of Lincoln-Douglas.

In situations where there may not be time to read the whole textbook prior to competitions, Chapters 3, 4, 5, and 6 are especially useful.

Chapter 1
The Nature of Lincoln-Douglas Debate

Learning Objectives

This chapter teaches the general nature of Lincoln-Douglas debate. It presents the general boundaries and parameters of this event, and introduces the principles upon which the event is founded.

After completing this chapter you should be able to:

1. **Define Lincoln-Douglas debate and explain its nature and structure.**

2. **Explain the nature of Lincoln-Douglas resolutions and how topics are given to debaters.**

3. **Understand the basis for argument in Lincoln-Douglas debate.**

4. **Explain why Lincoln-Douglas is an important activity that deserves respect.**

New Terms

Lincoln-Douglas debate
Esoteric
Resolution style
Resolution
Affirmative debater
Negative debater

Constructive
Cross-examination period
Rebuttal
Preparation time
Persuasion
Case

What is Lincoln-Douglas Debate?

What is *Lincoln-Douglas debate?* Is it a series of oratorical speeches? Or is it two people arguing with each other over *esoteric* topics? In a way, Lincoln-Douglas is a little bit of each of these. Lincoln-Douglas is a *persuasive* speaking event in which two contestants on opposing sides deliver persuasive presentations concerning ethical dilemmas in an effort to persuade the judge that one position is better than the other. Each match between two debaters is called a round.

In Lincoln-Douglas, a *resolution* (a topic of discussion) is provided to the debaters some time prior to the debate tournament. Each tournament will use only one resolution for all the rounds. Throughout the year, however, the resolution will change from tournament to tournament. Resolutions concern value dilemmas facing our world today. For example, a Lincoln-Douglas debater may face the following questions:

- "Should we value the preservation of our natural resources or should we value the development of our natural resources?" (A decision of social action)
- "Should we value censorship over the right of the free press?" (A decision of social preference)
- "Should we value national security over the individual's right to know?" (A decision of a social issue)

Notice that in each of the above examples, the topic to be discussed makes a question about our values: Which values or ideals do we hold most dear? Exploring the answer is the most fundamental lesson in Lincoln-Douglas.

Lincoln-Douglas is first and foremost a discussion about a given topic that evaluates the relative worth of two values.

Lincoln-Douglas topics are generally formulated in a certain style called a *resolution style.* The resolution style essentially takes the dilemma (the topic) and resolves the question for us. For instance, in the above examples, the resolution style suggests which part of the dilemma is preferable. For example:

- "Resolved: We ought to value the preservation of our natural resources over their development."
- "Resolved: We ought to value censorship over the right of the free press."
- "Resolved: We ought to value national security over the individual's right to know."

So where does debate come in? With the dilemma "solved" by the framers of the resolution, **the debaters argue whether or not the resolution (the solution) was the correct one**. For example, one debater, called the *affirmative debater*, upholds the resolution. The other debater, the *negative debater*, argues against the resolution.

Lincoln-Douglas debate is analogous to traveling down a highway in a car and coming to a fork in the road. Once the fork is reached, you must chose one pathway. The debate ensues when one person in the car chooses to support the decision to travel along one fork in the road, while another person in the car chooses to argue against the decision to travel down that fork in the road. (This may be familiar to many who experience family vacations!)

Lincoln-Douglas debate's "fork in the road" is the social dilemma discussed as part of the debate. The decision is arbitrarily made (the dilemma is "resolved" into a resolution), and the debaters argue whether the resolution should be "affirmed" (supported), or "negated" (contested).

The Structure of Lincoln-Douglas

Debate is an interactive process. This is what sets Lincoln-Douglas debate and cross-examination team debate apart from other forensic events. It is not enough to deliver one "side of the story" in Lincoln-Douglas debate. It is not enough to state your position for why the "left" fork in the road was chosen. You also must refute your opponent's reasons for why the "right" fork in the road should have been chosen. Thus, Lincoln-Douglas earns its surname: **debate**.

Lincoln-Douglas uses the following format or organizational pattern:

Affirmative Constructive Speech	6 minutes
Negative Questioning of the Affirmative Debater	3 minutes
Negative Constructive Speech	7 minutes
Affirmative Questioning of the Negative Debater	3 minutes
Affirmative Rebuttal	4 minutes
Negative Rebuttal	6 minutes
Affirmative Rebuttal	3 minutes

Each debater has the same amount of time to present the case (13 total minutes). It may look as if one side or the other has an unfair advantage. For instance, some people think having the last word is an advantage for the affirmative. Do not worry. The statistical odds of winning a debate round are exactly 50-50.

Each debater has one speech, a *constructive*, to make a *case* (see chapter 13). After the constructive speech, the opposing debater has an opportunity to ask questions of clarification or make initial confrontations. This period is the *cross-examination period* (see chapter 19).

Following the cross-examination periods, debaters rebuild their cases and make attacks upon their opponent's case. Appropriately, these periods are termed *rebuttals*. At first inspection, it appears that the affirmative not only has the advantage of the last word, but also an extra rebuttal! Structurally, this is true, but functionally, it is not. Note that the negative constructive is seven minutes long. This extended time is used in Lincoln-Douglas for presenting **both** the *negative case* (supporting the negative position to contest the resolution) and the *first negative rebuttal* (refuting the affirmative's claim to agree with the resolution). As a result, the negative debater has the same number of rebuttal speeches as the affirmative debater (see Chapters 14-16 for a discussion of rebuttals).

If the thought of having to develop ideas in response to opponent's attacks frightens you, you are not alone. With practice, you will come to anticipate what will be asked of you. In addition, throughout the round, you are given three minutes to collect thoughts, prepare for the next speech, and relax. These three minutes are collectively called *preparation time*, and they can be used between speeches (see Chapter 20).

A common question among debaters is, "How will I know whether I am going to be affirmative or negative in the debate?" Whether you begin negative or affirmative at a tournament is variable. You will alternate from round to round. Thus, in each tournament you will be asked to support the negative position as well as the affirmative position of the same resolution. For this reason, the Lincoln-Douglas debater must be prepared to defend both positions.

The Function of Lincoln-Douglas

Unlike other speech events, Lincoln-Douglas debate is debate. It is grounded in the intellectual confrontation of one contestant with another. It is the development and delivery of ideals, but it is also the refutation and defense of ideals. It is founded in planned, persuasive speech, but it is also built upon spontaneous, unrehearsed speech. It is oration, and it is debate. This component of Lincoln-Douglas is the focus of the next section.

The Attitude of Lincoln-Douglas Debate

Lincoln-Douglas blends debate and oratory; deliberation, refutation, structure, and technique of debate join the delivery, analogy, and persuasion of oratory. As a consequence, this event deserves and demands respect and integrity.

Lincoln-Douglas requires the skill of fluent, persuasive speech coupled with the ability to comprehend diverse and far-reaching human dilemmas which may have no real solutions. Lincoln-Douglas contestants are asked to delve into human politics and human thinking that extend to a number of dimensions. This is no easy task. The questions asked do not concern finite solutions (as in policy debate). They are resolutions that have no answers; they try our patience and rattle the very foundation of our beliefs. It is an event for those who wish to address the fundamental questions of our human existence.

Respect is the key to success. You must respect Lincoln-Douglas if you wish to win consistently. This means that you must care if you win or lose. You must show respect for those against whom you compete. You must take your research and case writing seriously (consistent winners don't write cases on the way to a tournament). Finally, you must show enough respect for the event to further its standards. Continue to better yourself, and by doing so, make the event more competitive. Guard against people who seek to "cheapen" the event. Lincoln-Douglas may not require as much evidence as does policy debate, but it certainly mandates original and authentic thought. It's easy to develop a set of links to make evident the possibility of nuclear war as is done in policy debate, but it is a little more difficult to twist John Locke's theories on the individual and the state.

Finally, Lincoln-Douglas asks for the ultimate in totally responsible, one-to-one competition. The nature of the event requires thought on issues that contestants do not necessarily want to address, forcing new inquiries and, ultimately, responses to difficult questions. It takes a unique individual to find the true excitement in such an undefined test of individual strength and desire that probes the unknown.

Suggested Activities:

1. Take the following questions and rewrite them in resolution form:

   a. Should we prohibit genetic engineering because of potential harms?

   b. Should equality be valued over liberty?

   c. Should drug testing be allowed in the workplace?

2. Using the current topic or one listed in this chapter, choose the affirmative or negative position and develop a one-minute speech explaining why you support or negate the resolution.

3. Write a short essay describing a value conflict you had to decide and how you decided it.

Chapter 2
Lincoln-Douglas and Its History

Learning Objectives

This chapter teaches the history of Lincoln-Douglas debate. It discusses the origin of the term and the history of Lincoln-Douglas as a forensic event.

After completing this chapter you should be able to:

1. **Explain the history and roots of Lincoln-Douglas debate.**

2. **Understand the fundamental, history-based concepts of today's Lincoln-Douglas debate.**

3. **Explain the components of the two theories of Lincoln-Douglas debate.**

New Terms

Lincoln-Douglas senate debates
National Forensics League (NFL)
Pragmatic

Being a Part of the History

Where did Lincoln-Douglas come from? Where is it going? And will I be there, wherever it ends up? For both the novice and the advanced debater these are good questions. The answer to the first one is easy; the second one is nearly impossible. Your own involvement with Lincoln-Douglas, however, is largely up to you.

The purpose of this book is to help individuals looking for a successful experience in Lincoln-Douglas Debate to realize their goal. The key then, is this: **If you have a driving desire to succeed in debate, this book will help you**.

It is crucial that Lincoln-Douglas debaters understand its history if they are to be successful. Just as a successful scientist could not feasibly find new discoveries without knowledge of past work in a field, neither can a Lincoln-Douglas debater succeed without knowledge of the past. The importance lies in the fact that Lincoln-Douglas is a relatively young event, and as a result, its history has a significant impact on where Lincoln-Douglas will go in the future.

The History of Lincoln-Douglas

It is a well-known fact that Abraham Lincoln was the 16th president of the United States. As you might have guessed, Lincoln-Douglas debate bears his name as a portion of its title. What is less well-known about Abraham Lincoln was that he had a fascinating political career prior to his successful bid for the presidency.

In 1858 Abraham Lincoln opposed Stephen Douglas for a U.S. Senate seat from Illinois. It was in this campaign that the roots of Lincoln-Douglas debate began. In an effort to demonstrate strengths, each candidate agreed to participate in a series of debates. These were candidate-against-candidate forums, in which each individual took a stand on the issues of the day.

While the original Lincoln-Douglas debates do not reflect today's time limits (the debates lasted hours) or the content of the original *Lincoln-Douglas senate debates* (the slavery versus states' rights issues), they do provide the foundation of several fundamental concepts in Lincoln-Douglas debate.

Each candidate worked to persuade the audience to support his position. Persuasion, more than anything else, is the key element in today's version of Lincoln-Douglas debate. The one-on-one nature of the debates is retained in current Lincoln-Douglas, as is the structure allowing for speeches, confrontations, and rebuttals.

Last but not least, current Lincoln-Douglas debate focuses on evaluating topics that are of fundamental interest to the lives of its audience. The topics in 1858 were not to be taken lightly. Neither should the topics in today's Lincoln-Douglas debates.

The History of Lincoln-Douglas in Forensics Competition

Lincoln-Douglas debate became a forensic event as a function of forensic officials' attempts to bring persuasive speaking back into debate. Persuasive speaking, as they saw it, was not being represented in team debate, and this warranted a new event. Thus, the first lesson of Lincoln-Douglas history is apparent: **persuasive speaking is the rule**. The extent to which Lincoln-Douglas contestants do not use a persuasive style of speech is the extent to which they will not succeed. (See how history proves to be important?) If you wish to succeed in Lincoln-Douglas debate, you must be not only logical, but also persuasive.

Lincoln-Douglas debate was offered in a few states prior to 1976, but it had nothing close to a national reputation. In 1976 it was prominent as a part of the Bicentennial Youth Debates—one of many activities commemorating the bicentennial of the Declaration of Independence. Following that experience, individuals involved in forensics became more interested in expanding the two-person debate concept as a way to overcome the problems of too much speed, too much evidence, and too much mechanical refutation in cross-examination team debate.

Because of its instant appeal, the *National Forensic League* adopted Lincoln-Douglas debate as a new national event in the summer of 1980. Since that time, coaches, students, and even the officials of the National Forensic League have struggled to define what is supposed to happen in Lincoln-Douglas debate. To date, that discord has separated Lincoln-Douglas philosophies into two main divisions. The history of Lincoln-Douglas debate, then, has evolved into a separation of expectations of the event. Understanding this division is imperative to succeeding in Lincoln-Douglas debate.

Throughout the nation, the way in which a winning Lincoln-Douglas debater presents a case may vary greatly. A successful debater in Baltimore, for example, might debate with a philosophical, oratorical approach while an equally successful debater in Des Moines might debate with a structured, *pragmatic* approach. As a result of this division in the event's philosophy, both of the two main theories are included in this text (see chapters 7 and 8).

This leads to the answers to the last two questions: "Where is Lincoln-Douglas going?" and "Will I be there?" The debater who takes hold of and respects the unbroken nature of Lincoln-Douglas debate will guide it to its final destination. Lincoln-Douglas debaters should not be discouraged with its uncertainty. In the end, Lincoln-Douglas' ambiguity may be its true salvation and justification. Welcome to the world of Lincoln-Douglas!

Suggested Activities

1. Research the original Lincoln-Douglas debates and write a short essay on the series of debates between Abraham Lincoln and Stephen Douglas.

2. Re-create one of the debates between Lincoln and Douglas. Use the issue of slavery as the point of contention and try to develop the arguments that were appropriate for that time.

Chapter 3
A Consideration of Values

Learning Objectives

This chapter teaches about values in Lincoln-Douglas debate. This chapter explains the term, "value," and how values fit into the scheme of Lincoln-Douglas.

After completing this chapter you should be able to:

1. **Define value and explain why it is the essence of Lincoln-Douglas debate.**

2. **List the three rules of values and explain how values derive from resolutions.**

3. **List the four sources of values and examples of common values.**

4. **Explain the concept of a value hierarchy.**

New Terms

Value
Value determination
Value hierarchy

Introduction

The concept of a *value* is the single most important facet of Lincoln-Douglas debate. Lincoln-Douglas debate relies upon the value concept in order to make decisions from its resolutions. Instead of centering on what should be done (as in cross-examination team debate), Lincoln-Douglas asks its contestants to determine what underlying values should influence our choices. In essence, Lincoln-Douglas asks us to determine what value we place on different ideals in relation to society's future.

While Lincoln-Douglas debaters do not offer or discuss policy actions or present plans, the values they debate are what influence our policy choices. It is important to understand this relationship between values and policies since values influence the choices a society makes. Lincoln-Douglas debaters often refer to the policies that result from a value to make an argument for why one value is preferable to another. Historically, the concept of a value has always been a method for making decisions concerning human social dilemmas. This competitive event operates on the same principle.

Definition

Initially, it is worth describing what is meant by a value. Value can be defined as:

The preference placed upon an action, object, idea, or person based upon individual or social worth.

In terms of Lincoln-Douglas debate, we can limit the above definition to get an operative definition. Since Lincoln-Douglas debate will rarely, if ever, allow for discussion of individual preference of persons or objects, we can eliminate these. As a result, we are left with a new definition which reads:

The preference placed upon an action or idea based upon individual or social worth.

In most resolutions, the value will be used to determine comparative worth of ideas in relation to social preference. Essentially, two or more ideas are compared in relation to how society (defined as a collection of individuals) would choose each in preferential order. The value determines which of the two different ideals is more preferable to society. It is important to emphasize that values are judgments based on our experiences—religious, social, educational, or cultural. As such, values are neither right nor wrong. They are better or preferable ideals which guide our decisions in given situations.

Values are usually categorized as moral or ethical, artistic, pragmatic or practical, and political. Moral values include what is right, good, or just. Artistic values refer to what is original, structured, and expressive.

Pragmatic values include what is practical or efficient. Political values include freedom, democracy, liberty, and rights.

Values in Everyday Terms

In the general sense, the word "value" has many different meanings. As a noun, the word has meaning as a concept of worth. For example, it is not uncommon to hear the expression, "This object has considerable value." In these terms, the word "worth" could easily be substituted for "value," and the sentence would have the same meaning. As a consequence, value can be regarded as synonymous with worth.

In terms of verb usage, the word value takes on a slightly different meaning. For example, "I have always **valued** individual rights" implies that we give preference to a certain object or concept. Once again, we can substitute the verb phrase "placed high preference on" for "valued," and the sentence holds basically the same meaning. As a consequence, the word "value" can be regarded as synonymous with the phrase "to place high preference on."

We can now combine the two to achieve a new definition.

Value= "worth"
    "to place high preference on"

Value= "An idea or concept that is worthy of placing high preference upon."

In the course of making one value preferential to another, we establish *value hierarchies* or an ordering or ranking of values. We hold many values, and often our values come in conflict with one another. We cannot always uphold two values simultaneously or to the same degree. For example, a person is not free to yell "fire" in a crowded theater when there is no fire. In our society we value both freedom of speech and security, but in this circumstance, we value the safety of many over freedom of speech. Thus, our hierarchy is guided by the value that guarantees the most to the many. In placing one value over the other in making a decision, we do not eliminate a value; we merely give it a less important standing.

A value hierarchy also suggests that for some values to be upheld, another value must be realized first. For instance, peace may be our ultimate value, but to ensure peace we might first need to pursue equality, justice, and cooperation. Milton Rokeach refers to this type of hierarchy as instrumental and terminal values. Peace is a terminal, or ending point value; equality, justice, and cooperation are instrumental values that help us achieve the terminal value.

Values in Lincoln-Douglas Debate

In Lincoln-Douglas debate terms, the word value is used as a noun. This is especially appreciated in the way the word is treated. For example, it is not uncommon to hear the word "value" in terms of: "What is your value?", "This is my value," "My value remains superior," etc. In another sense, preference is placed upon certain ideas and concepts that draw on using value as a verb. The question remains, however, "What do I mean when I say I have a value?"

A value is nothing more than an action, concept, idea, or belief that has social or individual worth. A value is an idea upon which society places considerable preference. That is to say, certain actions, ideas, beliefs, or concepts are more important to each of us as individuals and to society as a whole than other actions, ideas, beliefs, or concepts. Determining which actions, ideas, beliefs, and/or concepts are more important to each of us as individuals and to society as a whole involves the process we call *value determination.*

Value determination is the process of deciding which actions, ideas, beliefs, and/or concepts are more important to each of us as individuals and to the society as a whole.

Deriving a Value

It is important to note that every action, idea, belief, or concept can be considered a value. This point is not debatable. There is someone somewhere who will value just about anything. While the issue of whether something is or is not a value is **not** debatable, it is debatable as to what a given action, belief, idea, or concept actually is worth in relationship to other values. The right to safety is valued more than the right of free speech in the example of yelling "fire" in a crowed theatre. So how do we determine which value is more important to each of us as individuals and to society as a whole? That process is known as value determination, and it involves three rules:

Value Rule 1

A value is the preference placed upon an action, idea, belief, or concept based upon relative worth to each of us as individuals and/or the society as a whole.

Value Rule 2

Every action, idea, belief, or concept can be a value. Whether something is a value or not is not debatable.

Value Rule 3

The debatable portion of Lincoln-Douglas debate is not in whether something is or is not a value, but instead, is in how a given action, idea, belief, or concept is valued in relationship to other values."

Understanding these three rules is imperative. If there is a problem understanding them at this point, re-read the beginning of this chapter.

Examples of Common Values

Anything can be considered a value; however, some things are preferable values because they have a greater magnitude of importance to society and/or to individuals. For this reason, some values (the ones with the greatest magnitude of importance to society and/or to individuals) are commonly discussed in Lincoln-Douglas. After all, when we decide to make a decision about critical social dilemmas, we want to do so based upon the most important values to society.

The following list represents some of the more common values discussed in Lincoln-Douglas debate. At this stage, do not worry about the relative worth of each of these values. This is addressed in the next chapter.

- Aesthetics
- Acceptance
- Achievement
- Democracy
- Equality
- Family
- Free Expression
- Free Press
- Free Speech
- Freedom

- Individualism
- Justice
- Knowledge
- Leisure
- Liberty
- Life
- Love
- Majority Rule
- National Security

- Peace
- Privacy
- Progress
- Pursuit of Happiness
- Quality of Life
- Safety
- Security
- Self-Actualization
- Work

This list is long as well as diverse, but it is also incomplete. These values can be further diversified to more specific values (i.e., freedom of expression). Note, however, that the above values are acceptable values to Lincoln-Douglas judges. Be creative in determining which values to support in different resolutions, but also be sensitive to what your judge will accept as a legitimate value.

Suggested Activities

1. Prepare and deliver a three-minute speech on something you value.

2. As a class, brainstorm and list all of the things or ideals society or individuals value.

3. Listen to an audio tape of a Lincoln-Douglas debate round and write a paragraph critique of the debate.

Chapter 4
Value Determination:
Selecting the Best Value

Learning Objectives

This chapter is designed to explain (1) how the various values in Lincoln-Douglas debate are evaluated; (2) the process of value determination, which is the process of selecting the best value from a given resolution; (3) how to decide upon a value; (4) the "rules" of Lincoln-Douglas, specifically with reference to how these rules apply to values; and (5) the direct methods for comparing values within a round.

After completing this chapter you should be able to:

1. **Define value determination and explain the process of deciding on a value.**

2. **Explain the responsibilities of the Lincoln-Douglas debater in regard to values and the components for value testing.**

3. **Define presumption and explain its role in Lincoln-Douglas debate.**

4. **Explain the various methods for comparing values.**

New Terms

Value testing   Status quo
Litmus test   Dialectic resolutions
Continuum   Hierarchy
Presumption   Criteria

The Definition of Value Determination

In the previous chapter, we discussed values in relation to an action, idea, belief, or concept. In addition, we discussed that almost anything can be a value, and that questioning whether something was or was not a value is futile. This section delineates what makes one value better than others, and how a Lincoln-Douglas debater arrives at selecting the "best" value from a resolution.

In order to define a difference between values, it is essential to understand the process of value determination. One of the two great tasks that faces every aspiring champion Lincoln-Douglas debater is to determine which values are inconsequential and which values are important to the resolution being discussed. To accomplish this, you should first review the definition of value determination.

Value determination is the process of deciding which actions, ideas, beliefs and/or concepts are more important to each of us as individuals and/or to the society as a whole in relationship to other values.

The Process of Determining Relevant Values

There are no set rules as to which value is most important to individuals or society as a whole. In one resolution, the value of "life" may be the best value. In a different resolution, the best value might be the value of "individual choice." **It is the responsibility of the debater to not only set forth which value is supported in a round, but also to provide criteria supporting this value as the most important one in the round.** In order to lay claim to a victory in Lincoln-Douglas debate, the debater must derive a value or values from the resolution and supply support to the value's importance.

Now that you have been exposed to a list of values (Chapter 3) that may be used for a resolution, and you understand your responsibility as a debater (selecting and supporting a value or values), you are now ready to answer the question: "How do I choose which value is right for the resolution I am debating?" The answer to this question is straightforward: **The best value is the one that fits your line of argumentation.** In many resolutions, the choice is clear. For instance, the resolution, "Resolved: the right to a fair trial should be valued over the right to free press," has an affirmative orientation toward the value of "justice," and a negative orientation toward the value of the "free press/free expression." Other resolutions, however, are more complicated. The resolution, "Resolved: the development of natural resources should take precedence over the protection of the environment," does not have a clear link to one specific set of values. As a result, a certain amount of creativity is required to establish the link to the value of choice.

One of the best ways to determine a value from a resolution is to look at the resolution at face value, and make a list of the reasons why you would personally affirm the resolution. Another way is to work with a group of debaters to discuss and take notes on what the topic means to each person. Keep a list of the values identified from the topic. For the resolution on the development of natural resources, you might list the following: development equals progress, progress enhances our quality of life, progress saves lives, etc. From this list you can begin to identify underlying themes that run through the list. In the list provided, "progress" is an underlying theme for all of the reasons supporting development of natural resources; thus, progress is a logical value to support.

Once a value is chosen, test that value. This process is called *value testing*. (Note that "value determination" is the process of selecting a value from a resolution, while "value testing" is the process of seeing if the value withstands scrutiny.) Determine if adequate support for that value's importance to society can be found, why that value is enhanced by affirming the resolution, and why further enhancing that value will provide additional benefits to society. In the natural resources example, seek out evidence supporting why progress is important to society, or to us as a collection of individuals. Furthermore, find evidence for why affirming the resolution (developing our natural resources) actually enhances the value of progress. Finally, find evidence for the benefits progress offers society and the greater benefits it could provide if it were even further enhanced. If you can find adequate evidence for each of these three tiers, your value of progress is a strong value to be used for the resolution.

In addition to the above *litmus test* you should discuss this value with your teammates and your coach to receive input as to its worth. Others may be able to point out weak spots in the value or reaffirm your choice. Of course, the ultimate in value testing is done via practice rounds. If you can adequately support and defend the value through the course of a practice round, it is a good value for the given resolution.

The Rules of Debate

Before proceeding further with the concept of values, it may be helpful to take a more pragmatic look at Lincoln-Douglas structure. In doing so, it will become clear that the structure of Lincoln-Douglas mandates the use of values, value support and defense, and value evaluation skills. A brief discussion of some of the rules of Lincoln-Douglas debate follows.

1. The debate shall consist of two debaters. One debater shall support the resolution's statement, while the second shall oppose it.

This standard is relatively straightforward. In order to have a discussion of ethics, it is imperative there be two opposing sides. Unlike the nature of team debate, Lincoln-Douglas pits one individual against another. The judge of the round determines which debater is more convincing. The conflict in the round is between two individuals and not between two plans or cases. This is much like the original debates between Abraham Lincoln and Stephen Douglas in which each individual represented a position.

This rule is important because it sets the round's structure, but it is more important because it sets the environment for the round. Essentially, this standard mandates the evaluation of the debater instead of a mythical policy. This personal evaluation enhances the event's humanism. This standard of humanism is itself a value.

2. Each debater must name, support, and defend a value or values.

This standard has more implications than initially apparent. In policy debate, which is modeled after a trial, there is a *presumption* of "innocence" in which the affirmative must prove a case against the *status quo* (negative) in order to win. The negative, or status quo, is presumed to be the correct policy unless it is shown to be unworkable and disadvantageous. In Lincoln-Douglas there is no presumption. Both the affirmative and the negative are required to name, support, and defend respective values. The negative not only must attack the affirmative value, but must also present and support a value. This lack of presumption furthers the importance of the value in the round. Both debaters must support a value, and because this results in two values or sets of values in the round, both debaters must be prepared to defend a value.

In Lincoln-Douglas debate, the question posed within the resolution must be answered. In essence, if it is not yes, it is no. If object A is not placed above object B, then object B is placed over object A. There is no option of refusing to answer the resolution. The negative is responsible for presenting a counter value that would justify the negation of the resolution. Lincoln-Douglas resolutions are *dialectic resolutions*, meaning they have two "sides" built into the question. If the resolution is, "Resolved: Equality should be valued over liberty," the sides are "Affirmative=Equality," and "Negative=Liberty."

This standard also implies that each debater has the same presentational responsibilities. Both the affirmative and the negative must present a "value" case that supports their stances on the resolution. If the entire society were traveling down a road with a fork in the path, which path would be chosen? It is at this fork (the resolution decision) that two options are available. Choosing the right fork is the affirmative; choosing the left fork is negative. Each debater represents a "fork in the road," and then continues to provide the "benefit of choosing a fork" (the value). It is not enough for the negative to claim that we should not choose the right fork, and then leave the society with no direction. The negative must seek to diminish the "values" of traveling the right fork, but must also seek to convince the judge of the benefits of traveling the left fork.

The complex nature of Lincoln-Douglas resolutions makes answers to questions imperative. It would be fine to decide not to continue policies on space exploration, as society would continue without space exploration. Society could not continue to function, however, without making ethical decisions concerning "equality versus liberty," "the right of the individual versus the protection of society," or "protecting the environment versus developing natural resources." If the philosophy is not established, the society has no direction, and it will stagnate.

It may be helpful to relate Lincoln-Douglas resolutions to a shark. If a shark does not continually move forward, it will die. If society does not make continual progress it, too, will die. If the negative simply claims that the affirmative "fork in the road" should not be chosen, and then does not offer an alternative option (the negative value), the whole of society is left standing at the fork in the road. There is no option of travel. Like the stationary shark, the stagnating society, which has no philosophy upon which to make its decisions is left to die. The importance of this standard must be remembered. Each debater must uphold a value in respect to answering the resolution.

3. Each debater must address the opponent's value and make subsequent attacks.

This standard is what separates Lincoln-Douglas debate from Original Oratory. It is not enough to support one "fork in the road." Instead, it is necessary to make clear why the "left fork" is preferential to the "right fork." It would be safe to argue that silver is a valuable metal. It is possible that the affirmative value (silver) is a good value, but if an opponent upholds a more beneficial value (such as gold) he or she will win the round despite the merits of the affirmative value. To argue for silver over gold, an affirmative would have to do so within a context such as for photography. Compare your value to the value upheld by your opponent. It is important that you are able to show why your value is important to society, and how furthering that value (enhancing the value via the resolution's decision) will create greater benefits for society. In value decisions, it is not the choice that has benefits; rather, it is the choice with the most benefits. A good value will not be chosen when placed against a value of greater good. This comparison requirement makes it a necessity to "test" a value as to its social merit, and its ability to provide increased benefits if it were to be further enhanced.

Direct Methods for Comparing Values

This section establishes the methods of comparing values by developing a measuring device. There are several methods that provide us with this evaluation capability. This section discusses five methods of evaluation.

Before going forward, it is important to restate that values can be just about anything. It is possible for a society to value everything, from rain to a monkey. As humankind has progressed from simple to more progressive cultures, the "idea" has gained prominence as a value over tangible objects. Even the mark of currency is of little importance outside of the idea for which it stands (i.e., the removal of the gold standard did little to decrease the importance of U.S. currency for most Americans). In almost all cases, the values that society upholds are those that are mental constructs. The nature of values as mental constructs (thoughts or ideas) creates the possibility of an infinite number of values.

It is because of the large number of values that we must develop some way of evaluating which of the infinite number of values is most important to society. Certain values are indeed more important than others. There is no "black and white" in Lincoln-Douglas, only variable shades of gray. Establishing the relative "grayness" is the object of the following five methods.

The Inclusive Method for Comparison

This method rests upon the premise that the value applying to all humankind (past and present) is the best value. If you are given a resolution that is not specific to the United States, it would be a valid comparison of values to rank a value that applies to all people over a value that is specific only to the United States.

For example, if you were to choose the value of equality and your opponent was to argue the value of democracy, it would be good to state that most individuals in the "human race" value equality over democracy. As a consequence, equality is the better value of the two. In regard to the resolution, it should be argued that most resolutions are not limited to one specific nation, and, therefore, are applicable to all societies. It follows that when values are compared in the round, the value that affects all societies is the most important value. It is also important to note that even when both values apply to all of humankind this standard can be used. For example, if it could be established that all people benefit from equality more so than from liberty, the value of equality would be the greater of the two values.

In "closed ended" resolutions that are specific to the United States, this method favors the resolution that applies to all generations in the U.S. The value that is upheld by past, present, and future citizens that have been subjected to the dilemma (the resolution) is the greatest value in the round. For example, development of natural resources may allow for the value of progress, but only for the present generation. Future generations may not be afforded that value as resources are depleted. In contrast, if present and future generations are given the value of safety (from pollutants), safety has an edge when compared to progress. The value that applies to more societies or generations allows more people to enjoy its benefits. It is important, however, to note that this final comparison applies only to generations that are subjected to the conflict in the resolution. It is not applicable to state that the U.S. population of the 1920s could make a valid decision in regard to genetic engineering, since the dilemma arising from genetic engineering did not affect that society.

The inclusive method applies to the application of values to all societies. A later method addresses the application of values to all people within these societies. There is a subtle, but important distinction to be made here. It is plausible that all societies may find two values important, but only one of these values applies to more people within each of the societies. For example, all societies might value silicone computer chips and food, but food might be considered a greater value since it is more fundamental to survival.

The Contextual Method for Comparison

It is important to consider the resolution's intent when evaluating values in a round. Certain values apply better when considered in the proper context. Although all values can be somewhat applicable, the value that fits the resolution's context will ultimately be the better of the two values presented in the round. Although this sounds obvious, it is often overlooked.

For example, the values of national security and quality of life are both impressive in regard to society's well being. When considering a question of genetic engineering's worth, however, quality of life fits the resolution better than protection of the national security. A resolution concerning genetic engineering is obviously oriented toward the values of "life" and "ethics in science." The value that best fits the heart of the resolution's dilemma is the value that takes precedence.

The Additional Value Enhancement Method for Comparison

Although promoting a policy out of values is unacceptable in most people's views of L-D, it is a valid argument to claim that preserving one particular value will preserve or enhance other important values. There is merit in considering the impacts of placing one value above others. The value that enhances other values is greatly advantageous. On the other hand, the value that limits or destroys other values is not as advantageous.

For example, claiming that progress is an important value may be a correct statement. If it can be established that progress diminishes the values of safety and liberty, it would be considered a value of lesser importance. A cleaning product that cleans a house is valuable, but if it somehow kills members of the family, destroys cabinets, and stains rugs, it is not advantageous to have around the house.

The converse to this point is also true. A value that enhances other values will itself be more important to society. For example, upholding the value of individual rights is important. It is even more important, however, when we consider that it enhances liberty, freedom, equality, and a greater quality of life. Using the previous analogy, the cleaning product that cleans is a great product. If it can disinfect and deodorize as well as clean, it is much more valuable.

The Value Realization Method for Comparison

In terms of value evaluations, the number of individuals giving preference to a particular value should be considered. In simple terms, **the value that is realized by the most people in a society is the better of the two values in the round.** This method may seem identical to the inclusiveness method, but there is a distinct difference between the two.

The value realization method applies not to the most societies or the most generations of a society, but applies instead to the number of people within each society who realize the value.

It is sometimes helpful to think of this method in the same way one would think of buying a present for a parent. A present that one person can use, a shirt for example, is valuable. But a present that the whole family can use, a stereo or CD player, is inherently more valuable. Why? The answer is because everyone in the family can enjoy it, not just the parent. It is helpful to consider inclusiveness method as determining which value is better for the most families, and the value realization method as determining which value is better for the members of each of those families.

The Maslow's Hierarchy Method for Comparison

In addition to the above conditions, there are several hierarchies of human needs that define some values as more important to the human experience than others. A hierarchy is a standard that establishes some values as more important than others. Probably the finest of hierarchies is one defined by Abraham Maslow. Maslow's hierarchy seeks to define the importance of all human values in regard to how they relate to a progression of human needs. Maslow says that human needs fit on a hierarchy as follows: physical needs, safety or security, belonging, self-esteem, and self-actualization.

Maslow's hierarchy is much more complicated than simply listing value A as important, and value B as less important. Maslow's hierarchy explains our human needs and what motivates us. Because physical needs are primary, we must fulfill those needs before we are motivated to pursue others on the hierarchy. According to Maslow someone who is starving is more concerned with finding food than with fulfilling aspirations to become a great musician. Once basic needs are met, a person can aspire to higher level needs.

As a Lincoln-Douglas debater, Maslow's hierarchy can help you classify values according to which level of needs they satisfy. Thus, values relating to lower order needs may be the better value in the round. Preserving life may be more important than allowing individual freedoms.

However, when one reaches a point at which lower level needs are satisfied, a person may consider the higher level need more important as a way of actually preserving life. The famous Patrick Henry statement, "Give me liberty or give me death," suggests that life is meaningless without freedom. Thus, physical safety is sacrificed for a higher ideal.

Maslow's hierarchy does not offer a simple means for comparing values. The debater who understands this concept is able to dominate Lincoln-Douglas debate rounds. What perspective you bring to Maslow's hierarchy determines whether you use it to value basic needs or higher ideals.

If both you and your opponent are familiar with Maslow's hierarchy, it is possible no decision will be made concerning Maslow's hierarchy. The debate will regress into a circular argument that is ultimately solved by issues other than Maslow's hierarchy. In these scenarios nothing is lost. It is much better to understand Maslow's hierarchy and settle for a "no decision" on that particular method of comparison than it is to not understand it and have it cost you the round. Be familiar with this hierarchy in the event that an opponent attempts to use it.

It should also be noted that a hierarchy of any form is the debater's best friend. Apart from Maslow, there are many hierarchies developed by different authors. If you find a respected hierarchy that applies to your resolution, by all means, use it. However, due to the contradictory nature of hierarchies, a debater should make sure he or she knows every facet of the hierarchy. Maslow's hierarchy has endured more tests than any other; thus, when there is a comparison of hierarchies, Maslow's hierarchy generally predominates.

Summary

The five methods discussed in this section are regarded by many debate judges as the most acceptable in a round. All judges will not agree to all five methods all of the time, but this is a good starting point for value comparisons.

Criteria Introduction

In addition to the methods that are used primarily for "head-to-head" value comparisons, there is another important concept that is critical in evaluating a round. This concept is called the criteria and is used to evaluate a round. *Criteria* is simply the standard by which a judge evaluates the round. As a debater, you offer the judge criteria on which to base his or her decision.

Suppose you go to a local auto dealer and inquire about buying a car. The auto dealer offers two choices, a sports car and a mini-van. Each has great attributes which set it apart from all others in its class. The mini-van is roomy, safe, has low insurance rates, and can easily hold five kids, two dogs and groceries. The sports car, on the other hand, can go from zero to sixty in five seconds, is fuel efficient, and is stylish. Which do you choose? Each vehicle has considerable value, but one is an "apple" and one is an "orange." How do you compare the two? The answer lies in standards for choosing a vehicle. If your standard is a spacious, practical vehicle, you choose the mini-van. If your standard is speed and style, you choose the sports car.

Sports Car	**Mini-Van**

Benefits:	Benefits:
Speed	Spacious
Fashionable	Safe
Fuel Economy	Low Insurance

Most people would like to have both vehicles, just as the judge sometimes wants to have both values, but that is not possible. A judge must choose between values (vehicles), and must have a criteria on which to make that decision. Chapter 5 discusses criteria.

Concluding Remarks on the Importance of Values

In the minds of many Lincoln-Douglas students there is a question as to why so much time is devoted to the discussion of values. Many debaters often ask, "Why do I need to understand all of this information on values and value determination? I've won (or have known people who have won) plenty of rounds without using any of this." It may be possible to get by without using values and still win some rounds, but debaters will **not** win consistently at a higher level of skill without fully understanding values and value comparisons. But more importantly, since Lincoln-Douglas is value debate, a debater cannot fully participate in the activity without an understanding of values. For these reasons, it is important to begin to develop an understanding of values and value comparisons. The final message is simple: have faith in the understanding of values and the power that this understanding can bring. Then the phenomenon of winning in Lincoln-Douglas debate becomes much less the result of luck, and much more that of skill.

Suggested Activities

1. Using the following list of resolutions, determine the value conflict for each resolution:

   Resolved: That national security is more important than government honesty.

   Resolved: That the right to strike should not be denied public employees.

   Resolved: That the advantages of genetic engineering outweigh the disadvantages.

2. Write an essay on how to compare values.

3. Select random values out of a hat, pair up with another student, and deliver a short debate explaining why your value is more important than your partner's value. Be sure to explain the situations under which your value is preferred.

Chapter 5
Criteria: The Mechanism for Evaluating Values in the Round

Learning Objectives

This chapter teaches the general nature of Lincoln-Douglas. It explains the general boundaries and parameters of this event, and introduces the principles upon which it is founded. To gain a comprehensive grasp of the event, this chapter introduces three different facets of Lincoln-Douglas: the general nature, structure, and function of Lincoln Douglas debate; the attitude of Lincoln-Douglas debate; and the history of Lincoln-Douglas debate.

After completing this chapter you should be able to:

1. **Define criteria.**

2. **Explain the three levels of Lincoln-Douglas debate.**

3. **Explain the four categories of criteria and how they can be integrated.**

4. **Understand that the criteria can be challenged and are debatable.**

New Terms

Criteria

Cost benefit analysis

Futurism

Utilitarianism

Deontological theory

Means

Ends

Consequences

Introduction

Lincoln-Douglas is a debate about values. These values are used to establish which philosophy of the resolution (affirmative or negative) is more ethically correct in the round. Yet, at times, this value comparison becomes confusing. For this reason, it is necessary that a debater not only define a value upon which a case rests, but also define the standard upon which the judge should evaluate the arguments presented. The set of standards that is used to determine which value is most applicable to the resolution and most "valuable," is called the *criteria.*

In Chapter 4 we discussed five different methods for comparing values in terms of their relative importance. Criteria is in a class by itself. This section discusses how it is possible for a debater to give the judge a set of standards that helps determine the preferable value in the round.

In this section four main forms of criteria are discussed: cost benefit analysis, utilitarianism, futurism, and deontology. These forms are the most common in debates, and are the criteria that most debaters find easiest to use and understand.

Defining Criteria

In the context of making decisions outside of debate, criteria is a well understood concept. In everyday situations, criteria is nothing more than the standards used to make a decision. For example, if you were to ask, "What am I looking for in a car?" you would be inquiring into the criteria for buying a car. By the same token, if you were to say, "When I finally decide on a car, what will be the basis of my decision?" you would be beginning the process of creating criteria.

Criteria: The Standards Used to Make a Decision

To better understand this concept, remember the example presented in the previous chapter comparing the sports car and the mini-van. Both have benefits. In its own way, each is a good choice, and the decision as to which should be chosen is almost impossible without criteria. Yet, in the real world, these decisions are made all of the time. Why? The reason is because people universally employ a criteria to choose one "good" thing over another. The debater's responsibility is to outline the round's decision standards to allow the judge to make a decision on the values presented. The debater essentially presents a criterion that entices the judge to choose his or her value. This bias is the source of conflict between the two debaters, but it is also the factor that allows one debater to win and one to lose.

Before the discussion of criteria is continued, let's re-evaluate the above analogy. To begin, place yourself in the position of the judge. This is the scenario: you, the judge, must choose a value (vehicle) in the round. This is a necessity. Someone has to win the round. Placed before you are two debaters (auto dealers), one representing value A of individual rights (the sports car), and one representing value B of society's rights (the mini-van). In diagram form, it looks something like the following:

Sports Car   ## Mini-Van

Benefits: Benefits:
Speed   Spacious
Fashion   Safe
Fuel Economy   Low Insurance

Individual Rights   ## Society's Rights

Benefits: Benefits:
Liberty   Protection
Freedom   Equality

Both options have considerable benefits. The choice is difficult, but must be made. What standard will you use to make this decision?

Let's suppose one auto dealer informs you that the vehicle the family can use is the best to purchase. Furthermore, let's suppose the other dealer informs you that the vehicle that has fewer costs versus its expenses will be the best to operate. If you believe the first standard, your choice will be the mini-van, since more kids, pets, etc. can fit into the van. If you choose the second standard, you may choose the sports car, since its gas and maintenance costs are less. The choice depends upon what you are looking for in transportation.

The same is true for the value decision in Lincoln-Douglas debate. The choice that is made depends upon what a judge is looking for in a value. One debater claims that the value of the greatest good for the greatest number is the best value. The other debater claims that the value that creates the greatest benefits versus its relative costs (harms) is the greater value. If the judge believes the first debater's standard of the greatest good for the greatest number, he or she will be inclined to choose societal rights since more people are protected. If the judge chooses the second debater's standard, he or she would choose individual rights as a value since more benefits are created by protecting individual rights.

As a consequence of the above example, a new definition of "criteria" is possible:

Criteria: The standards that are presented by a debater to illustrate the relative importance of a value. When two good values are presented, the criteria is the set of standards that the debater presents to show that one value is a "better choice."

Presenting a value is not nearly enough to convince a judge to vote for a philosophy. Establishing criteria for the judge is essential if he or she is to choose between values.

Criteria Varieties

Although the number of standards is infinite, there are four major forms of criteria that seem to dominate Lincoln-Douglas debate. The following four subsections present an explanation and example of each. It is important to become familiar with each criteria. It facilitates your use of them, and allows a solid understanding of each in the event that they are used against you.

Cost Benefit Analysis

The *cost benefit analysis* criteria, often called CBA for short, is probably the most widely used criteria in debate. The nature of cost benefit analysis is described in its title. The debater who uses CBA simply weighs the costs of a value versus its benefits. In most "real world" ethical and pragmatic decisions, cost benefit analysis is employed to reach the decision. In the analogy used earlier concerning the vehicles, cost benefit analysis was used to decide which would have the most benefits to the buyer as opposed to the costs incurred by the buyer.

In debate, cost benefit analysis is used to measure the relative benefits of a value when compared to society's costs. For example, "Resolved: An individual's right to privacy ought to be valued above the protection of society," might have "privacy" (affirmative) and "security" (negative) as conflicting values. The debater upholding privacy might contend that while the benefits of security are great, they are outweighed by the great costs "security" inflicts on individuals in society. In addition, the debater might claim that the benefits of preserving an individual's right to privacy are greater than the harms caused by this value. In this manner, the affirmative can concede harms associated with the right to privacy, but these harms are outweighed by its benefits. If given a choice between an ice cream cone and a frozen yogurt dessert, which would you choose? While ice cream has a slightly better taste, it also has many more calories. Choosing the frozen yogurt dessert makes sense, because, although it has fewer benefits in terms of taste, it has considerably fewer "harms" in terms of calories. Making this decision employs the CBA criteria. A choice is made between two options based upon which has the most benefits and least harms.

Utilitarianism

A second form of criteria is the concept of *utilitarianism.* John Stuart Mill wrote that "An ethical decision is right if and only if it produces the greatest happiness for the greatest number." Understanding this concept helps you understand the underlying theory behind this criteria. In some situations, the temptation to make an ethical decision based upon personal attitudes and emotions are too great to be ignored. Mill attempted to alleviate this temptation by saying that what we feel and/or personally believe as ethically correct should be subject to what the greatest number consider is ethically correct. Without question, this concept has some serious flaws, but it also has some grand advantages when applied to Lincoln-Douglas debate theory.

In Lincoln-Douglas utilitarianism is advantageous when used with a value that encompasses a large portion of society. In certain situations the value that affects the most members of society is the most advantageous. Utilitarianism is appealing in that a great number of people, not an exclusive minority, enjoy the value. For example, a resolution that reads, "Resolved: The individual's right to know should be placed above national security," might have "knowledge" and "security" as its conflicting values in a round. The negative might argue that because the right to a secure society is enjoyed by everyone, it is of greater importance than the right to knowledge enjoyed by only a few. Because more individuals can enjoy the value of security it is, therefore, a greater value.

The downfall to this criteria is that it has the potential for creating an oppressive majority. If slavery is considered, for example, it can be stated that slavery benefited more people than it harmed. This, however, did not make slavery defensible ethically. An opponent who can point out the tyranny of majority oppression, will have a distinct advantage in destroying this criteria and any justification of value comparison that uses this criteria.

There are adequate responses to the claims of the oppressive majority, however, and these allow for functional use of utilitarianism as a criteria. In addition, it is possible to state that not all of the oppressive majority gained a "great happiness" from the enslavement of African-Americans. Economically, it may have been beneficial, but when all factors are considered (moral, ethical, etc.) the greatest "happiness" for the greatest number sways the decision to a negative (no slavery) ballot. The greatest good is as much a part of this criteria as the greatest number.

Thus, even though a decision might affect the greatest number, if it does not create the "greatest good" for the greatest number, it is not the ethical decision.

A debater should always be prepared to defend the criteria's merits on ethical grounds. This is crucial to winning a round when value comparisons are on the line.

Futurism

In addition to CBA and utilitarianism, there is another, less prevalent form of criteria, *futurism*, that is quite effective if used correctly. Friedrich Nietzsche contended that man's only responsibility is to create a society/human race that is superior to the one that exists at present. Nietzsche claimed that the standards with which we judge ethical decisions are "mediocre" (without creativity), "intellectual" (without emotion), "provincial" (without question), and "collective" (without concern for individualism). In this respect, Nietzsche claimed that our only "true" option in ethical decision making is to consider how we can improve the society that follows ours.

In "Resolved: Protection of the environment ought to be valued over development of natural resources," "security" and "progress" might be the conflicting values in the round. In this example, the affirmative might claim that by the standard of tomorrow (Nietzsche), the only ethical choice would be to preserve the environment. The need to perpetuate our existence is illustrated by the many monuments and memorials we construct to demonstrate to future generations that we are, indeed, a part of their history. It is the most noble of actions for a parent to sacrifice the benefits of today a child's future. Inherently noble, by definition, is that which is socially ethical and socially correct. In this respect, the ethical choice in a resolution such as the above example is the one that perpetuates the next generation's survival.

The natural argument against futurism is, "Why should we always live for tomorrow, when life is worth living today?" Nietzsche's answer would be that today's life is important, but to fully appreciate and increase the meaning of today's life it is important to make decisions that supersede today's expectations and approximate the relative high expectations we have for tomorrow. Making decisions that are concerned with tomorrow's good creates a society that goes beyond its own expectations (the provincialism, collectivism, mediocrity, and intellectualism) and makes "true" ethical decisions. The value of lives guided by these "higher expectations of preservation and perpetuation," is the value that best enhances today's society.

Deontology

Unlike the utilitarian theory espoused by Mill, Immanuel Kant proposed that the ethical decision in any value dilemma is the one that provides for "respect for persons." In the *deontological theory*, actions are right or wrong for reasons other than their *consequences*. The *means* by which we reach the consequences (the way in which the goal is achieved) are inherently more important than the *ends* achieved.

Several real life decisions illustrate this decision making criteria. Consider the search of a criminal's home by police officers. Even if there are drugs on the premises, the correct decision is not based upon the greatest good for the greatest number (utilitarianism). If it were, the police officers would immediately knock down the door and seize the drugs. This, of course, would keep the drugs off the streets and the greatest number would receive the greatest good. The correct decision, however, is for the officers to obtain a warrant for searching the premises. Why is this decision made? Essentially, our justice system is founded upon the deontological criteria of ethical decision making: the means for reaching the correct decision are as important as the consequences of that decision. Searching the criminal's house without a warrant is a violation of the right to privacy. As a consequence, if the means by which the drugs are seized is "bad," then the whole decision is bad.

Kant essentially contends that we cannot justify an action after it is completed. We cannot, for example, justify a violation of the right to privacy **after** we have already searched the criminal's home—even if we find drugs on the premises. According to Kant, we make ethical decisions to protect the "respect for persons." In summary, Kant contends that the means by which we make the decision are of greater importance than the ends.

This criteria is especially well suited for resolutions that involve issues of individual rights, particularly those involving the right to privacy. Consider the resolution, "Resolved: Drug testing ought not be allowed in the workplace." "Privacy" and "safety" are the conflicting values in the round. In this example, the affirmative might claim that by the criteria of the deontological theory, even the great benefits of drug testing (safety) do not justify the invasion of privacy. Since the means by which the benefits of drug testing operate violate the "respect for persons" rule, the whole action is not justified.

Application of the Four Types of Criteria

To fully appreciate the four types of criteria and their differences, look at the following resolution and compare how each criteria would intersect with the resolution in a fictional debate scenario: "Resolved: The right to know ought to be valued over national security."

The affirmative debater is Jon, and he chooses to defend the value of the individual's right to know. The negative debater is Kristin, and she chooses to defend the value of national security.

Let us assume that each debater presents, as part of the first speech, an argument that establishes his or her value as important to society. Holding a value, however, is not sufficient. Instead, we are interested in which of the two values is more important to society.

At this stage in the debate, each debater has fulfilled the requirements of the first level of debate. Namely, each debater has derived a value from the resolution, and each debater has shown that the value is important to society.

To appreciate the concept of criteria let us consider a scenario in which only Jon provides a criterion by which to evaluate the values in the round. Assume that Jon chooses cost benefit analysis as his criteria. Remember that under this criteria, the value that has the most benefits with the least costs will be the value that is given priority. Therefore, the costs and benefits of the individual's right to know are compared to the costs of national security.

Let us now consider the situation of Jon presenting utilitarianism as a criteria. Under this standard, costs and benefits are not an issue, but instead, the issue is how the costs and benefits relate to the greatest number of people in society. In the previous criteria, Jon may well have won the round by comparing the relative costs and benefits of the individual's right to know to those of national security. Under the utilitarian standard, however, Kristin might win the round by presenting the fact, that while the individual's right to know has many merits, these merits are not appreciated by the greatest number of people. Kristin might continue by saying that national security is the value providing the greatest good for the greatest number, since everyone can appreciate security. Therefore, it is the better value.

Now consider the situation of Jon presenting deontology as a criteria. Under this standard, Jon upholds Kristin's claims that everyone might benefit from national security, but not at the expense of using the individual as a means to this greater end. Remember, the premise of deontological thought is that decisions should not be made by looking solely at the consequences, but instead at what sacrifices are made in reaching those end goals. In this situation, Jon might claim that the individual is used as a "bad means" (the individual's right to know is sacrificed) to reach a socially desirable goal. Thus, it really makes little difference whether the value of national security is good, or even good for the greatest number. Instead, it is important only that this decision be made with reference to what harm it brings to the individual (the means) in the process. Under this criteria, then, Jon can prove that his value of the individual's right to know should be paramount, since we should not sacrifice the "respect for persons" (the means) in achieving even the best of goals (national security).

Finally, consider Nietzsche's standard of futurism as a criteria. Kristin might argue that the advantages of negating the resolution in favor of the value of national security represent the greatest benefits for "tomorrow's society." Kristin might agree that it is important to the individual's right to know, but it is not critical to the success of tomorrow's society. The value of national security, however, is both important to today's and tomorrow's societies. Thus, under the standard of futurism, the value of national security is the superior value.

Two final points should be made about criteria application. First, **criteria is debatable**. One debater might present a criteria only to have the opponent contend that the criteria is ridiculous and not the best mechanism for deciding between the two values in the round. At this point, the debater must defend the criteria or forfeit it.

Second, it is critical to recognize that **your opponent may be able to use your criteria against you**. In the final scenario, Jon could have used the argument: "Since extreme oppression results from restricting the individual's right to know, all we can promise our future society is a totalitarian (oppressive) society." Therefore, using Kristin's criteria of futurism, we can conclude that the best alternative, in reference to tomorrow's society, is a decision for the value of the individual's right to know. As you can tell, presenting and adequately defending a criteria does not mean you will win the round based upon that criteria.

This leads to the most important observation about criteria. Rounds are not won on the basis of criteria. They are won because the winning debater makes a stronger case on the virtues of his or her value. The judge may accept your criteria as the best mechanism for evaluating the two values in the round, but may then decide that your criteria reveals your opponent's value as superior. The bottom line is that you should be conscious of criteria and how it facilitates the judge's decision in the round, but your primary attention should be focused on the values in the round.

Summary of Criteria Varieties

Regardless of what criteria is used, it is critical that debaters understand what the criteria says and, more importantly, what it means. If you quote ethical philosophers in support of your criteria, be prepared to field questions about the extended philosophy of those individuals. It is useless to use the criteria of futurism without understanding the philosophy that goes with this standard, and with Nietzsche's philosophy in its entirety. During breaks between topics, it is to your advantage to study philosophers who deal specifically with ethical decision making. Knowing the work of these philosophers not only allows effective application of usable and creative criteria, but also affords you the advantage of questioning and weakening an opponent's criteria.

Objections to Criteria Distinctions

A common objection raised by debaters as well as ethicists is whether there is a distinction among the criteria. Isn't Nietzsche's standard of creating a better society for tomorrow (futurism) equivalent to the greatest good for the greatest number (utilitarianism)? There are different situations in which the criteria used to make an ethical decision results in completely different results. Recognition of this fact is paramount in succeeding in the use of criteria.

Consider, for example, the tremendous good done for our society in the expenditure of fossil fuels. They heat our homes, power our transportation, and save lives. However, fossil fuel expenditure depletes natural resources for the future. For this reason, the further expenditure of fossil fuels is an ethically correct decision under a criteria of utilitarianism, while it is not an ethically correct decision under a criteria of futurism.

Also, consider the battle between the First and Sixth Amendments. The Sixth Amendment provides the accused the right to a fair trial. The First Amendment guarantees freedom of speech. These two amendments may conflict if unfair pre-trial publicity makes a fair trial impossible. Under the deontological criteria, the Sixth Amendment appears to be the greatest of the two amendments, since it upholds the "respect for persons" as an end in and of itself. Yet, while the rights of the accused are good for us all, the "relative happiness" the Sixth Amendment provides the great majority (the greatest number) is not nearly equal to the magnitude of the benefits (happiness) the First Amendment provides in the form of public information. Under the utilitarian criteria, the most ethical decision would be in favor of the First Amendment (the value of "freedom of the press").

As you can see, the best value under one criteria is not necessarily the best under another criteria. This is the reason a debater must both produce, and defend, the criteria in the round. And this is also the reason a debater must be prepared to respond to various criteria.

The Levels of Lincoln-Douglas

Lincoln-Douglas debate is an event of many facets. As a consequence, there are many levels of Lincoln-Douglas that have to be understood in order to "truly" win a round. These are described in the following three subsections that should help you understand how the resolution, the case, the values, the criteria, and the value comparisons all fit together for a winning case. Keep in mind that these are levels, and while they relate, each level has its own integrity.

Level One – The Resolution Linked to the Value

The first level of Lincoln-Douglas is linking the resolution to the value. Each debater must derive a value from the resolution to support and defend. In simple terms, the debater must present a case stating that it is necessary to affirm (or negate) the resolution in order to enhance or protect a particular value. All harms and benefits listed in the case result from this value. All benefits are also linked to this value.

Using the example, "Resolved: The benefits of genetic engineering outweigh the harms," the affirmative could state that the benefits of genetic engineering outweigh the harms when we consider the value of progress. The value of progress, then, justifies the affirmation of the resolution.

Because social progress is needed, we must affirm the resolution: "Genetic engineering's benefits outweigh its harms." The resolution relates directly to and is derived from the value. This is often difficult for debaters in Lincoln-Douglas debate to recognize. Given the resolution, "Resolved: Development of our natural resources ought to take precedence over the protection of the environment," the affirmative debater might make the link by choosing the value of progress.

The way that either the affirmative or the negative justifies the resolution is based upon the value that is chosen. The proper attitude is, "I believe the affirmative should be upheld because of the importance of the value of ___(insert value here)___ ." The improper attitude is, " I believe the affirmative should be upheld because this is the round I must go affirmative."

The first responsibility for a Lincoln-Douglas debater is to demonstrate that a value justifies the resolution. This level derives a value from a resolution and then establishes it as in important value.

Level Two – The Comparison of Values

After the value is derived from the resolution, it is important to compare values in the round. The second responsibility a winning debater must fulfill is to show how his or her value is the most important one.

The second point of argumentation deals with which value is the most important in the round. If a debater claims that censorship or restriction of free expression is a value, many of us would expect that debater to lose against a debater who supports individual freedom and demonstrates that value's superiority compared to censorship. There is no such thing as an obvious comparison in debate. Failure to support the superiority of one value over another should lead to a loss. Nothing can be assumed to be correct in and of itself unless that claim is supported.

The previous discussion on criteria shows how to establish a comparison. The criteria establishes what the judge will be looking for in "purchasing" a value, and if your value fits this criteria the best, your value is supreme in the round. The first two levels of a debater's responsibility are illustrated as follows:

Debate Level 1-

Debater 1 claims that value A justifies (is the reason we should affirm) the resolution.
Debater 2 claims that value B justifies (is the reason we should negate) the resolution.

Debate Level 2-

Debater 1 succeeds in proving that value A is more important (should be chosen as superior) than value B because of the standards set forth in his or her criteria.

As a consequence, Value A > Value B, and, thus, Debater 1's justification for the ballot > Debater 2's justification for the ballot.

Debater 1's justification for affirming the resolution is greater than Debater B's justification for negating the resolution. Thus, Debater 1 wins the round.

Level Three- The Case

In addition to the value and the criteria, you must make your case, which means defending the link between the value and the resolution. In the case, the affirmative presents harms that are leveled against the value when the resolution is not affirmed and benefits that result from supporting the value. In addition, the affirmative presents arguments that show how the value is enhanced or protected by affirming the resolution. Each of these arguments is debatable, and, thus, another level of debate is opened.

Of all the debate tiers, this one is most adequately addressed by debaters. In a resolution on drug testing, the affirmative addresses the harms caused by drug testing, and the benefits of avoiding drug testing. Yet, the mere definition of "harm" requires that something of "value" has been violated. The same is done in the attacks against the opponent, as the affirmative claims that the benefits of the negative case are not that meaningful.

In essence, this level establishes the quality of the "product" being defended, and downplays the quality of the opposition's product. The case establishes that the action of the resolution (affirmative or negative) will enhance or diminish the quality of the value chosen. If the case is strong, then it will prove that the value is enhanced by affirming or negating the resolution. This enhancement then continues to strengthen the value's appeal in the round. As a consequence, the case serves to strengthen the value, which in turn, proves to justify affirming the resolution.

Summary of the Three Levels

In a step-by-step method, the responsibilities of a debater can be summed up in the following outline form:

I. The Resolution Linked to the Value
    A. Derive a value from the resolution
    B. Prove that the value supported is important to society
II. Value Comparisons
    A. Compare your value to your opponent's using the five
       methods of value evaluation presented in Chapter 4.
    B. Compare your value to your opponent's using the
       round's criteria

III. The Case
    A. Establish that affirming or negating the resolution
       causes benefits that enhance the value.

The criteria is an essential ingredient to the whole scheme of Lincoln-Douglas debate. Without it, level two falls, and there is no possibility of comparing values in the round. Even though your case may demonstrate a quality value, the judge may still choose a value of a totally different nature. In the event that your value is an "apple" and your opponent's value is an "orange," the criteria ensures that the judge is "in the market" for your value.

Suggested Activities

1. Write an essay explaining the three major forms of criteria.

2. Place all of the values listed in Chapter 4 under the criteria form to which they would best be suited.

3. Pretend that you have a choice between an apple and a hammer. Write a paragraph explaining your choice and illustrate your criteria for choosing one over the other.

Chapter 6
Research in Lincoln-Douglas Debate

Chapter 6 teaches how to research Lincoln-Douglas topics. The case, the value, the criteria, the rebuttal extension evidence – have their origins in quality research. This chapter introduces the process that goes into conducting quality Lincoln-Douglas research.

After completing this chapter you should be able to:

1. **Explain why research is important in Lincoln-Douglas**

2. **List the types of research.**

3. **List the phases of research and explain the goals and processes of each.**

4. **Identify the components of source citation.**

5. **Identify sources appropriate and inappropriate for Lincoln-Douglas research.**

New Terms

Handbook research
Type I research
Type II research
Cause and effect claims

Why Research?

Research is a term that often causes debaters to "cringe" at the mere mention of its name. After all, the time spent sifting through "endless" amounts of material is not as enjoyable as the actual debate rounds. Recognize, however, that research is the foundation upon which everything in the actual round is built. Without quality research, the Lincoln-Douglas debater stands to be punished in debate rounds. Remember, you must support and defend your claims in Lincoln-Douglas, and without the research to establish this support and defense, debate rounds are nearly impossible to win.

You should also recognize that research is not torture. While at times it can seem tedious, there will be other moments when you'll find a great piece of evidence in an obscure book! And while the beginning of the research process may seem overwhelming, you gradually become an expert on the topic you study. Research in Lincoln-Douglas can be exciting and rewarding, as long as it is approached with the proper attitude.

The Two Types of Research in Lincoln-Douglas

There are two types of research in Lincoln-Douglas. The first type is research needed to link a value to the resolution being debated. For example, with a resolution concerning censorship, the debater needs to have evidence showing that censorship causes a degeneration of the value of the freedom of the press. This link is established by what we call *Type I research*. Type I research focuses on the actual resolution, and provides support for *cause and effect claims* that are made by the debater about the topic of the resolution. In the above example, the debater made a cause and effect claim: "Affirming a resolution in support of censorship will result in degeneration of the freedom of the press."

Type II evidence supports the merits of the value, regardless of the resolution. For example, Type II evidence would support the merits of the value of the freedom of the press, regardless of the resolution debated. As you might guess, Type II research takes place all year, since it is not dependent upon the resolution being debated at one particular time.

The Three Phases of Research

Research in Lincoln-Douglas is best considered in the form of three separate phases. Each phase has its own distinct responsibility, and each phase naturally occurs at a different time in the research process. Thinking about research in this way not only helps you find support for attacks and defenses, but also assists you in developing quality arguments and contentions.

The following three phases of research apply more to Type I research since Type II research should take place all year.

1. The Development of Background Knowledge

After a resolution is announced, begin research by investigating the general nature of the topic. The best way to begin is by selecting and browsing through several sources on the resolution (from magazines, books, *Facts on File*, etc.). At this phase, you are not interested in finding specific information about the topic; nor are you interested in finding case arguments. This phase should generate some interest in the topic, and more importantly, should help you start thinking about ways to approach the topic.

Because the goal of this phase is to build your background on the topic, this phase is the shortest of the research phases. No more than two days should be invested in this research phase. The short nature of this phase does not, however, lessen its importance to the research process. It is critical that a debater gain a general appreciation for the "whole" topic prior to beginning Phase Two, since doing so will ensure that you're headed down the correct path. Many hours of research time are often lost because a debater assumed a meaning of the topic, only to find out that the assumption was not in line with the true intent of the resolution.

2. The Development of the Case Structure

The second phase of research is focused on the development of arguments. The proper development of the case begins with "brainstorming" (collecting as many ideas on the topic as you can). This collection of ideas comes from learning about the topic. Whereas the first phase of research is used to gain a general understanding of the topic, the second phase of research is designed to generate possible arguments.

The process of phase two is relatively simple and will be explored in detail in Chapter 12. For now, it is important that you recognize that the goal of this phase of research is to find arguments that could be used to support each side of the resolution. Once you find these arguments, you can begin writing the case.

3. Finding Support for Case Contentions

Once the case writing process has begun, the final research phase should be initiated. The goal of Phase Three is to find specific documentation to support the arguments that are a part of the case. This is the phase most debaters think of when they hear the word, "research."

The methods for accomplishing this goal vary, but one way is to make photocopies of each of the sources from which you wish to obtain evidence. Once you find the piece of evidence, you can photocopy it, and then cut and paste the piece of evidence onto a note card. Immediately copy the source from which the evidence was obtained onto the top of the card.

The source is as critical as the piece of evidence itself. The source should include the following information:

- title of the article (if from a magazine or other periodical)
- title of the source (title of the book or magazine)
- author's name (as well as his or her qualification if this can be obtained)
- date the source was published
- page number from which you copied the evidence.

If it is not possible to make multiple photocopies, hand copy or type the evidence onto a note card, and proceed with the above process. It is important, however, that the card be neatly copied, since this evidence will be read in debate rounds. You can type several quotations from a single source into a word processing program and then cut and paste them to cards. You can also prepare briefs or blocks of evidence on sheets of paper. These are commonly used arguments with quotations from several sources.

Many debaters often ask: "How much evidence is enough evidence?" The answer depends upon how much support the case requires. Since Lincoln Douglas debate does not depend heavily upon evidence (simple logic is equally important), it is possible that you could get by with no evidence. For most cases, however, there will be some controversial contentions that should be supported by an expert opinion. Review your case once it is completed, and assess each contention's need for evidence support. In addition, attempt to anticipate arguments an opponent might use against your case. Also, seek out evidence to support your responses to arguments you anticipate facing from your opponents. The rule of thumb is one to three cards for each important and controversial contention.

Sources for Lincoln-Douglas Research

Although there is an infinite number of sources to research, there are some sources particularly helpful in Lincoln-Douglas debate. Because many topics will reflect modern ethical dilemmas, periodicals are a good place to begin. The best periodicals are the ones that present the facts of the dilemma, but also give some opinionated views in their editorials and articles. These opinions allow a debater to experience some of the potential arguments on a topic. Some sources that contain this mix of "facts and opinions" include: *U.S. News & World Report, Time, Newsweek, Christian Science Monitor, The Atlantic,* and *The New Republic.* In addition, it is helpful to research the topic in philosophy books in order to gain a strong background on the topic. In resolutions that concern "hot, modern" topics, recent essays and position papers sometimes lend new and insightful ways to look at the topic. In addition, government and American Civil Liberties Union pamphlets are good sources for positions on ethical decision arguments that might otherwise be difficult to support.

If unfamiliar with debate resources, it is often beneficial to listen to the sources that other debaters use at tournaments. When you hear great evidence during a tournament, write down the sources and make a point to include them in future research.

Note that research should focus not only on the topic in the resolution, but also on the values and criteria used to support the topic (Type II research). The same rules that apply for Type I research also apply to Type II research (except that Type II research should continue year-round, since it does not depend upon the specifics of the resolution).

Remember, debate research does not necessarily mean finding great evidence cards. Some of the best sources will be those that give background on the topic and facilitate your ability to produce logical analysis.

The Use of Handbooks

Many universities and debate institutes offer debaters a short cut to research. Handbooks containing both Type I and Type II evidence are available for purchase. The use of published handbooks is not a good idea, however, for several reasons. First, the evidence in most handbooks is not of superior quality. You might argue, "But isn't some evidence better than no evidence?" The answer to this question is "no." Debaters who rely upon published handbooks for evidence will not do their own original research, regardless of good intentions. The simple fact is that the debater who knows he or she has enough evidence to "get by" will not feel the "fear of having no evidence" that motivates debaters into finding original evidence. In addition, the whole process of developing the case through the three phases of research is stifled by using handbooks.

Another reason for avoiding handbook evidence is that the debater who depends upon the handbook for evidence will never really fully understand this evidence. Remember that true understanding of a piece of evidence comes from understanding the context from which it came. Debaters will never fully be able to grasp the context of the evidence by merely reading random excerpts, some of which may have been taken out of context.

It should also be noted that handbooks are available to everyone. As a consequence, much of the competition has a copy of the evidence being used for your case. If you rely on this evidence, your opponents will have an easy time attacking your case, since they are already familiar with how it is established and what to do to defeat it. Finally, extensive use of handbooks defeats one of the major advantages of participating in Lincoln-Douglas debate—learning how to research. In our rapidly changing, competitive world, the person who knows how to locate information is more likely to succeed. Remember, the people who write the handbooks couldn't have done so if they had not learned how to research.

So how should handbooks be used? Handbooks can best be used to anticipate what the competition will present. By definition, your best competition will not rely upon handbooks (this is what makes them the best), but the remainder of the competition probably will use handbooks. Use this fact to your advantage by studying the evidence in debate handbooks, and by using this information to beat opponents who try to use this evidence against you.

The second use for debate handbooks is that they provide a good listing of sources. Take the source listings in the handbook, search out the actual documents, and begin the process of finding your own original research from these sources. This allows you to take advantage of these predetermined "great sources," while capitalizing upon the benefits of original research.

Best Source List

The following sources are useful on most Lincoln-Douglas topics. The complete citation is not given for the book titles, but you can locate them using the title cards in a card catalogue.

Current Periodicals

The Atlantic
Business Week
Changing Times
Congressional Digest
Current History
Discover
Ebony
The Education Digest
Facts on File
The Federalist Papers
Foreign Affairs
Harper's
Jet
Life
The New York Times Magazine
Natural History
National Geographic

National Review
The New Republic
The New Yorker
Newsweek
Omni
Parents
Popular Science
Prevention
Psychology Today
Scholastic Update
Scientific American
Science Digest
Science News
Time
Today's Education
U.S. News and World Report
The Wall Street Journal

Criteria and Value Sources

Civil Liberties and American Democracy by John Brigham
Concerning Justice by Lucilius A. Emory
The Constitution: That Delicate Balance by Fred W. Friendly
Democracy by Anthony Arblaster
The Economics of Justice by Richard A. Posner

Four Reasonable Men: Marcus Aurelius, John Stuart Mill, Ernest Renan, Henry Sidgwick by Brand Blansherd
Fundamentals of Philosophy by Errol E. Harris
Habits of the Heart: Individualism and Commitment in American Life by Robert N. Bellah
Health Care and Society by Arnold Birenhaum
An Introduction to Modern Philosophy by Castell
Liberty, Equality, and Fraternity by Joseph I. Shulin
Man and Society: Freedom and Liberty by Samuel H. Jameson
The Nature of Human Values by Milton Rokeach
Natural Law in Political Thought by Paul E. Sigmund
New Knowledge in Human Values edited by Abraham H. Maslow
On Being Free by Frithjof Bergmann
On Liberty by John Stuart Mill
The Paradoxes of Freedom by Sidney Hook
The Philosophical Dimensions of Privacy, edited by Ferdinand David Schoeman
The Politics of Unreason: Right-wing Extremism in America by S. M. Lipset
Progress and Its Discontents edited by Almond, Chodorow, and Pearce
The Quest for Equality in Freedom, by Francis M. Wilhoit
Respect for Life in Medicine, Philosophy and the Law by Owsei Temkin
The Right and Wrong of Compulsion by the State by Auberon Herbert
The Right to Live, The Right to Die by C. Everett Koop
Six Great Ideas: Truth, Goodness, Beauty, Liberty, Equality, Justice by Mortimer Jerome Adler
Speech and Law in a Free Society by Franklyn Saul Haiman
Twentith Century Social Thought edited by Robert P. Cuzzort and Edith King
Two Treatises On Government by John Locke
The Way of Philosophy by Milton K. Munitz

Other Useful Sources

Black's Law Dictionary
The Random House Dictionary
Webster's Dictionary
Peter's Quotations
The Universal Almanac
Paul Harvey's "The Rest of the Story"
More of Paul Harvey's "The Rest of the Story"
That's Not What I Meant! by Deborah Tannen

Useful Authors

Henry Adams
Thomas Aquinas
Hannah Arendt
Aristotle
Peter Berger
Hildegard Bingen
Buddha
Winston Churchill
John Calvin
August Comte
Charles Darwin
Rene Descartes
Emile Durkheim
Ralph Waldo Emerson
Frederich Engels
Sigmund Freud
Mahatma Gandhi
G.W. F. Hegel
T. Hobbes
David Hume
Thomas Huxley

Thomas Jefferson
Immanuel Kant
Suzanne Langer
Martin Luther King, Jr.
John Locke
T.R. Malthus
Abraham Maslow
Thomas Merton
Karl Marx
John Stuart Mill
John G. Neihardt
Friedrich Nietzsche
William Paley
Thomas Paine
Milton Rokeach
Jean Jacques Rousseau
Oswald Spengler
Henry David Thoreau
Alexis de Tocquville
Lao Tzu

Suggested Activities

1. Brainstorm, as a class, a list of books or periodicals that would be a good place to research the current L-D topic, or one listed in the previous chapters.

2. Bring a magazine or newspaper article to class which supports your position on a particular resolution. As a class, read each of the articles and discuss ways to cut appropriate material from them.

Chapter 7
The Oratorical Theory
of Lincoln-Douglas Debate

Learning Objectives

This chapter teaches one of the two main theories of Lincoln-Douglas. This chapter describes the "oratorical" theory and Chapter 8 will describe the "debate" theory of Lincoln-Douglas. Keep in mind that neither of these two theories is entirely correct. Rather, each theory has benefits and drawbacks. By understanding both theories, you should gain a grasp of the range of Lincoln-Douglas. In addition to the oratorical theory of L-D, two additional sections are introduced. One section highlights the synthesis of these two theories, and how the combination of the "debate" and "oratorical" theories work. The second section illustrates how to develop style. While Chapters 7 and 8 are distinct portions of the book, consider them together since the best debater will understand both theories.

After completing this chapter you should be able to:

1. **Explain the philosophy and rationale of the oratorical theory of Lincoln-Douglas debate.**

2. **Understand the nature of logic, evidence and delivery in the oratorical theory.**

3. **Explain the role of refutation, comparison, and deliberation in the oratorical theory.**

4. **Explain the Lincoln-Douglas spectrum and where the oratorical theory fits in.**

New Terms

The oratorical theory	Evidence
Realism	Deliberation
Logic	Refutation

The General Philosophy of the Oratorical Theory

The *oratorical theory* places faith in the belief that Lincoln-Douglas debate is an event of comparative orations. In essence, Lincoln-Douglas contestants present a series of five oratorical speeches. The basis of this theory rests in the initial intent of Lincoln-Douglas debate: persuasiveness. Remember that Lincoln-Douglas originated as a response to the lack of persuasiveness in cross-examination team debate. As a result, this theory contends that persuasiveness should be the end goal, and a string of orations best meets the requirement for persuasiveness. It is true that persuasiveness tends to be the end goal of Lincoln-Douglas debate, but there remains an important question: Is a series of "non-conflicting speeches" persuasive?

Comparison, Refutation, and Deliberation in the Oratorical Theory

The assumption that a series of orations is persuasive is questionable. When is the last time a friend persuaded you by a series of orations? Persuasiveness is best achieved through natural, yet organized speech. A series of non-conflicting orations fails to meet this criteria in its entirety. In addition, this theory fails to note that Lincoln-Douglas is still debate. And debate is a comparison, refutation, and deliberation of affirmative and negative contentions. Without such deliberations and refutations, Lincoln-Douglas debate is certainly no longer debate, but Lincoln-Douglas orations. This is the pitfall of the oratorical theory.

In essence, followers of this theory believe serious conflict between the two contestants detracts from persuasiveness. The history of Lincoln-Douglas as a debate event and that of the 1858 senate debates suggests otherwise. Furthermore, the topics discussed in Lincoln-Douglas debate require deliberation and refutation of ideals. Merely discussing emotion about the affirmative case or the negative case is not enough. You must offer counter-arguments against the opposition's statements. This theory strives to instill persuasiveness, and that effort is important.

Rate of Delivery in the Oratorical Theory

The rate of delivery in the oratorical theory is slower than the rate of the debate theory. Just as it is difficult to believe that a friend can persuade you by a set of flowery orations, it is equally unbelievable that a friend speaking at 300 words a minute would persuade you. True persuasion rests in the ability to talk in a manner that is familiar and comfortable with the judge.

It should be noted that while a slower rate of delivery is good, it does not require you to speak like a third grader. The key word in this discussion is "reasonable." This does not mean that what the debater considers reasonable is the rate at which to speak. A reasonable rate, like so many other things discussed later, should be considered in reference to the judge's opinion. It may be equally damaging to speak too slowly. The rule is simple: look to the judge to give clues as to how fast you may proceed, and do not exceed this limit. If no clues are apparent, however, it is always better to proceed at a slower pace instead of the reverse. You may not cover as much material, but you, at least, will be persuasive.

Logic Versus Evidence in the Oratorical Theory

The oratorical theory has another characteristic in that it relies heavily upon *logic* instead of documented evidence to support its propositions in a debate round. As Chapter 12 illustrates, evidence is important to support and validate contentions. Proponents of the debate theory call upon this need for documented evidence in support of Lincoln-Douglas ideals, and subsequently criticize the oratorical theory for its lack of evidence support. Evidence, however, should never replace logic in building and supporting a case, and this is where the oratorical theory has a distinct advantage. Even though a piece of evidence says that the closing of a Native American museum in New York will cause a global nuclear war, it isn't very logical. As a consequence, it shouldn't (and usually won't) hold much weight in a Lincoln-Douglas contest. While evidence as support is important, logic is equally, if not more, important in the final analysis of the round. The pure logic of the oratorical theory and the pure documented evidence of the debate theory are not the solution to supporting propositions in Lincoln-Douglas rounds. Instead, the optimum solution is a combination of both logic and evidence to support Lincoln-Douglas contentions.

Realism in the Oratorical Theory

Finally, the oratorical theory holds merit in the creation of realistic scenarios when analyzing resolution topics. The consequences of affirming or negating the resolution should be *realistic*. For example, contending that another U.S. Civil War will emerge from negating a resolution on censorship is somewhat unrealistic, despite what the evidence might say. The diminishment of individual rights and subsequent degradation of democracy is believable, but not war. Because the oratorical theory propounds the use of logic for supporting Lincoln-Douglas propositions, the scenarios produced are generally grounded in realism. Put simply, if logic is employed as the guiding force in a debater's decisions, realistic scenarios will follow.

Conclusion

The importance of this chapter is to get a feel for one approach to Lincoln-Douglas debate theories. In the next chapter, the opposite view will be presented. The specifics of each theory are not important. Instead, concentrate on the five characteristics of debate (rate of delivery, amount of deliberation and refutation, the use of logic and evidence, the degree of realism in discussions, and the amount of structure in the speech), and how each theory approaches these issues. At the end of the next chapter, you will be introduced to the development of your own style, at which point you will be asked to take the merits of each theory and incorporate them into your own style.

Suggested Activities

1. Practice delivering short impromptu case openings using the oratorical theory for the current resolution or one listed in previous chapters.

2. Write a paragraph describing your ideal judge. Explain the characteristics that this individual would have and why you would be most successful with this type of judge.

3. Select random evidence cards and practice reading them for maximum oratorical impact.

4. Develop and practice persuasive oratorical introductions and conclusions for each of your speeches.

Chapter 8
The Debate Theory
of Lincoln-Douglas Debate

Learning Objectives

This chapter teaches one of the two main theories of Lincoln-Douglas. While Chapter 7 described the oratorical theory, this chapter illustrates the debate theory of Lincoln-Douglas. Keep in mind that neither of these two theories is entirely correct. Rather, each theory has benefits and drawbacks. By understanding both theories, you will gain a grasp of the range of Lincoln-Douglas, and be able to synthesize the best portions of each theory into your style. The first section of this chapter explains the debate theory's benefits and drawbacks. The second and third sections teach how to combine the two theories into a style to make you a better debater.

After completing this chapter you should be able to:

1. **Explain the philosophy and rationale of the debate theory of Lincoln-Douglas debate.**

2. **Explain the role of refutation, comparison, and deliberation in the debate theory.**

3. **Explain the stock issues in the debate theory and why cross-examination debate stock issues do not belong in Lincoln-Douglas debate.**

4. **Understand how and why the oratorical and debate theories can be combined for judge and opponent adaptations.**

New Terms

Artificial reality	Significance
Stock issues	Solvency
Topicality	Judge adaptation
Inherency	Debate style

The General Philosophy of the Debate Theory

In contrast to the oratorical theory, the debate theory offers a different account of Lincoln-Douglas' purpose. This philosophy contends that Lincoln-Douglas is similar to cross-examination debate. However, it employs one person on a team instead of two and advocates value decisions instead of policies. Beyond these two exceptions, the debate theory contends that the intent of both Lincoln-Douglas and cross-examination team debate is basically the same. Both events use a significant degree of structured conflict to refute the opponent's case, and both utilize similar speed, evidence, and *artificial reality* to persuade the judge.

The obvious drawback to this theory is that significant structure, rapid delivery, and artificial reality are not always persuasive. Just as the oratorical theory is not necessarily persuasive with its nebulous, flowery speech, neither is the debate theory with its fast-paced, structured speech. As you might suspect, the optimum persuasiveness is a marriage of the two.

Refutation, Comparison, and Deliberation in the Debate Theory

This theory has merit in that it advocates many of the intentions of debate: refutation, comparison, and deliberation of issues. Debate, by definition, should rely upon the comparison of ideas to reach a conclusion regarding a value resolution. If the ideas in the round are not compared, it is difficult to reach a solid decision. The debate theory contends that each debater should be encouraged to develop original thought on the topic. The culmination of the thoughts presented by both debaters sheds light on the best solution to the resolution. This theory holds that in the process of responding to direct attacks, the debater is forced into original thought on the resolution. The attacks and refutations inherent in this theory force the debater to discuss the resolution in an authentic and realistic manner.

Reality in the Debate Theory

The word choice in the case is designed to convey one meaning and only that meaning. This is in contrast to the nebulous nature of the oratorical theory, which often uses elaborate, unnecessary words to impress the judge. It is imperative to note that the importance of Lincoln-Douglas resolutions should not be bypassed in an effort to use "twenty-five cent words" to impress the judge. The debate theory advocates a common and concise language in deliberating on an issue. Success comes from developing theories that illustrate the magnitude of social problems, not from the memorization of large, cumbersome words that confuse and circumvent the importance of the resolution. In this philosophy, what is said is what is meant, which lends considerable honesty to debate and exemplifies the standards worthy of Lincoln-Douglas debate.

Stock Issues in Lincoln-Douglas Debate

There are several concepts in cross-examination team debate that guide that event's progress. These concepts are called the *stock issues*, and are critical in deciding who will win the debate round. For a cross-examination debate team to win the round, it must fulfill these stock issue requirements:

- *Topicality*   the case presented by the affirmative must be "topical," or relevant, to the resolution

- *Inherency*   the case must be an essential part of the present system or system being proposed

- *Significance*   the case must prove a significant reason for change

- *Solvency*   the affirmative case must "solve" the current issues or problem and gain the advantages

As you might suspect, the debate theory, which evolved from cross-examination debate, often tries to institute these stock issues into Lincoln-Douglas. However, stock issues are often inappropriate. Consider each stock argument below for a discussion of why it does not apply to Lincoln-Douglas.

Topicality. This stock issue argument makes the affirmative responsible for presenting a plan that is relevant to the topic. There are no plans in Lincoln-Douglas, which is the first reason this stock issue does not belong. Furthermore, recognize that both the affirmative and the negative debaters have a responsibility to prove their cases in the resolution. As a consequence, it is not sufficient for the negative to merely say "the affirmative is not topical" and win the round. The negative debater must also show why he or she is correct in negating the resolution. Finally, recognize that when a general concept is discussed, anything can be presented. If a debater's argumentation is not relevant (not topical) to the resolution, the judge merely ignores the argument. The debater is not penalized by losing the round, but instead is penalized in that he or she wastes time, makes little or no sense, and is not very logical or persuasive in presenting the case. If debaters aren't logical and persuasive, they lose the round. It is that simple.

Inherency. Because Lincoln-Douglas resolutions deal with value decisions, and not policies, inherency is not applicable in Lincoln-Douglas debates. There is no "present system" or a "system being proposed," since Lincoln-Douglas is not place or time bound.

Solvency. Since there are no plans in Lincoln-Douglas, there are no advantages to be achieved by the plans. As a consequence, the process of proving that a plan will gain an advantage is not applicable in Lincoln-

Douglas debate. Lincoln-Douglas considers the relative importance of two values. It does not ask the debaters to introduce a plan to institute policies which result from these values; it only asks them to determine which of the two values in the round is the most important.

There are a number of debaters who will try to hold you to proving these stock issues in a round, and you should be able to justify why each stock issue does not belong in Lincoln-Douglas.

Structuring Speeches

In this theory the method of organizing speeches is highly structured. As mentioned before, the nebulous, oratorical style is not persuasive because it is not realistic. The extreme debate theory is also not persuasive, but for a different reason. Overly structuring a speech with twelve to twenty points (with several subpoints under each) is not realistic, and, thus, not persuasive. Just as the judge finds nebulous, flowery speech uncommon and unrealistic, he or she will also find highly structured, non-fluent speech uncommon and unrealistic. The overly structured speech in the debate theory is as much a pitfall as the non-structured style is in the oratorical theory. The important point to recognize is that there is an advantage debate theory offers in organization, but organization, when taken too far, can lose its realistic (and persuasive) effect. A good Lincoln-Douglas speech is organized around the responsibilities discussed in Chapter 5, and a good speech follows a logical progression of arguments.

Combining the Two Theories

It should be obvious that choosing one theory over the other is not a wise idea. Each theory has advantages, but each theory also has sizeable disadvantages that can greatly reduce persuasiveness. A marriage between the two theories, in which the deliberation, refutation, structure, and technique of debate join the delivery, analogy, and persuasion of oratory, is best. The winning debater is usually the individual who is able to take the persuasiveness and logic from the oratorical approach and combine it with the reasonable organization and honesty of the debate approach in presenting a case.

After examining each approach, it is advisable to take into account which theory is more prevalent in the area of the country where you are competing. *Judge adaptation* is dependent upon your ability to recognize the philosophy of the judges in your area. While you should not completely favor one theory over the other, your style will undoubtedly be closer to one theory than the other. In making the decision as to which theory to favor you should consider which style the judges in your area prefer. Some parts of the country prefer the debate theory, while other areas advocate the oratorical theory.

Recognize that debaters naturally develop a feel for a *debate style* that more closely resembles one theory over the other. Since each philosophy presented is a representation of the extreme end of a spectrum, the tendency to lean towards one end more than the other is natural. Both styles can be equally successful. Therefore, it makes little difference which style you adopt as long as you take into account which style is more comfortable and which style judges find more acceptable.

The following chart summarizes the benefits and disadvantages of each theory. Use elements of each theory, and your own thinking, to create your unique and effective style.

Key Concepts to Be Included In Your Style

- Oratorical theory
- Persuasiveness
- Slower rate of delivery
- Dependence on logic
- Realistic Scenarios

- Debate theory
- Organizational skills
- Refutation skills
- Use of good supporting evidence
- Realistic manner of speech

Key Concepts NOT to Be Included In Your Style

- Oratorical theory
- Nebulous speech
- Words "meant to impress"
- Too slow of a rate of delivery
- Avoidance of conflict/refutation

- Debate theory
- Excessive structure
- Non-Logical/unrealistic scenarios
- Excessive rate of delivery
- Reliance on evidence only

Suggested Activities

1. List and discuss in a paragraph the important features of the oratorical theory and the debate theory of L-D debate.

2. Line up your class from shortest to tallest. Discuss the concept of a spectrum with the debate theory represented at one end and the oratorical theory at the other.

3. Develop a three-minute speech on the current L-D topic or other topic listed in this text in two ways: one utilizing the oratorical theory and the other the debate theory. Have class members discuss which was more persuasive.

4. Write a short paragraph explaining why L-D should use both debate and oratory techniques.

Unit II
DEVELOPING
A LINCOLN-DOUGLAS CASE

Unit II is devoted to explaining the elements of a successful Lincoln-Douglas case and the thought process that is a part of developing a successful Lincoln-Douglas case.

Chapter 9 develops the idea of the case opening and its function in establishing rapport with the Lincoln-Douglas judge. Chapter 10 logically follows, and explains the concept of the interim, the elements that link the rapport generating opening to the case contentions. Chapter 11 is devoted to the proper use of definitions, including standards for introducing alternate definitions by the negative debater.

The actual case and its contentions are addressed in Chapter 12. This chapter focuses on the responsibilities of the case as well as strategies for creating cases. This unit concludes with a discussion of the specific and unique characteristics of both the negative and the affirmative constructive speeches. Special emphasis in these sections is given to strategies of integrating all of the concepts of this unit into practical speeches.

In situations where students may not have time to read the whole textbook prior to going to competitions, this unit is particularly useful since it provides the bare essentials of writing and presenting a Lincoln-Douglas case.

Chapter 9
Case Openings

Learning Objectives

Chapter 9 is designed to teach case openings. The case opening is the introduction to the debater's presentation of the case. This chapter explains what should be included in a case opening as well as things that should be avoided.

After completing this chapter you should be able to:

1. **Explain the qualities and importance of a good case opening.**

2. **Understand the importance of establishing rapport with a judge.**

New Terms

Case opening
Rapport
Spontaneity
Analogy
Flipped analogy
Personal overview

Introduction

The beginning of the case is generally not recorded in the judge's notes, but it is nonetheless one of the most important segments of Lincoln-Douglas debate. With the *case opening*, a debater makes a first impression upon the judge. Since the object of evaluation is you as a single person, it is critical that you use this initial impression to influence the judge. From the minute a debater begins a round, the judge is forming a first impression. The first words in the opening of the case will either confirm or deny the judge's expectations. Remember, in Lincoln-Douglas debate, the debater is as much a focus of evaluation as are the case, value, and criteria presented.

While the judge is forming his or her first impressions, your opponent will also be forming an impression of you. While it is not critical that you impress your opponent, it is worth noting that the impression you give your opponent will give him or her either a feeling of intimidation or a feeling of momentum. Giving an opponent momentum at the beginning of the round is dangerous as this can instill irrecoverable self-confidence. Conversely, a smooth, well-rehearsed opening can give the advantage of intimidation over an opponent. Before the game has truly begun, you will already enjoy an advantage.

The Qualities of a Good Case Opening

What goes into a good case opening? While the number of things that can constitute a successful case opening are limitless, there are a few common qualities that make up each successful case opening. Below is a list of the qualities that should be incorporated into both affirmative and negative case openings since both debaters try to establish rapport with the judge.

The Case Opening Should Build Rapport

The purpose of the case opening is to establish an impression with the judge, and present the debater as a person to the audience. Understand that the goal is to establish and maintain *rapport* with the judge throughout the round. This rapport begins in the case opening, and it is imperative that you present a case opening that develops this relation with the judge. It will be easy for the judge to vote against your case because your case is only a collection of ideas with no emotions. It is more difficult, however, for the judge to vote against you if the judge feels the vote will be against you as a person. Establish a connection with the judge, and make it difficult to vote against you.

Failure to establish rapport in the opening will make developing rapport during the rest of the round almost impossible. Focus efforts on the one goal of establishing a good impression. Do not worry about the actual substance of the debate until the interim and the case. During the introduction, keep the goal of building rapport consciously in the front of your mind.

Memorize the Case Opening

The first quality in establishing rapport is presenting a case opening that is memorized and not read as part of a script. Having the opening memorized does three things. First, it allows a debater to step away from any physical distractions (podiums, desks, tables, etc.) and speak with the judge, person to person. Second, it allows the debater to have direct eye contact with the judge, which is essential in rapport building. Finally, having the opening memorized allows presentation of an image of sincerity. Hearing a debater present a memorized and fluent opening is impressive and the debater is showing the judge that the debater honestly believes what he or she says. Sincerity is the essence of persuasion, and this sincerity shines through in memorization.

Spontaneity in the Case Opening

The second quality in a great opening is a degree of *spontaneity* in the presentation. Spontaneity essentially means "non-rehearsed, fresh." Every great opening should incorporate a small portion of you as the person in it. Allow yourself to be a little spontaneous in the presentation of the opening to prevent the case opening from appearing as if it were an impersonal "canned" speech. The general content of the opening should be memorized, but the opening should also be full of the life that comes from "spontaneous" speeches. This does not mean that the opening should be made up as it goes. On the contrary, the general content of the opening should be memorized, but the opening must seem like real and normal conversation that is not totally rehearsed. Hearing a debater who sounds like a casette tape is not persuasive. There is a delicate blend of memorization and spontaneity that goes into great openings, and debaters should strive to achieve that blend. Accomplishing this feat is not easy, and takes a great deal of practice. As a rule of thumb, if openings are not fluent, memorize more of the openings. If, on the other hand, openings become lifeless and boring, try to add more spontaneity to the presentation.

Time Considerations of the Opening

The final general component of the opening is time consideration. Remember that the opening is designed expressly for the purpose of establishing rapport with the judge. It is not a time to start deliberating the case or responding to an opponent's contentions. The establishment of rapport must be quick, to the point, and followed by the interim of the case (see Chapter 10). A long opening will bore the judge, and defeat the purpose of the opening. As a rule, the opening should not exceed thirty seconds. This ensures enough time to make a good first impression, but also guarantees that a debater will not spend too much of the speech on the opening.

Sources of Good Case Openings

Quotations as Case Openings

A highly effective way to open a case is through the use of a quotation. If a quotation is used as an opening, there are several considerations to make. First, it should be interesting. A boring quotation sounds boring. Second, the quote should tie into the topic being discussed. If the material is irrelevant, the judge may become so preoccupied with trying to figure out how it applies to the resolution that the rest of the opening is missed and rapport building is lost. Third, it should be short enough to be memorized. It really makes little difference where the quotation comes from, only that it is attention-getting, relevant, and makes sense. The source of the quote should be given. Do not use the quotation as a piece of evidence to argue against the opponent. Save all argumentation for the actual case deliberation.

Stories as Case Openings

Using a story or allusion as a case opening is also effective. The disadvantage to using a story is that it must be short in order to make it under the thirty second time guideline. Stories longer than thirty seconds can leave the judge lost or bored, and render rapport building useless. A good, short, memorable story, however, is an effective way to gain the judge's attention. Some of the same considerations for the quotation as an opening also apply. The story should be short, memorized, interesting, and relevant to the resolution. The use of a story has an advantage in that it allows the debater to bring it back up in the last rebuttal of the round and reinstitute the feeling of rapport the debater established in the case opening. This is an effective way of bringing the round together, and leaves a positive impression with the judge as the debater exits the round.

Analogies as Case Openings

An *analogy* is one of the most effective ways to begin a case. An analogy uses a familiar set of circumstances or events to explain or describe a more complicated set of circumstances or events. Since the use of analogies is also discussed in Chapter 26, discussion here is limited. It is important to note, however, that the same considerations that accompany stories also apply to analogies. The analogy should be short, memorized, interesting, and relevant to the resolution. Take care that the analogy is not too complex. Remember, only thirty seconds are available to present and explain the analogy. A complex analogy can do more harm than good in that it can thoroughly confuse and bewilder the judge, again destroying rapport building efforts. Like stories, analogies can be tied to the ending of the last rebuttal as a nice way of bringing the round together. Analogies have an additional advantage in that they can be tied to the case portion of the round throughout the round's duration. Exercise extreme caution in using analogies, however, since a *flipped analogy,* an analogy you present which is overturned on you by your opponent, can be devastating.

Personal Overviews as Case Openings

Sometimes the simple approach is the best approach to introducing a case. While it is the least extravagant of the four methods of opening a case, providing a *personal overview* of the topic can be equally effective in establishing rapport with the judge. A personal overview is a simple presentation of yourself that is done in a tone of voice that is slow, harmonious, natural, pleasing, and seeks to provide your assessment of the resolution. The personal overview can be the most effective way of establishing rapport with the judge. Because judges are familiar with hearing people talk to them in a natural, everyday voice, this method is effective. The other advantage of this technique is that it presents a no-nonsense, honest approach to the debate. Some judges find it refreshing for a debater to be willing to discuss the resolution in "real world" fashion.

While this method is effective, its effectiveness is reserved only for those debaters who continually practice using it as an introduction technique. Voice inflection, nonverbal communication, and eye contact are critical components of an effective "personal overview" opening approach. The debater lacking these qualities often falls flat in this approach.

As with the other techniques of case openings, the substance of the overview is not as critical as the way that it is said. The overview should apply to the resolution and make reasonable sense. It does not, however, have to be a great analytical discourse to be effective. The goal is to present the speaker to the judge and establish a relationship. As long as the overview accomplishes this goal, it is effective, regardless of the "worthiness" of the analysis.

Conclusion

The case opening is one of the most important moments in Lincoln-Douglas debate. Because Lincoln-Douglas debate is as much the presentation of one's self as it is the presentation of a debate case, the first impression a debater makes in a round is critical to the overall performance. The opening is essential to establishing good rapport with the judge. Like all aspects of Lincoln-Douglas debate, the development of a good case opening comes only with practice. The debater must establish the balance between memorization and spontaneity, and must be able to radiate a feeling of comfort and confidence as a first impression. The bad news about these qualities is that they must be learned; no one is born with this talent. Practice developing these skills to be outstanding in the area of presenting a first impression. The good news about these skills is that everyone can achieve equal success in making positive first impressions during the delivery of a case opening through sufficient practice.

Suggested Activities

1. Deliver short impromptu (30 seconds) case openings over the current topic or one listed in the book.

2. Working in small groups, prepare case openings using each of the different types decribed in this chapter. Deliver the openings to the class and have them identify each type.

Chapter 10
The Interim

Learning Objectives

Chapter 10 is designed to teach the interim. The interim is the portion of the debater's presentation that provides a transition from the case opening to the case presentation. This chapter explains what should be included in the interim and provides some hints on creating an effective interim.

After completing this chapter you should be able to:

1. Define interim.

2. Understand the importance of stating the resolution and the debater's position on it.

3. Give examples of effective transitions for use in the interim.

4. List the elements of a good case preview.

New Terms

Interim
The statement of position on the resolution
The statement of the resolution
Preview
Slug

Introduction

That which is said between the opening and the case itself is an extremely important portion of the constructive speech. It is useless to spend time on an effective and persuasive opening if it is stranded from the main substance of the speech. In fact, if there is not a smooth transition between the case opening and the case itself, a debater is better off deleting the opening altogether.

The *interim*, the section of the speech that connects the opening and the main points, makes or breaks the quality of the opening and sets the tone for the case points. More importantly, the interim maintains the persuasive tone created in the case opening. A smooth interim undoubtedly casts an impression of organization and control. Of course, the contrary is also true; a choppy interim will create a disorganized impression. As a consequence, it is important that we spend time discussing what distinguished a great interim from a poor one.

Preparing the Interim

Definition of Interim

The best place to start is to correctly define what is meant by the interim.

Interim: The section of the speech that connects the opening to the main points.

Everything between the opening and the case points can be considered as the interim. Frequently, a debater discusses many things in the opening that have nothing to do the case points. Although this is an ineffective transition between the case opening and the case points, it is still considered the interim, since it appears between the opening and the case.

A great interim, however, contains only those things that serve to link the case points to the main case—and nothing more! An average to poor interim includes a great deal of extraneous information. This extra information may be pertinent to the case being discussed, but does not necessarily belong in the interim position. The placement of what is said is as important as the content of what is said.

The sole purpose of the interim is to the opening and the main points. Extra information only serves to cloud the transition, and confuse those who must sort through its content to find the reason for the opening's existence.

What Goes Into the Interim

If we know what not to put into the interim, what do we put in it? Let's return to the definition of the interim and re-define in practical terms what the interim must do. In practical terms, the interim should be a collection of six main components:

•the transition between the opening to the resolution
•the statement of position on the resolution
•the statement of the resolution
•the transition between the resolution and the preview
•the preview
•the transition between the preview and the case points

Everything that does not serve to perform one of these purposes should be left out of the interim.

In graphic terms, we have the following:

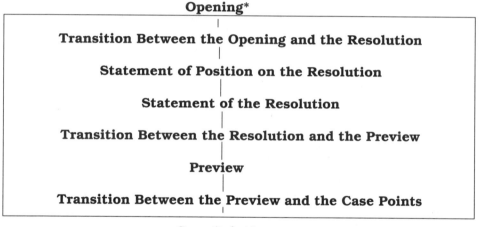

Opening*

Transition Between the Opening and the Resolution

Statement of Position on the Resolution

Statement of the Resolution

Transition Between the Resolution and the Preview

Preview

Transition Between the Preview and the Case Points

Case Point*

*Indicates portions of the speech that are **not** considered part of the interim, and are discussed in other chapters of this book.

Sample Transitions from the Case Opening to the Resolution

With the structure of the interim established, let's examine each part of the structure and determine what makes each piece effective. Initially, assume that we have finished the case opening, and are now ready to proceed into the interim. The first step is the initial transition from the opening to the position on the resolution (see diagram). This portion of the interim will vary depending on what opening you choose. Below is a short list of opening types, along with sample transitions to the resolution. This should give some idea as to what works well to make a succinct transition. Please keep in mind that the best transitions are the ones with which you feel comfortable. Do not memorize these examples, but instead use them to develop your own transitions.

1. History of the Resolution as the Opening. If you start with a history of the resolution and how this "social dilemma" has come about, it is sufficient to say:

> "Because I believe the social dilemma that has evolved from... (the history you just presented)... must be solved before it expands into a larger social issue, I stand in favor of/against the resolution."

2. General Commentary or Analysis of the Resolution as the Opening. If, instead, you make a commentary on the issues surrounding the resolution, or you simply want to make an initial analysis of the topic for an opening, it will suffice to say:

> "For all of the reasons I have just presented, I stand resolved that. . . should be affirmed/negated," or "Because of the foreseeable consequences of not taking action on this resolution, I believe that. . . should be affirmed/negated."

3. Using a Quotation as an Opening to the Resolution. If a quote is used, it is necessary to link it to the resolution. This is often effectively done by superimposing the person quoted onto the present Lincoln-Douglas debate round. For example, a debater quoting Thomas Jefferson in the case opening might say:

> "If Thomas Jefferson were sitting here today, he would cringe at the thought of censorship in the name of decency. As a result I thus oppose/affirm the resolution which states. . ."

4. Using Stories, Anecdotes, Analogies as an Opening to the Resolution. Finally, if eloquent anecdotes, stories, or analogies are used to open the constructive, find some clever way to link the analogy to the resolution. This is generally done by explaining how the analogy fits the resolution. It is not enough to hope that the judge can see the parallel; it must be explained. Furthermore, it must be explained in a way that is time-efficient and concise. It is often useful to take a direct approach and plainly say:

> "Because in this day and age, Hester Prynn's Scarlet Letter is equivalent to mandatory drug testing in not only marking a person but limiting freedoms, I stand opposed to the resolution on drug testing."

The initial difficulty of analogies, as explored in Chapter 26, is making clever analogies fit the topic. The second obstacle is the application of the analogy to the resolution. A very complicated thought must often be explained in a matter of seconds. In short, analogies, although potent, are not easy weapons to fire, and should be used with caution. Time will be spent in a later section discussing the merits, dangers, and skills needed to use analogies effectively.

The Debater's Position on the Resolution

The second phase of the interim is the *statement of the debater's position on the resolution.* For example, the affirmative must state that he or she affirms the resolution, while the negative must state that he or she negates the resolution. It may seem silly to devote discussion to such a small sentence, but the impact of tying the opening directly to a position statement has an important effect on persuasion. In each of the examples, the link between the opening and the resolution contains a key element of the debater's statement of belief. Either the statement is worded to support the resolution, or it is worded to negate it. This statement of belief is vital to starting a feeling of sincerity. If the message is portrayed with honesty, your persuasiveness will increase several fold. This sincerity begins with being able to look the judge in the eye and say quite plainly, "I **SUPPORT (NEGATE)** this resolution."

In all actuality, this is not a tough segment of the debate. It takes nothing more than a few moments of planning ahead and being prepared to lead from an opening to a statement of belief. In fact, all that must be done is to state:

"For these reasons, I stand **opposed to** (in support of) the resolution that. . ."

The implications of this simple sentence can have significant ramifications when it comes to sincerity, and ultimately, persuasiveness.

The Statement of the Resolution

The *statement of the resolution* naturally should follow the position statement. It is important that the resolution be stated for several reasons. First and foremost, stating the resolution establishes a broad-based sense of authority in the analysis. Not stating the resolution creates a feeling that something is being hidden, or that the debater is afraid to discuss the "whole resolution."

Second, knowing the resolution establishes the fact that the debater cares enough about the topic to memorize the wording and establishes sincerity. A football player takes time out to understand the parameters of the game of football, and it makes little sense for the Lincoln-Douglas debater not to do the same in regards to the parameters of debate. Take time out to give attention to the event's parameters, i.e., the exact wording of the resolution.

In addition, knowing the resolution has obvious benefits in preventing "traps" later in the round. An opponent who plans on trapping you by a technicality within the resolution's wording will often abandon such plans when you demonstrate mastery of the wording of the resolution.

A well memorized resolution impresses the judge. Most Lincoln-Douglas debate judges struggle to keep up with which stance on an issue is negative and which is affirmative. Presenting a complicated sentence with mastery may make the judge want to ask **you** questions about what should be placed where in the round. Obviously, a judge will not make such an inquiry, but if it seems that the debater might have a better mastery of the resolution than the judge, the debater appears more impressive when it comes to signing the ballot.

It is also important to memorize the resolution so you have easy access to it throughout the round. If there is ever a need to refer specifically to the wording of the resolution in a heated rebuttal, knowing the resolution verbatim lends fluency and effectiveness.

Memorizing the resolution provides the debater with a fluent transition from the opening into the case and it allows the debater to respond to a "wise-crack" cross-examination question. You lose a great deal of credibility when you cannot repeat the resolution, or have to go to a briefcase for reference. To avoid such embarrassment, take time to memorize the resolution.

The Transition from the Resolution to the Case Preview

Before actually presenting your case, it is important to provide the judge and your opponent with a road map to make note taking easier. The *preview* becomes the judge's "game program" to following and understanding your arguments. Your judge is able to take notes with greater accuracy. It also enables your opponent to keep more accurate notes and avoid wasting your time asking for clarity.

It is relatively simple to make the transition from the resolution to the preview. In all actuality, it should contain nothing more that the following:

"In supporting the resolution, therefore, I offer the following three (two) contentions. (Read the main title of each of your contentions.)"

The Case Preview

At this point, we arrive at the preview to the case. Regardless of multiple subpoints, the main contentions of a case will almost always win or lose rounds. As a consequence, include only the main titles of case points in the preview. Ideas sound more familiar when heard twice, and consequently, the preview is a vital portion of persuasiveness.

A good preview should be just that: a preview, and not a detailed explanation. The goal is to convey only the main points of argumentation. Details come later.

Considering that a full constructive is six or seven minutes, fifteen seconds is hardly a waste of time. The preview is essential because without it a major contention could be lost. It is also important to keep in mind that previewing the information demonstrates you have confidence in what you say. It is as if you project the sentence, "These are the things that I have to say. If need be, I will say them as many times as possible without fear of being attacked by my opponent, because I feel what I have to say cannot be logically refuted."

The preview does not have to flow like the "opening to resolution" transitions. It should however, be something more than, "Point one will be A, Point two will be B, etc." Remember that a judge is not a data entry base to a computer terminal. Give an outlined structure in a reasonably fluid style. For example:

"In looking at the resolution we will decide today, I will first give attention to how affirming the resolution perpetuates the value of A. In similar fashion, I will show that support for the resolution will equal B. And finally, in contrast, I will show how negating the resolution will cause significant reduction in value C."

Notice that a strategy is played out before the judge. Do not just list the *slug* titles or key words for each point, but talk in a reasonable (and persuasive) tone of voice to present a simple plan of action. There is nothing hidden or elaborate; simply state what the judge can expect in the first constructive. Being able to come front stage with this approach lends, once again, considerable authority.

Transition from the Preview to the Definitions

Finally, after all of these steps are completed, it is essential to set the parameters of debate. Although Chapter 11 discusses the uses of definitions, it will suffice to say that after the preview, you should define your terms.

Some people argue that definitions should come before the preview, but when the definitions come after the preview the judges can use this time to catch up in writing the previewed points. As a consequence, some of the definition time can be used to "double ensure" that main points, via the preview, are translated into the judge's notes.

The natural response to this philosophy is, "What about the definition time? Don't the judges lose time in writing definitions down?" This may be true, but consider that the use of definitions in Lincoln-Douglas debate is rarely a point of decision making. Unlike team debate, the exactness of word use is not crucial. Since there is no topicality in Lincoln-Douglas debate, it makes little sense to spend a great deal of time trying to tie an opponent down to strict definitions. Assume that the judge is going to make a decision on the values presented in the round, and not on the definitions, and plan the interim accordingly.

Definitions in Lincoln-Douglas debate will never be as important as in team debate. Furthermore, when both debaters are reasonably close to the intent of the resolution, definitions rarely win rounds. Finally, Lincoln-Douglas debate judges rarely flow definitions. Parameters for the round must be established, but it's unnecessary to spend a large amount of time on definitions.

Once again, the more simple the transition, the better. In fact, after presenting the preview to the last point of your case, it is enough to say:

"However, before I begin, I would like to define a few crucial terms."

Following this transition, begin defining the resolution.

Conclusion

Although it is difficult to believe that so much attention could be given to what appears to be such an insignificant portion of the constructive case, the interim creates initial and lasting impressions. For this reason, devote time to practicing interim skills. Mastery of transitions, resolutions, previews, and definitions helps win rounds. Good debaters may win without using good interim skills, but great debaters refuse to win without them. Remember, in a close round, the ballot always go to the debater who pays closest attention to the little details. The interim, not a piece of evidence, may be what separates you from a state tournament victory, or a national tournament berth. The choice, of course, is up to you.

Suggested Activities

1. Write sample interims to fit the case openings developed in Chapter 9.

2. Divide the class into pairs and have them practice delivering interims with case openings to each other.

Chapter 11
Using Definitions Properly

Learning Objectives

Chapter 11 is designed to teach the proper use of definitions. As this chapter explains, it is important to define certain words in the resolution in order to set the debate's parameters. Many resolutions have words that are either ambiguous or can be interpreted in a number of different ways. For this reason, definitions are a critical part of a successful Lincoln-Douglas presentation. This chapter shows how and where to find good definitions, and how definitions should be used in the round.

After completing this chapter you should be able to:

1. **Explain the role and importance of definitions and list the six rules governing their use.**

2. **Determine which words or phrases require definition and locate definitions from a variety of sources.**

3. **Understand the importance of preparing for and recognizing unusual and biased definitions.**

4. **List the four standards for negative definitions.**

5. **Explain how and when to present definitions.**

New Terms

Setting parameters
Ad absurdum argument
Resolution phrases
More inclusive
   definition standard
Inclusive

More sources agree definition
   standard
More applicable to the
   resolution definition standard
Biased definitions
Dice

Introduction

Definitions, in the strictest sense, should accomplish only one purpose—to clarify ambiguities in the resolution. It is wise to take definitions at face value and nothing more. In many rounds, debaters attempt to win Lincoln-Douglas rounds by cleverly manipulating the definition of one or more words. In almost all of these rounds, the individual attempting to win the round with the definitions usually loses. There is a lesson to be learned: **Definitions are designed to set the parameters of the debate, not win debate rounds**. Attempting to gain a victory through definitions usually equals a loss.

Definitions are designed to *set the parameters* of debate, that is, to establish just what should be talked about given the resolution. When asked to debate a resolution concerning genetic engineering, define what "genetic engineering" means. In this way, the topic is clear, and the boundaries of the debate are established.

The Rules of Definitions

1. Do Not Rely on Definitions to Win the Round.

The best and safest method of debate simply is to debate the resolution. To spend a large amount of time on definitions is risky, since it may imply that you have nothing to say about your case, which, in turn can hurt your image in the judge's eyes. There is also the possibility that the judge will find the extraordinary time spent on definitions somewhat obnoxious. As a consequence, any valid points presented later in the round might be considered less serious because of initial attempts to avoid the resolution by relying only on definitions. It is possible to win a round on definitions, but the probability that you will lose the round is much higher. With those odds, it is not worth the risk.

2. Definitions Should Be Used To Establish Preferential Ground For the Rest of the Round.

Although definitions should not be used as a means to win a round, they are, on occasion, an aid in tilting the scales. It is worth investing time to research closely how certain words and, more importantly, certain phrases of a resolution can be defined. Definitions are used to clarify words in the resolution that are ambiguous or have multiple interpretations. For this reason, it is possible that a debater may be able to define a word or phrase in the resolution to help the case. Selecting a definition that incorporates good aspects of a concept (i.e, genetic engineering) or that leaves out bad aspects of a concept, can go a long way in winning the round. For example, defining censorship as "the protection of the public from damaging or slanderous statements" leaves out the bad aspects of censorship (namely, the limitation of knowledge) and selectively incorporates the positive aspects of the concept. A definition should be complete and supported by a documented source, but there are multiple definitions for each concept or topic. Finding those that help your case is an important step.

3. Investigate Definitions That Come from Larger Sources Rather Than Just Those from a Dictionary.

At times the way in which society or a court defines something may be entirely more realistic and pertinent to the resolution than a definition from a standard or specialized dictionary (such as a law dictionary). For this reason, investigate other sources that define the word or phrase in question within the context of the resolution. The fourth and fifth rules of definition suggest alternatives to standard dictionaries. Even when standard or specialized dictionaries provide adequate definitions, continue to search out other sources.

4. Prepare for Unusual Definitions.

It is a good idea to research even the most unusual interpretations of different elements of the resolution. Although you may never use these definitions, there is always the possibility that an opponent will. Knowing the background of these definitions keeps you from being surprised by them. Having this knowledge also adds merit to counter-arguments as to why the unusual is too far off-base to apply to the intent of the resolution.

5. Do Not Define Every Word in the Resolution.

Usually only two or three words in a resolution require definitions. It is a waste of time to define words such as "an" or "the." Doing so wastes time and bores the audience.

In policy debate, the exact nature of the wording is critical to the final outcome. In Lincoln-Douglas, however, the debate is based upon logic and the general principles underlying the resolution. As a consequence, stick to the logical interpretation of words such as "ought," "should," "preferable," etc.

But what if an opponent uses a ridiculous, illogical definition against you? In these cases it is generally sufficient to respond to the opponent's definitions with an *ad absurdum* argument which merely states that the definition is absurd and not logical such as defining "a" as meaning "three or more." Keep in mind that it should not be difficult to beat "ridiculous definitions," so the time used here should be minimal.

Usually, resolutions compare two ideals or positions. The terms of the ideals or positions should be defined. As mentioned earlier, definitions that add "social insight" to these terms are advantageous. Since a definition will almost never win a round in Lincoln-Douglas, multiple definitions of the same term are usually unnecessary.

6. Define Resolution Phrases as Phrases, Not as Individual Words.

At times a phrase is assigned to represent an ideal or value instead of just one word. For example, "individual rights" may not be spelled out in the resolution. Instead, the phrase, "the individual's right to know" may be how the value of "individual rights" is incorporated into the resolution. In these instances, which are very common, the phrase in its entirety should be defined. A standard dictionary is probably not a good source for definitions of this sort, since it does not define phrases. It is possible to break up a phrase such as "the individual's right to know" into its smallest divisions (i.e., "the," "individual's," "right," "to," and "know"). To do so, however, risks breaking the true meaning of the phrase. In addition, attempting to define each word of a phrase can waste a great deal of time and sacrifice a great deal of credibility in the definitions. As a consequence, make every effort to define phrases as phrases. A good source for phrase definitions is *Black's Law Dictionary.*

Sources of Definitions

If preparation time is limited, *Black's Law Dictionary* is probably the best source. In fact, in most cases, a definition from *Black's Law Dictionary* is difficult to defeat. If, however, you have extra time to invest in value definitions, the resources of great philosophers (such as Kant, Locke, Nietzsche, Jefferson) are of great benefit. *Six Great Ideas* is also one of the best collections of resources for value definitions.

Periodicals and Journals

At some point, however, you will be asked to debate a resolution that is more modern in context. The best resources on technological ideas, such as genetic engineering, are found in professional journals and/or the more respected science magazines such as *National Geographic, Science Digest, Discovery* and scientific journals, such as *New England Journal of Medicine.* The reputation of a magazine is generally proportional to a librarian's opinion. Thus, if you have a question about a source's credentials, ask your librarian or teacher. If a periodical is well known and will be recognized by a judge, it is probably a good source for definitions.

Major periodicals are often used for definitions. *Time, Newsweek, U.S. News and World Report, The Atlantic, The New Republic, The New York Times, The Wall Street Journal,* and *The Christian Science Monitor* are all periodicals that carry a respectable national reputation. In addition, there are other resources, such as *Facts on File* and *Editorial Research Reports* that are beneficial in defining some of the more controversial issues in the limelight of public debate.

U.S. Society Definitions

Debaters are often asked to debate issues that are related to U.S. policy or laws. Particularly, issues concerning the Supreme Court's decisions and the Constitution are popular and are encountered with regular frequency. The *Congressional Record* and other similar periodicals are advantageous in this position. In many cases, references to the Constitution and amendments can best be defined from a book discussing the Constitution.

Finding Definitions from the Same Source

In finding a source for definitions, keep in mind that it is wise to define your resolution terms from the same source. Doing so lends credibility and consistency to your case analysis. In addition, this saves time since you do not have to re-quote a different source title, which can cost you time. If a source for definitions happens to be indicted or challenged as to its credibility, it is also easier to defend definitions if they come from one or two sources. This can save valuable time in rebuttals.

Negative Definitions

The above advice is particularly useful for the affirmative portion of the debate. In the negative case it is important to have a good understanding of what it means to contest a definition and what it means to do it successfully. This section explains the negative definition strategy. The first thing to remember before beginning discussion of negative definitions is the cardinal rule for definition use: **Too much time spent on definitions is a waste.** Understanding this is the foundation for negative theory on definitions.

The first rule of thumb is to establish a field of play in the debate round that is fair to your side. "Fair" means that you must establish a set of parameters that allows the negative case to be a viable alternative for the judge to accept in the round. In most cases, standard definitions given on the part of the affirmative are fair ground for the negative as well. In other cases, you may have to make some minor modifications in the affirmative's definitions in order to allow for effective debate. The following examples should serve to define the difference:

In example A, we discuss the resolution, "The rights of the individual should take precedence over the rights of society." The scenario is as follows: The affirmative debater defines the following terms:

- •Individual rights - Rights afforded to the individual in general accordance with the first amendment.

- •Society's rights - Rights afforded to the society, the sacrifice of individual rights in order to protect the social institution.

In example B, the resolution is the same. The difference is that the affirmative defines the following terms as:

- •Individual rights - The preservation of human meaning and purpose. Life, liberty and the pursuit of happiness. The basis of all social interaction.
- •Society's rights - The restriction of individual rights for the purpose of social maintenance.

In example A the negative debater should grant the definitions of the affirmative case. It is hard to believe that the negative debater will find definitions that are any more "fair" than those given by the affirmative. Using these definitions, the negative can easily accomplish his or her goals in the round. As a result, it is not worth wasting critical negative constructive time in redefining the definitions. The first negative speech must be used for not only presenting the negative case, but also for arguing against the affirmative case. All of this must be done in seven minutes, and, thus, conservation of time is critically important.

In example B the affirmative is clearly "stacking the deck" to give an unfair advantage to the affirmative in the round. It is now imperative that the negative redefine the terms to include a more reasonable assessment. Particularly, the definition of individual rights offers an inherent "goodness" to the concept of individual rights, giving the affirmative case an advantage, and it should be redefined. This set of definitions implies that the negative case's substance (the social institution) is dependent on the affirmative case's substance (individual rights). Such an implication is necessarily detrimental to the negative case. This merits a redefinition. Deciding on when redefinitions are warranted is generally not that difficult. If definitions appear neutral and fair, they are generally acceptable definitions for the round. Keep in mind that whenever the affirmative attempts to define the definitions in such a manner that limits the negative's ability to fairly debate the resolution, the negative should redefine the terms.

Standards for Negative Definitions

How does the negative successfully defeat and replace biased affirmative definitions? Answering this question is not as difficult as it may seem. The negative must, however, follow some standards in warranting a replacement of the affirmative's definitions.

Contrary to popular belief, the negative does not have the automatic option to redefine the definitions and hope they are accepted. If a negative wishes to redefine a word in the resolution, there must be a substantial reason to do so. In almost every case, the negative must meet at least one of the following standards to warrant a redefinition.

More Inclusive Definition

The first way the negative can justify a better definition is by claiming that the alternative is more *inclusive*. Inclusive means that the negative definition applies to all situations related to the resolution. Non-inclusive means that the definition unfairly limits the resolution to a few preferential scenarios. In the case where an affirmative presents a non-inclusive definition, the negative should argue that his or her definition applies to all possible scenarios, while the affirmative's definition has been designed to unfairly limit the debate. The negative should claim that the resolution was meant to be debated on all scenarios, and the negative's definition includes more of these scenarios than does the affirmative's definition. The negative must then present an alternate definition, and demonstrate, either by logic or evidence, that this definition is more inclusive or incorporates more of the "possible scenarios" in which the resolution is debated. Put simply, the resolution is designed to make value judgements that will, in most cases, affect all individuals. Limiting the resolution to only one country, or only one part of a society, is not fair to both debaters, and not true to the intent of the resolution.

More Sources Agree

Occasionally, the affirmative presents a definition that slants the debate in a direction favorable to the affirmative case. This is not beneficial to the negative case and makes it necessary for the negative to introduce an alternate definition. The trouble arises when the affirmative presents a perfectly legitimate definition for a section of the resolution. In these situations, the negative must present an alternate definition with substantial support from research sources. It is easy to find one piece of evidence to say whatever it is you need to say, but it is much more difficult (and much more valid) to find and present two or more definitions that agree with your statement. Do not spend too much time on this, but do invest enough time to protect yourself. If the opponent presents a legitimate definition that unfairly hurts your case, present an alternate definition, and substantiate that definition with multiple sources.

More Applicable to the Resolution in Question

In general, the less a definition is *diced*, the more applicable it will be. If an affirmative insists on defining "mandatory drug testing" by dicing the resolution into subunits, i.e., "mandatory," "drug," and "testing," it is worth redefining the resolution by offering a comprehensive redefinition for the phrase, "mandatory drug testing." In doing so, you create a more reasonable definition on which to stand. An affirmative who relies upon the *dicing effect* probably does not have much ground to stand on, and as a consequence offers a definition that is not fair to the resolution. Be prepared to redefine the resolution in terms of the meaning of the phrase instead of individual meanings of words.

Occasionally, the affirmative uses definitions that do not apply to the resolution being discussed. At times you will be asked to debate specific resolutions that concern specific topics. This set of resolutions will inevitably hold phrases such as "genetic engineering" or "mandatory drug testing." The great theorists and philosophers from history won't have specific comments on such issues. Beware of debaters who attempt to use dated definitions to define current issues. While an old definition is not a justification for redefinition (since Lincoln-Douglas is not time bound), topics that discuss current issues deserve current definitions. While Aristotle can comment on the rights of the individual versus the rights of the society, it is not credible to use Aristotle to define terms such as genetic engineering. This does not bar using older theorists within the debate; instead it merely mandates that current definitions be used to fit the specifics of the resolution.

Affirmative Definition is Biased by Source

Occasionally, a definition presented by the affirmative is biased by the source from which it comes. For example, a great definition against pornography and censorship coming from *U.S. News and World Report* based upon Gallup polls is difficult to beat. The same definition coming from *Playboy* magazine, however, has considerable source bias. If pornography were illegal, *Playboy* magazine might become subject to censorship under some individuals' standards, and would stand to lose money. Thus, it is a biased source. The key question to ask is, "What else is this source supposed to say? Is this source an interested party in either side of the resolution?" If so, definitions using that source would be less credible.

In other cases, the source may simply not be capable of adequately defining the topic being discussed. Using a source that doesn't contain expert opinions on the topic is absurd. Debaters who attempt this are opening themselves up to negative definition challenges. Remember, everyone outside of his or her field is an amateur and not qualified to make authoritative statements. A good rule of thumb is to question every debater encountered about the validity of a particular person defining terms. If a debater cannot give reasons why the person defining terms is an expert in that field, it is safe to say that the definition warrants redefinition. By the same token, be prepared to defend all of your sources, both on the affirmative and the negative. In all cases it does not hurt to inquire about an opponent's sources and qualifications.

The Affirmative Use of Negative Definition Standards

While the above strategy is almost exclusively used by the negative, the affirmative at times may find use for the redefinition standards. Occasionally, the affirmative definitions are challenged by the negative. If the negative does not meet any of the above standards, the affirmative should be able to use the above standards to demonstrate why the negative's redefinition is not valid. The affirmative may find it advantageous to be familiar with what the negative has to prove so that the affirmative can substitute alternate definitions.

The Time Allocation for Definitions

Definitions are an important part of the round, but they are not the component that ultimately wins the round. As a consequence, they should be given enough, but not too much time allocation. In short, definitions should not receive a large portion of either constructive or rebuttal speech time. Use only what time is necessary. More than thirty to forty-five seconds on definitions is too much.

The Timing of Definitions

Finally, it is important to note that the timing of definitions is critical. After the constructives, whatever definitions prevail are the ones that set the parameters for discussion in the remainder of the round. If the negative does not offer reasons for redefining terms in the negative constructive, it is too late to do so in rebuttal.

Conclusion

Definitions are not a crucial portion of the debate round, but should be treated with proper respect. Definitions should only set the parameters of the debate. Define what terms are needed for the context of the debate and leave them alone. It is also advisable to keep definitions on the affirmative side relatively in line with the intent of the resolution. When you are the negative, watch for unfair affirmative definitions and be prepared to defeat those definitions. While definitions do not usually win rounds, they can cause you to lose rounds if they are mishandled. Be confident and conscious of the power of definitions.

Suggested Activities

1. List three or four resolutions on the chalkboard and pick, as a class, which terms should be defined in a round.

2. Practice delivering case openings and interims with definitions.

3. Write out definitions for the major terms in the current resolution or one of those listed in the text using each of the four sources listed in this chapter.

Chapter 12
Writing and Building the Case

Chapter 12 is designed to teach case writing. Previous chapters have introduced the areas of Lincoln-Douglas that precede the case and facilitate its effective presentation. The case opening and the interim should have established the rapport and persuasiveness that allow arguments about the resolution to be effective in winning the judge's approval. This chapter explains the essential components of a successful case, and highlights some of the pitfalls commonly encountered by Lincoln-Douglas debaters.

After completing this chapter you should be able to:

1. List and explain the three functions of a case.

2. Understand the 11 components of an effective affirmative or negative case.

3. Understand the process of writing and polishing a case.

New Terms

Case   Brainstorming
Specifics of the resolution   Dream case
Purification of the value   Extension evidence
Major source of conflict   Dialectic mind-set
                    Case spike

Introduction

The comparison of values is essential in Lincoln-Douglas debate. Equally as important is the analysis of the actual topic delineated by the resolution. If, for example, the resolution includes the topic of drug testing you should discuss values in relation to drug testing. The resolution has a built-in hidden deliberation between the rights of the individual (anti-drug testing) and the rights of society (pro-drug testing), but the fact remains that the specifics of drug testing must still be addressed. The round was not meant to be a discussion **exclusive** to the rights of the individual versus the rights of society; if it were, the resolution would delineate only the rights of the individual versus the rights of society and not drug testing. The *case* is the place where Lincoln-Douglas addresses the specifics of the topic in the resolution.

In addition to the intent of the resolution, there is another critical reason the topic should be discussed in its entirety. If you remember, the first "level" of Lincoln-Douglas debate is the link between the resolution and the value that is upheld. This "level," like all others, is debatable in that if the value selected by one debater is "off-base," it is open to criticism by the opposing debater. The case is designed to make the link between the resolution (drug testing) and the value chosen (individual rights/society rights). The case essentially exists to prove that affirming or negating the resolution will result in the enhancement or diminishment of one or more values. The case, then, fulfills the responsibility of the first debate level. There must be a strong link between the resolution and the value selected, and the case is responsible for making this connection.

The case is the portion of the constructive speech that addresses the specifics of the topic in the resolution, makes the link between the resolution topic and the chosen value, and establishes the value chosen as a "truly" important value (purification of the value). The case further proves that affirming or negating the resolution will result in the enhancement or diminishment of this important value.

The Three Functions of the Case

1. Addressing the Specifics of the Resolution

As was discussed in other sections, the first duty of a case is to address the *specifics of the resolution*. It is important to note, however, that "specifics" means general facets of the issue being discussed in the resolution. It does not imply a policy discussion as in cross-examination team debate. Lincoln-Douglas does not seek to solve policy, nor even address policy. Instead, it seeks to evaluate the values that underlie value decisions (which, incidentally, are reflected in policy making). Therefore, focus on aspects of the topic, but not upon policies surrounding that topic. For instance, in the example used above (drug testing), the debater is expected to focus upon the real world application of drug testing (i.e., Does it work?, Is it safe?, etc.), but the debater would not be expected to evaluate whether a government policy should be accepted, modified, or rejected. The distinction between specifics and policy is a critical element to be mastered. As a rule of thumb, if you are not addressing the merits of the resolution's decision i.e., what value comes about from drug testing, you are too vague and your case is missing the first critical element. If, on the other hand, you are focusing only upon a certain policy or law, you are too specific and your case is not addressing the general values that underlie those and other policies.

2. The Fulfillment of the Link Between the Resolution and the Value

The second function of the case is the establishment of the link between the resolution and the affirmative/negative value. The first function of the case is to establish that the position a judge takes on a given resolution (voting affirmative or negative) has an impact on the enhancement or degradation of a certain value. If the judge votes affirmative, then the value upheld by the affirmative is enhanced. If the judge votes negative, the affirmative value is degraded in importance. For example, if the judge votes to affirm the importance of drug testing in the workplace, the affirmative's value of "safety" is enhanced. If the judge votes to negate the importance of drug testing in the workplace, then the affirmative value of safety is degraded. As a consequence, the second function of the case is to establish the link between the value and the resolution. Notice that affirming the resolution has impacts on the final state of both values in the round.

3. The "Purification" of the Affirmative or Negative Value

The second function of the case is to establish the value as "pure." The case does this in two ways. First, the case should illustrate that the value is pure in its derivation from the resolution. The case must prove that affirming the resolution results in affirming the value behind the resolution. In the example used above, the case must prove that affirming the resolution on drug testing results in an increase in the value of safety. A debater can make the greatest case for the importance of the value of "safety," but it is a fruitless effort if he or she cannot show that "safety" is actually enhanced by affirming the resolution. Second, the debater should establish that the value chosen is actually important to society, and, therefore, worth making a decision to "enhance it." For example, in a drug testing topic the value of "safety" should be established as having relatively few harms and relatively great benefits when the judge votes to affirm the need for drug testing. If affirming the resolution on drug testing, the case should illustrate that drug testing in the workplace supports the value of safety and is not harmful to the individual's right to privacy in such a magnitude as to outweigh the benefits of employee safety.

The Components of a Great Affirmative or Negative Case

In building a case, remember that an intuitive approach to the resolution produces a more successful case. The more creative you are in developing the case, while still remaining realistic and rational, the greater the difficulty your opponent has in defeating your case. Creative here means cleverness and knowledge of the topic. It is not enough to list the first three ideas that come to mind while constructing the case. To develop a great case, either affirmative or negative, a debater must devote diligent hours of research to the topic. In doing so, it is important that you conduct research on the general topic area. It is important that you understand the background of the case so that you can be creative and responsive to your opponent's arguments.

The actual components of a case are dependent on the topic. As a consequence, actual cases are not provided in this section. What is discussed, however, is the thought process that is involved in creating any case. It is far more important that you learn the process of creating a case, instead of learning someone else's case. The ability to write and understand your own ideas on a topic enables you to better defend and extend arguments in rebuttals. An average case you designed, wrote, and understand is far better than an excellent case that someone else has written for you. In the following sections you'll find listed the top 11 guideposts in learning to develop effective affirmative and negative cases.

1. Develop the Right Attitude

The most important facet to developing good case structure is the attitude toward the resolution. Researching the topic is impossible if you cannot muster at least some degree of excitement about the topic. A positive attitude produces positive results. The ability to sound persuasive while discussing a topic depends on your attitude about the topic. If you had to persuade your parents, with which of the following topics would you be most effective: 1) "The time of your curfew," or 2) "The wisdom of the U.S. leaving the gold standard?" The answer should be obvious. You could be equally persuasive in both areas after adequate research, but the lack of personal interest in the second topic area prevents a tone of sincerity. In the first topic area you have a vested interest, and, thus, you are more persuasive in your delivery. Because you are interested in a topic, your attitude towards research and delivery is much more positive, and much more effective. It is important that you create an attitude of personal attachment to the resolution. If the resolution is poor, as some are, just remember that everyone has to deal with the same resolution. If it is a difficult topic, you should be greatly inspired to work that much harder, since all of the weak debaters will be weeded out because of its difficulty. If it is an easy topic, you should be able to create a case early, and then expand on some ideas of your own to make the resolution difficult for your opponents. Either way, remember that everyone must debate the same topic, and it is a waste of time to be frustrated and intimidated by its degree of difficulty. Develop a positive attitude, and go with it.

2. Decide Your Value and Prepare to Defend It

You must choose the value on which you base your case. This part of Lincoln-Douglas works much like a circle. You must choose a value to defend in your case, and then your case must show that your value is derived from the resolution. A proper link will allow you to claim that affirming the resolution enhances your value A in society. Furthermore, you will be able to claim that negating the resolution will diminish your value A in society. The five standards in this section describe the values that are not only easily defended, but also easy to use in competition. Deciding your value is the first step, and this is largely arbitrary. It is important, however, that your value is derived easily from the resolution. For example, a resolution concerning the protection of the environment versus the development of natural resources easily leads to the values of progress, safety, life, quality of life, etc. It is not, however, easy to link them to the values of democracy, privacy, knowledge, etc. As an affirmative or negative you may choose any of an infinite number of values. This step in case development is easy. The second step in case development is making the link between the value chosen and the resolution. How does protecting the environment (affirming the resolution) produce the value of "life"? In all cases, answer how affirming the resolution (if you are affirmative) produces the chosen value.

3. Choose Criteria

The next step in creating the case is to choose the criteria for the round. What standard should the judge use to compare the values in the round? Will the value that delivers the greatest good to the greatest number of people be the best value to choose? If so, you will choose utilitarianism as your criteria. Will the value that produces the most benefits with the fewest corresponding harms be the best value in the round? If so, you will choose cost benefit analysis as your criteria. Will the value that helps the future generations the most be the best value in the round? If so, you will choose futurism (Nietszche) as your criteria. The criteria you choose should give an advantage to your value. For example, the value of security is a good match with the criteria of utilitarianism because it applies to many people in the society. Thus, you should tell the judge from the outset that the value that delivers the greatest good to the greatest number of people (utilitarianism) will be the best value in the round. Then you will give an advantage to your value of "security." Notice that your value already has an advantage in helping you defeat your opponent. It is also important that you fully understand your choice of a criteria. The criteria should show the value that you uphold in the round is the better choice of values in the round. Even when your value is completely incomparable to your opponent's, the criteria should convince the judge that your value is the one that should be chosen. If you are still unclear on this point, refer to Chapter 5 for a better understanding. Not every resolution and/or value fits the same criteria. Be prepared to analyze which of the criteria given in this book (or some of your own) fits your chosen value.

4. Isolate the Major Source of Conflict

The major source of conflict is defined as the underlying conflict of values within the resolution. In many instances the underlying conflict in a resolution is the same as other resolutions previously debated. For example, a resolution on drug testing has as its major conflict the individual versus society. A resolution concerning the individual's right to know versus national security might also pit the value of the individual against the value of society. Thus, major sources of conflict coincide.

The ability to identify this major source of conflict enables you to draw upon any experience in regard to past topics. For example, if you had already debated drug testing earlier in the year, you may be able to use some of the same "generic" arguments about individual rights versus society's rights when you debate a topic about national security and the right to know. Being able to capitalize on this experience will give you an advantage over opponents.

In this example we have seen that the rights of the individual versus the rights of society underlies many topics. Mandatory drug testing, genetic engineering, freedom of the press versus the right to a fair trial, and many other resolutions have this underlying theme as its foundation. While the specific deliberations in each round differ from one topic to the next, each of these topics has common, generic arguments that apply to other resolutions. If you can identify the underlying theme in the resolution, you can use your past experience in debating some of these common, generic arguments from past resolutions.

Identifying this common theme will also help you recall some of the more effective arguments in other resolutions and how these arguments were or were not defeated. If a debater could have the same confidence at the beginning of a topic's season that he or she has at the end of the season, he or she would be unbeatable. Identifying this underlying source of value conflict from other related resolutions enables you to gain that initial "unbeatable status."

In addition, knowing the underlying theme of conflict enables the debater to better focus on the major theme of the resolution. This prevents you from drifting into tangents when you write the case which, in turn, makes you more persuasive. Some common themes include:

Individual Rights versus the Rights of Society
Right to Know versus National Security
Safety/Environment versus Technological Progress
Privacy versus Social Protection
Free Press versus Censorship (Morality)

5. Isolate Arguments That Are Major Conflict Points

You should not only isolate the major theme of conflict, but also isolate some of the major points of conflict. In each resolution there will be re-occurring battles over the same arguments. As you debate more and more rounds on the same topic, you should come to identify the re-occurring points of conflict. As you debate successive rounds, make a note of these arguments (points of conflict), and prepare your case for future rounds accordingly. For example, if you anticipate the negative debater will present argument A, build within your case the natural response to argument A. In this way you have the advantage of not only making a stronger argument of your own, but also of presenting your defense to the anticipated counter-argument. Including responses in a case prior to an opponent's arguments is called a *spike* in the case. Spiking a case is advantageous in that it takes away an opponent's argument. Spiking should be disguised so that it appears to be actual support for the case and not an obvious response to what is expected of the opponent. It should not be so obvious that it sounds like: "My opponent is going to say this, so I will say this . . ." The ability to build responses to an opponent's anticipated attacks rests upon the ability to isolate re-occurring points of conflict in the resolution.

Isolating the main points of the argument also can increase your research power. If you can identify which arguments will appear in many of the debate rounds, you can devote more time to researching and understanding these arguments. Some resolutions will have obvious points of conflict. Others will require that you call upon past experience to assist you in being persuasive. Practice rounds are an excellent source of developing the experience that is the foundation of anticipating certain attacks from opponents.

6. Build Your Dream Case of Arguments

If you recall the opening statements of this chapter, the greatest advantage a debater can have in a resolution is to be "clever and knowledgeable." Your creativity will upend opponents who have not invested sufficient time to know and understand the topic. You can best develop this creativity through *brainstorming* on the topic. Brainstorming is essentially the process of thinking out every possible argument that comes to mind, and writing those arguments down. Do not censor any argument because it is silly or because you don't think you could find adequate evidence to support it. After brainstorming, build your *dream case*. Pretend you can support any idea that you can conceive. After you have made this wish list of case arguments, begin your research. Determine which of the arguments are reasonable and for which of your ideas evidence can be found. Determine which arguments will require support from documentation, and which will be supported by logic.

Preparing for Lincoln-Douglas debate is not like writing a book report or a research paper. Lincoln-Douglas debate is a mixture of documented knowledge and unique ideas and logic. Combine research, present and past theories and philosophies, and individual logic to create new and persuasive arguments on the topic. This creativity depends on the brainstorming/dream case process. If you use this process, you will be surprised at how many arguments you will develop. The obvious argument will never win a big tournament. Capitalize on your own creative abilities!

7. Organize Your Case Points

After completing Case Point Six, you should have a general list of arguments that support one side of the resolution. Now you must organize these ideas so your audience or judge can follow your train of thought. There is no need to put everything into discrete points, subpoints, and double subpoints. Instead, design an organization of ideas that effectively groups similar arguments and creates a natural progression through the case.

When writing your case, use no more than four and no fewer than two main contentions. Most debaters seem to find three contentions best. In general, the first contention should address your value and how it is linked to the resolution. How does affirming a resolution advocating mandatory drug testing create the value of "safety"? The first point should answer this question. The second contention should deal directly with the resolution's topic, in this case, mandatory drug testing. What types of benefits will result from affirming the resolution on mandatory drug testing? What harms can be expected to resort from affirming the resolution? How do these harms relate to the benefits of "mandatory drug testing?" The third point largely is up to you. Some debaters use the third point to support the value. Others use the third point to support the criteria or the value or both.

The order of these points can be switched around. It is not mandatory that the suggested point be first. The order should, however, follow a sequence of logical progression. Each point should make a smooth transition to the next point. It is absolutely crucial in the organization of the case that related arguments be grouped together, and that the following questions be answered:

- How does your value derive from the resolution?
- What benefits can be expected from the resolution, i.e., why should we affirm the resolution?
- Why is your value and criteria more important and more appropriate than your opponent's?

8. Collect Evidence

At this point in case construction, begin looking for evidence that supports the arguments established in Case Points Five, Six, and Seven. After completing Case Point Seven, you should have a rough sketch of the case construction. Now attempt to find documentation to support each claim. There will be some arguments that will require more evidence than others, namely the "hot topics" described in Case Point Five. Use ideas from Chapter 6 to assist in gathering support for case arguments.

9. Polish the Case

After developing the case's structure and support, you are now ready to try the case on for size. Practice rounds are a critical component of this stage. Do not think that once you have designed a case you are ready to go to a tournament and win. First, debate teammates or debaters from other schools. After several practice rounds, you will see the obvious weak spots in the case. You may also discover some of your opponents' points that were difficult to beat. You should be eager to delete points in your case that were easily destroyed, and incorporate into your case your responses to your opponents' tough argument. Writing the case is not a one time event; instead, it involves continual revision. The amount of polish put on the case is directly proportional to the number of practice rounds prior to a tournament.

The more you practice the more you will realize which points need extra support in rebuttals. Begin finding *extension evidence* to help these points survive your opponents' rebuttals. Extension evidence is vital to the debater who wants to finish the round with strong momentum, and it is an essential part of building the case. You will find that some points are so strong that logic alone carries them through the round. Other points, however, require additional support as well as reasoning. Extension evidence is discussed in Unit III, Refutation and Rebuttals.

10. Sensitize Yourself 24 Hours a Day to the Topic

Each day you should be conscious of everything you hear and see concerning the topic. While watching the news, hearing a history teacher lecture, or reading the newspaper be conscious of any new idea that might add to the case. You will be surprised how much pertinent information comes your way. Some of the best arguments come from some of your teachers, so be attentive.

It is advantageous to ask different people what they think of the topic to get their perspectives on the ethical dilemma. Anyone can provide a fresh look at a complicated topic that just might spur a new argument. Understanding as many of these perceptions as possible gives you a greater advantage in debating your opponent. If you can understand your opponents' thought process, you can predict what he or she will say, and pre-empt his or her arguments. This ability, however, rests in understanding a number of different perceptions from a number of different people.

It is also a good idea to carry your case notes with you at all times. When you have a few extra minutes during the day, take the case out and think about what could be added, what the opponent might say to each of your contentions, or what could be said to better illustrate a point. Constant attention to the case can generate a number of new and refreshing ideas for even the most tired and worn-out cases.

11. Write the Opposing Case

The initial case you decide to write, affirmative or negative, should be based on the philosophy closest to your own. This ensures that you have momentum going into the topic and that you maintain the proper attitude while starting research. There will come a time, however, when you must start developing the other case. Developing the opposing side will strengthen your case.

As you might guess, the above ten suggestions should all be used in writing the opposing case. As you proceed through these ten steps, note that your previous case is a great tool in developing your present case. Occasionally, it will help to use your first case to start the brainstorming process in developing the second case's structure. Begin by looking at the first case. Try to come up with arguments that refute all of the contentions in the first case. This should get you started in the process of developing the second case.

When writing the second case, attempt to beat the initial case, and assume that first case is the best case you will ever compete against. Design each case so that it can stand up to the other. The negative should be designed to beat the affirmative, and vice-versa. The wisdom in this approach is two-fold: first, this process prevents writer's block and keeps you focused on the main point; second, this process allows development of the second case at the same time you are challenging your first case's contentions. This technique can expose any weak arguments in your initial case. This procedure also allows development of a *dialectic mind-set* (the ability to think of two sides of an issue at one time). This technique allows you to succeed within the actual round, because you are better able to anticipate your opponent's attacks on both sides of the resolution.

After you develop the second case, you will have both an affirmative and a negative case. Continue going back and forth between the affirmative and the negative cases. Use the affirmative case to challenge the negative case. How well does the negative respond to the claims made by the affirmative? How well can the affirmative refute the claims of the negative? In essence, the affirmative is built in response to some of the claims your negative case makes, and the negative is built in response to the affirmative arguments. Conduct "mini-debates" between your affirmative and negative cases within your own mind. If done properly, this exercise can be as valuable as actual practice rounds since you will begin to get a feel for what it takes to defeat each of your points. This is advantageous in that you also will know what you can do to prevent these attacks if your opponent uses them against you. You will also have a solid line-up of "attacks" of your own to launch against opponent's contentions that are similar to your own.

It should be noted, however, that both the negative and the affirmative should be separate and unique cases. The affirmative is not based on the same philosophy as the negative case. Instead, the intent of Case Point Ten is to facilitate thought on one philosophy by examining that philosophy and arguing against the other philosophy. Essentially, you are taking the initial case and arguing against it. As you argue against it, you will begin to understand the alternate philosophy upon which the opposing case is based. Once you have gained that understanding, and have developed some key arguments against that philosophy, proceed to the other case and start its original construction. The affirmative and the negative should not be a point by point reflection of each other, but instead should be used to discover the strong and weak points of each opposing philosophy.

Conclusion

The affirmative and negative constructive case processes are similar. As a consequence, the above 11 steps should be used with both sides. In addition, a debater never outgrows the need for creative thought on a resolution. Good debaters use the above steps to become good, and then stop using them once they are there. Great debaters continue to use them for the rest of their debating careers. No one ever outgrows the need for creativity in a debate case.

Suggested Activities

1. As a class, brainstorm a dream case over the current topic or one given in the text.

2. Make a list of sources from which evidence can be collected.

3. Write a report that details the responsibility the student has with a given resolution to each of the following debate responsibilities: value, criteria, and underlying conflict.

Sample Affirmative Case

(This case does not include all transitions or previews as the writer had these memorized.)

Matt Schmitz*

Mortimer J. Adler was quoted in 1963 as saying that "According to the individualist view, it is the fulfillment of the individual that comes first. The state is merely an instrument to serve the individual good." It is in concurrence with this statement that I stand firmly resolved: **"That society benefits more from individuality than it does from conformity."**

Society: an association of persons united together for the benefit of the individual,

Individuality: the quality of state of existing as an individual, and finally

Conformity: Correspondence in form or manner, imitation

Now, for philosophical clarification I offer the following value contentions:

Value Contention 1: The purpose of a society is to better the individuals therein. When societies are founded their main purpose is to increase the individual's happiness. Without individuals we would have no societies. John Dos Passos tells us in his work, *A Question of Elbow Room*:

"Protection of the individual's happiness—the assurance of the elbow room he needed to reach his full stature—was the reason for the state's existence."

Therefore, a society is best benefited when the individuals comprising it are best benefited. Keep this point in mind, this is key. With this in mind we now need to look at:

Value Contention 2: Where we see that the individual can only be benefited through the expression of individuality. Only with this expression can a person be fulfilled. If someone conformed to what everyone else was doing merely because others were doing it the person gains no practice in either discerning or in desiring what is best. Without this choice; without this individuality a person can never be strengthened. Imagine a person's faculties as being a muscle. They can only be improved by being used, but if a person merely imitates everyone else these never get used, nor do they get worked. Only through being an individual can a person develop to the fullest. John Stuart Mill, a famous philosopher, expounds in his essay "On Liberty":

"But different persons also require different conditions for their spiritual development; and can no more exist healthily in the same moral, than all the variety of plants can in the same physical atmosphere and climate. The same things which are helps to one person towards the cultivation of his higher nature, are hindrances to another."

We can obviously see that the individual can only be benefited through individuality, therefore society can only be benefited through individuality. When these individuals are benefited they are also more capable of helping the ones around them and helping society as a whole. Again John Stuart Mill explains to us in "On Liberty":

"In proportion to the development of his individuality, each person becomes more valuable to himself, and is therefore capable of being more valuable to others. There is a greater fullness of life about his own existence, and when there is more life in the units there is more in the mass which is composed of them."

Furthermore, I feel it essential to turn to:

Value Contention 3: Where we see that individuality is imperative for adaptability. Frequently, when analyzing different societies, the most successful ones are the ones that are able to adapt to different problems. In free societies, emphasis is placed on individuality. In turn, this leads to the development of new ideas and innovations. Free thinking people are paramount for the flexibility to respond appropriately to threats to our civilization. If everyone conformed to everything a society did, they would risk slipping into a type of "mechanical" existence. There is always a need to discover new practices, to uncover new truths. Without free thinkers continually solving problems and adapting to new ones, a society would probably stagnate and die. Again John Stuart Mill observes:

"There is too great a tendency in the best beliefs and practices to degenerate into the mechanical; and unless there were a succession of persons whose ever-recurring originality prevents the grounds of those beliefs and practices from becoming merely traditional, such dead matter would not resist the smallest shock from anything really alive, and there would be no reason why civilization should not die out, as in the Byzantine Empire."

We constantly require these original thinkers for our society to be benefited. However, individuality is important for other reason as stated in:

Value Contention 4: Where we see that individuality is essential for other fundamental values. First, the value of freedom. Individuals are necessary to keep a society in check. If everyone conformed to what a government dictated, then it would be very easy for that government to slip into tyranny and restrict the necessary freedoms of the people. Secondly, please consider the value of happiness and the right to pursue it. Under conformity a person is unable to pursue individual happiness. As we can see in value contention two, individuality is needed for self-fulfillment. It is also only through self-fulfillment that a person can truly be happy. John Stuart Mill again explains to us in "On Liberty":

"Such are the differences among human beings in their sources of pleasure, their susceptibilies of pain, and the operation on them of different physical and moral agencies, that unless there is a corresponding diversity in their modes of life, they neither obtain their fair share of happiness, nor grow up to the mental, moral, and aesthetic stature of which their nature is capable."

Now, thirdly, consider the value of progress. Without creativity, without originality, progress is impossible. The prosperity of a society is dependent on the fresh ideas and innovations of its individuals. Historically, this has proved to be true. Generally, the successful societies, and the ones which experience the greatest amount of progress, are the ones which place emphasis on individual thought and action. Albert Einstein, noted thinker and scientist, wrote in "Ideas and Opinion":

"Without creative personalities able to think and judge independently, the upward development of society is as unthinkable as the development of the individual without the nourishing soil of the community."

My four value contentions make your decision a simple one. We must realize that society can only be benefited through individual development. And only through this individual development can we adapt to our problems. We must realize that individualism is necessary for freedom, the pursuit of happiness, and progress. Obviously, we can see that only through individuality can a society truly be benefited. I thank you and now yield to any questions the negative might have.

Sample Negative Case
Matt Schmitz*

(The negative case is shown in outline rather than manuscript form. This allows a debater to adapt the introduction and transitional material throughout the speech to the affirmative case points to allow for comparisons.)

Value Contention 1: The purpose of a society is to maintain social order. A society is best benefited when social order is maintained. James S. Campbell explains in the book *Law and Order Reconsidered*:

"A society, whether primitive tribe or modern nation, may be looked upon as a complex of human institutions whose purpose it is to secure some measure of social order. These institutions may have other purposes and fill other needs; but the achievement of order is a fundamental part of their function."

Value Contention 2: Conformity is needed for social order.

1. The definition of society proves this:
     -*Black's Law Dictionary:* An association or company of persons united together by mutual CONSENT in order to deliberate, determine, and act JOINTLY for some COMMON purpose.
     -We cannot act jointly without conformity.

2. Obedience to law and standards imperative for social order.
     -New York example
     -if no one followed rules we would have ANARCHY
     -only through conformity can order be attained
     Immanual Kant, a famous philosopher, tells us in *The Philosophy of Law*:

"Resistance on the part of the people to the supreme legislative power of the state is in no case legitimate, for it is only by submission to the universal legislative will that a condition of law and order is possible."

3. Criteria can only be meet through conformity.
     -society can only be benefited from conformity
     -Locke – would degenerate to the point of its collapse
     -order important as we will see in . . .

Value Contention 3: Social order is essential for fundamental values.

1. Survival needs
     -New York example
     -James S. Campbell again expounds in the book *Law and Order Reconsidered*:

"Why is social order so universally sought by groups of men? A number of answers might be offered. One important answer is that human welfare demands, at a minimum, sufficient order to ensure that such basic needs as food production, shelter, and child rearing be satisfied, not in a state of constant chaos and conflict, but on a peaceful, orderly basis with a reasonable level of day-to-day security."

-Cannot attain ANY other values

2. Justice
   -Law is essential for justice
   -No order = no law
   -In an unordered society justice is impossible
   David Hume, a famous philosopher, tells us in his essay "On Justice":

"Thus, the rules of equity or justice depend entirely on the particular state and condition, in which men are placed, and owe their origin and existence to that UTILITY, which results to the public from their strict and regular observance."

-Justice is essential
     -Central to our constitution and government
     -What we base our society on

3. Happiness
   -Individuals can only acquire happiness through an ordered society
   -Self-fulfillment is impossible without order
     -TOO BUSY WITH SURVIVAL NEEDS
   -Mortimer J. Adler expresses this view in his book *Great Ideas from the Great Books*:

"A well-constituted, and justly ordered state contributes to the happiness of the individuals it comprises. And a civic-minded and conscientious individual contributes to the happiness of others by fulfilling his duties as a citizen."

-Happiness is paramount.
-Basic right
-Declaration of Independence
-Always striving for it

*Matt Schmitz, from Silver Lake High School in Kansas, attended the National Forensic League National Tournament in 1990, 1991, and 1992. He placed 15th out of 200 debaters in 1992. He also attended the Catholic Forensic League Nationals in 1991 and 1992. This is his 1991 CFL speech.

Chapter 13
Affirmative and Negative Constructives

Learning Objectives

Chapter 13 explains the affirmative and negative constructives. The affirmative constructive is the first speech given in Lincoln-Douglas debate, and as such is critical in setting the tone of the round. The negative constructive is the first opportunity to present the negative's side of the resolution. The affirmative and negative constructives share many components, but the negative also includes the first negative rebuttal to the affirmative case. As seen in Chapters 9, 10, 11, and 12, the first speech on each side has many components. This chapter explains how to integrate each of these components into the first speech of the round.

After completing this chapter you should be able to:

1. **Understand the distinction between the case and the constructive.**

2. **Explain what information and elements should be presented in the affirmative and negative constructives.**

3. **Explain the negative constructive strategy when the affirmative and negative share the same value.**

New Terms

Constructive
Alternative definitions
Affirmative game plan
Block

Negative case
Negative constructive
Presumption
Prima facie

First negative rebuttal

Introduction

The affirmative constructive is the first speech of the round. The affirmative has the power to set the round's standards as well as the overall momentum. As a consequence, it is very important that the affirmative constructive be a persuasive speech.

The affirmative constructive is unique in that it is the only speech in the entire round that is not dependent upon what the opponent presents. While the first four to five minutes of the negative constructive are pre-planned, the last two to three minutes are dependent upon the affirmative's value, criteria, and definitions. Because of this self-sufficiency, there is no excuse why the affirmative constructive should not be absolutely polished. The affirmative has the opportunity to prepare a six-minute speech that will be delivered just as it was rehearsed. The judge also expects that the affirmative constructive will be well rehearsed.

Distinction Between the Constructive and the Case

As a matter of definition, there is a difference between the term "constructive" and "case." The term, *constructive*, is defined as the first speech in the round delivered by each debater. Note that the constructive is the speech time allotted to the debater, not what is actually said in this speech time. The case, on the other hand, is what the debater presents in this speech time to support the value, criteria, and contentions.

The constructive is the speech period, and the case is what the debater says within that period to uphold a position on the resolution. The distinction has little impact on the affirmative. The affirmative constructive and the affirmative are the same thing, since the affirmative has nothing else to present except support for the case and the related elements: opening, interim, etc. For the negative debater, however, the distinction is critical. The negative presents both a case and a first rebuttal to the affirmative case within the negative constructive. The case is only one element of the negative constructive; the first negative rebuttal is the other. Knowing and understanding this distinction is critical. The case is contained within the constructive. The case is what is discussed; the constructive is the time allotted to the debater to present a position.

The Difference Between the Negative Case and Constructive

There is a distinction between the negative case and constructive because the debater may say something other than about the case within a speech period. Not only is it possible, it is a reality in the negative constructive. The constructive contains not only the negative case, but also the first negative rebuttal.

After the affirmative case is presented, the affirmative constructive is completed. The affirmative case is perfectly timed to fit into the six minutes allowed for the affirmative constructive speech.

This book treats the *negative constructive* speech as having two parts: the *negative case* and the first negative rebuttal. Do not confuse the term *first negative rebuttal* with what most people call "the negative rebuttal." The "negative rebuttal" is the speech period that comes between the first and second affirmative rebuttals and is referred to in this book as the "second negative rebuttal." Note the format of a Lincoln-Douglas debate:

Lincoln-Douglas Debate

Affirmative Constructive

Negative Cross-Examination

Negative Constructive
  •The Negative Case
  •The **First Negative** Rebuttal

Affirmative Cross-Examination

First Affirmative Rebuttal

Second Negative Rebuttal

Second Affirmative Rebuttal

The negative philosophy has two total speeches: the negative constructive and the negative rebuttal. Within those two speeches, the negative has three things to present: the negative case, the first negative rebuttal (located within the negative constructive), and the second negative rebuttal.

Understanding this separation is vital to your ability to perform the necessary duties in the negative constructive. To be successful as a negative, you literally will have to shift gears in the middle of the negative constructive and perform an entirely different duty. Begin your negative case just as you begin your affirmative constructive (i.e., with your case). Unlike the affirmative, however, you should then shift from a "case mode" to a "rebuttal mode" and proceed to attack the affirmative case as a part of your first negative rebuttal.

Presumption

Both the negative and the affirmative share in the weight of *presumption*. This means that the affirmative debater and the negative debater each has an equal responsibility in proving his or her respective side of the resolution. It is not enough for the negative to contend that the affirmative is wrong; he or she must also contend that the negative side of the resolution is right. If the affirmative does not prove the resolution "affirmed," and the negative does not prove it "negated," the ballot goes to the more persuasive debater, not automatically to the negative. Considering this, it is easy to see why the negative case is as important to the round as the affirmative case.

To a certain extent, the negative case is similar to the affirmative case. The following section discusses the building of the negative constructive speech, and how this process is both similar to and, at the same time, different from building the affirmative constructive. Initially, it may help to review some of the essential concepts in the construction of the case. The following subsections list and describe the important elements of the negative case and the negative constructive speech. Keep in mind that there is a distinct difference between the negative case and the negative constructive.

Important Elements in the Case

This section illustrates the elements that must be present in affirmative and negative cases if they are to be successful. Each element begins with an explanation of the affirmative and common applications and is followed by the explanation of negative case applications when they differ from the affirmative.

The Value

The value supported by the case is the most important facet of the round. After all, Lincoln-Douglas debate, in its purest form, is "value debate." The basis of the affirmative case should be the value supported by the affirmative philosophy. The affirmative must identify and support a value in order to win the round. Furthermore, this value must be identified in the affirmative constructive. Otherwise, the debaters have nothing upon which to make a comparison, and the judge has nothing upon which to make a decision.

In some rare instances, both the affirmative and the negative will choose the same value on which to base their case. The affirmative should still maintain its value as **the** value in the round, but should not need to offer extensive proof of the value's merit since both sides have agreed on the value. Instead, the affirmative should devote more time to proving how affirming the resolution better achieves the value in question. All of this, however, is not known by the affirmative until after the negative constructive. For the purposes of the affirmative constructive, proceed with the assumption that the negative will offer a different value. Thus, it is important that you support the merits of your value in your affirmative case.

The basis of the negative case should be the value supported by the negative philosophy. If the negative does not support a value, winning the round is impossible. It is difficult to win an event based upon value comparison if you have no value with which to compare to your opponent's. For more information on the selection of values, review Chapter 4.

The Criteria

It is also important to establish a "mechanism" by which the judge is to evaluate the values in the round. The affirmative philosophy must provide a criteria with which the judge is to evaluate the round. Provide the judge with a voting standard of how to evaluate the values. In most cases, the negative will present a value that is entirely different from the affirmative value. The judge, therefore, is left with the difficult task of comparing two different values. Without a means of evaluation (the criteria) the comparison of two different values may not be possible. Therefore, it is necessary for the affirmative to present a criteria by which to evaluate the relative worth of the two values in question.

It is important for the affirmative to define its own criteria. If the affirmative relies upon the negative's criteria for evaluation, the affirmative value is disadvantaged. If you are selling the judge a "mini-van" based upon the criteria of speed, car performance, and fashion, you will have to do quite a sale. In order to make your "sale" of the value easier, it is imperative that you define your own criteria for the affirmative case.

To illustrate the importance of defining the affirmative criteria, consider the following example where the affirmative relies upon the negative criteria for evaluating the values in the round on the topic: "Resolved: The individual's right to know ought to be valued above that of national security." The negative has defined the criteria in the round to be utilitarianism. The negative has chosen the value of safety, while the affirmative has chosen the value of knowledge. The negative makes the claim that since safety is important to most people in the society, it is the better of the two values. The negative goes on to say that while the value of knowledge has its merits, it does not produce the "greatest good for the greatest number," which the value of safety does. The affirmative can show that the merits knowledge provides for a few individuals are significant, but this is insignificant in this situation. The benefits to a few people are great. However, the criteria in the round, utilitarianism, supports the value that helps the greatest number of people. Had the affirmative defined a criteria of cost benefit analysis, the value would have been supported by the argument that the benefits of knowledge outweighed the harms. Without a criteria, the affirmative is forced to prove that knowledge is a better value than safety under the standard of utilitarianism. Since the negative value was chosen to fit the negative criteria, the affirmative is forced to operate at a disadvantage from the start.

In the negative case, it is also important to establish a "mechanism" by which the judge is to evaluate the round. The criteria in the negative case is equally as important as it was in the affirmative case. The negative philosophy has to provide a criteria with which the judge is to the evaluate the round. Without this means of evaluation, the comparison of two different values may not be possible. If the negative must rely upon the affirmative criteria for evaluation, the affirmative value will have an advantage from the start. The negative, like the affirmative, should select a criteria that is partial to the negative value. Allowing the affirmative to define the criteria in the round can be disastrous. It is imperative to be conscious of the criteria supported by the affirmative, and be ready to redefine that criteria if it is not preferential to the negative cause.

The Introduction

It is important that both the affirmative and negative cases have an introduction that is attention getting and persuasive. The opening should not be too dramatic, as realism is the best way to establish rapport with the judge. The opening should reveal your personality as a debater. As is illustrated in Chapter 9, the opening's sole purpose is to establish rapport with the judge upon which the foundations of persuasion can be constructed. The introduction should not be elaborate in either its content or its length. It is to your advantage to keep the introduction short and to the point. Thirty seconds is usually adequate. Establish rapport with the judge in the opening, keep it short, and keep it to the point, and you will develop a perfect opening to either the affirmative or negative philosophy. For questions about case openings, review Chapter 9.

The Interim

The interim that is described in Chapter 10 should be used to connect the case opening to the case points for both the affirmative and negative. Make the transition from the opening to the resolution, recite the resolution from memory, state the position on the resolutions, give the definitions on the affirmative, and present the case preview.

The Definitions

As was described in Chapter 11, the affirmative has a responsibility to start the round with definitions of the key terms in the resolution. It is important that the affirmative define only the major terms in the resolution. Lincoln-Douglas does not hinge upon the technical wording of the resolution, but on the intent of the resolution; thus, definitions of every term are not necessary. The affirmative should define the important terms in a straightforward fashion. Trying to win a round on definitions rarely works in Lincoln-Douglas. As a consequence, defining the parameters of the resolution in a fair manner is the best way to approach definitions in the round.

In Chapter 11, the use of alternate definitions was discussed in reference to the negative case. The affirmative can also make use of these definition standards. If you have defined the terms fairly in the resolution, and the negative still insists on re-defining the terms, use the negative definition standards to ensure that your opponent fulfills his or her responsibilities in making re-definitions. Negative alternate definitions require that the negative present some standard of why the affirmative definitions are flawed, and why the negative definitions are superior. Just because your opponent wants a different definition does not warrant a justification for an alternate definition. If the affirmative has unfairly limited the parameters of discussion in the round by using unfair or biased definitions, the negative should redefine the terms. Doing so requires presentation of some standard explaining why the affirmative definitions are bad, and why the negative definitions are superior. A debater must show why that definition is superior, and you should hold the opponent to that responsibility. Review Chapter 11 for the reasons that warrant use of negative over affirmative definitions.

Even if the negative offers new definitions, the affirmative should not engage in extended argumentation over definitions as they are rarely critical to the round's outcome. Establish affirmative definitions, and then make the negative prove why counter definitions are superior.

If the affirmative definitions are fair and unbiased, the negative should grant those definitions. Granting fair definitions economizes time on the case and lengthens time spent on the negative rebuttal. Do not define your own definitions if they are the same as or similar to the affirmative's. Knowing whether you can accept or must challenge the affirmative's definitions requires that you listen closely to how the affirmative defines the standards of the resolution.

Case Points

A debater must present and support a case that upholds its justification for either affirming or negating the resolution. The negative case should be shorter than the affirmative case. The negative constructive is seven minutes long, which gives the negative one more minute than the affirmative constructive. The negative, however, has the responsibility of presenting the first negative rebuttal as well as the negative case within the negative constructive. It is crucial to leave time at the end of the negative constructive to attack the affirmative case. This is made possible only by shortening the negative case. In most cases, this means shortening or eliminating the definitions and limiting the evidence used for support under each argument of the negative case. This does not mean that the negative should shorten the number of arguments supporting a position, but instead should be conscious of the length or number of evidence cards supporting each point. This may result in the negative deferring some evidence cards until the second negative rebuttal when time permits.

The negative cannot win in Lincoln-Douglas without a case. Since there is no inherent presumption in Lincoln-Douglas, the negative has a responsibility to negate the resolution just as the affirmative has to affirm it. The negative must present and support a case that accomplishes this goal. The negative must attack the affirmative case. Typically, the case deals with four responsibilities. These responsibilities, if met, work in concert to establish the debate's value, the value's merits, the degree to which the value is achieved, and the merits of the criteria. These four primary issues are as follows:

First, both affirmative and negative cases should derive a value from the resolution. On the topic, "Resolved: The individual's right to know ought to be valued over national security," the affirmative must show that the value of knowledge can be derived from the resolution. The affirmative can accomplish this goal by showing that affirming the resolution and giving priority to the individual's right to know translates into knowledge for that individual. The negative must show that safety can be derived from the resolution. The negative can accomplish this goal by showing that negating the resolution and giving priority to national security translates into guaranteeing society the value of "safety."

The second case responsibility is to show that the significance of the value warrants choosing it over another value. In the above example of the individual's right to know versus national security, the value of national security is compromised if we affirm the resolution and choose the value of knowledge. As a result, the affirmative must show that the value of knowledge is achieved to a high degree by affirming the resolution. Because individual rights will be compromised by negating the resolution, we must be absolutely positive that individuals will receive necessary knowledge in order to justify this reduction in social safety.

Conversely, if the resolution is negated, the value of the individual's right to know is compromised. As a result, the negative must show that the value of safety is achieved to a high degree by negating the resolution. In other words, safety is achieved by negating the resolution. Because the individual's right to know is compromised by negating the resolution, we must be absolutely positive that individuals will receive necessary national safety in order to justify this reduction in individual rights. This responsibility is generally accomplished by addressing the actual issue in the resolution, and making specific arguments.

The third case responsiibility of the affirmative case is to support the merits of the chosen value. Assuming that both affirmative and negative values are achieved equally, why should we choose one value over another? The case must show why your value is superior to your opponent's. For further information on how to establish value superiority, see Chapter 4.

The fourth case responsibility is to establish and support the validity of the affirmative or negative criteria. In the above example, the affirmative would probably choose the criteria of cost benefit analysis because the benefits of affirming the resolution are far greater than the costs. Since the costs of national security (the sacrifice of individual rights) might outweigh its benefits, this criteria would discriminate against the negative case. If the affirmative can establish that cost benefit analysis is the best standard by which the judge should evaluate the values in the round, the affirmative will probably win. Why? Because knowledge is a better value under the standards of cost benefit analysis (i.e., the benefits are greater than the costs), the judge should choose knowledge as the supreme value in the round. The affirmative case must make the point through supporting arguments and evidence.

The negative would probably choose the criteria of utilitarianism because a great number of people would enjoy the value of safety. Since only a few individuals enjoy the value of the right to know, the criterion of utilitarianism works well for the negative to discriminate against the affirmative value. If the negative can establish that utilitarianism is the best standard by which the judge should evaluate the values in the round, the negative will win. Why? Because safety is a better value under the standards of utilitarianism (i.e., more people benefit), the judge should choose safety as the supreme value in the round. The negative case must make the point through supporting arguments and evidence.

The Conclusion

Finally, it is important to end the constructive with a strong personable ending. It is not persuasive to end the constructive in the middle of an evidence card; nor is it persuasive to finish a speech with, "I am open for cross-examination." In the last fifteen to thirty seconds, step away from the podium, lay down your materials, come closer to the judge, and summarize the essence of the resolution and your case. Allow the judge to see that the debater who has been philosophizing for six or seven minutes is indeed a person. It is much more difficult to vote against a person than it is a philosophy.

Note that there is one essential difference between the negative and the affirmative conclusions. The affirmative conclusion is the last thing in the constructive speech and directly follows the affirmative case. The negative conclusion is also the last thing in the negative constructive, but it does not directly follow the negative case. Remember that the first negative rebuttal comes between the negative case and this conclusion. You must pull both aspects of the constructive together.

Unique Features of the Affirmative Case

Necessary Information

The negative has only two speeches to respond to what the affirmative presents in the round. To be fair to the negative, there is an understood rule in Lincoln-Douglas that every argument that supports the affirmation of the resolution should be presented in the first affirmative constructive. This does not mean that everything you have to say in the round must be presented in the affirmative constructive. The two affirmative rebuttals are designed to give the opportunity to present supporting evidence and to respond to arguments presented in the negative case. Your affirmative case, however, should be *prima facie*, which means that in the absence of rebuttal it should be able to stand alone and support your claim to affirm the resolution prior to anything being said by the negative.

The requirements for achieving prima facie statı s are many. You must present a value, criteria, definitions, and all the supporting arguments that link the value to the resolution and defend its worth. All of this must be presented in the affirmative constructive. You do not have the option of introducing your value in the affirmative rebuttals; nor do you have the option of presenting half of your contentions in the affirmative constructive and the other half in the affirmative rebuttals. You must present it all in the constructive if you hope to win as an affirmative.

The Affirmative Constructive Should Be Familiar

Since you have sufficient time to prepare for the presentation of the affirmative constructive, this speech should be as familiar as your name. You should know which contention says what and which subpoint supports what claim. Knowing your case allows you to better view where your opponent is making attacks against your case and enhances your ability to respond to those attacks. Familiarity with the case also allows a more persuasive presentation of the affirmative constructive.

Establish the Affirmative Game Plan.

As will be seen in Chapter 23, the use of a game plan is critical to success. Each individual debates with a different style, and each debater is best in the style that is most comfortable. If you can get your opponent to debate your style, it will put him or her at a disadvantage.

While enticing your opponent into debating in your style is complicated, an affirmative constructive can start this process. The degree of structure used in the speech should reflect your abilities. If you are comfortable with a high degree of structure, your affirmative case should reflect this. Hopefully, your opponent will try to respond to that structure in the same way you present it. If he or she is not familiar with a great deal of structure, this will give you an advantage in the round.

The same is also true for the level of speed at which you proceed and the types of arguments presented. If you are good at talking fast while still being persuasive, your affirmative case should reflect this. If you are good at pragmatic, or real world, non-philosophical arguments, you should try to incorporate those arguments into your speech. If an argument sounds great, but you do not understand it, do not use it.

Proceed with your style of debate. If you try to alter your style to fit the opponent, you will set yourself up to play your opponent's game plan. If the opponent does not debate your game plan, there is no huge loss. Just proceed with the rest of the round, but don't try to beat the opponent's game plan.

Anticipate Negative Arguments

An affirmative should anticipate the potential negative constructive argument. Initially, anticipate which arguments you cannot win as an affirmative. Depending on the resolution, some arguments cannot be won by even the best of debaters. Do not do your opponent a favor by introducing those arguments before he or she does.

It is also possible to anticipate how an opponent will respond to your arguments. Try to diffuse any arguments you can anticipate your opponent making in response to your case. This must be cleverly done as you do not want to disrupt the natural flow of your case. You also do not want to give your opponent ideas. Do not give an affirmative contention, provide what you anticipate your opponent will say, and then give a response. This gives your opponent the arguments he or she needs to defeat your case. Part of your case time is spent enumerating negative arguments, which is a waste of time.

Instead, present your contentions in such a way that possible objections to these contentions are resolved. For example, if you are supporting the individual's right to know, you might anticipate that your opponent will respond by saying that very few people actually enjoy the right to know; thus, it is less of a value. A subpoint under your first contention might be: "A. Many people enjoy the right to know."

In this way, you do not give the argument away; nor do you spend part of your speech time discussing arguments your opponent has not even presented. If, however, your opponent makes the argument in the negative construct that very few people actually enjoy the right to know, you can refer to your first subpoint. In this way, your judge gets an early look at an important response.

Have an Outline Copy of Each Case

It is advisable to have a copy of the affirmative and negative constructives written in outline form. These copies should be placed in a plastic holder for all rounds..

The merits of having an outline copy of the case are numerous. First, an outline allows efficient location of contention (or subpoint). It is important in high pressure situations that you know which of your contentions claims what pieces of truth. If asked in cross-examination what your second contention states, you can look at your outline form instead of shuffling through the case. During rebuttals, this outline can serve as a road map in directing and organizing the rebuttal. This ensures that you will not miss vital points of the case in the midst of a heated rebuttal. Since you will be more organized with the neatly written case outline, you will also be more relaxed and collected for presenting rebuttals. This quick reference in pressure situations can make a difference, since you will be able to find quickly what contention to cross apply to the negative case.

The Distribution of Time

In cross-examination team debate there is what is called a *negative block*, where the negative team has back-to-back speeches—the second negative constructive and first negative rebuttal. Lincoln-Douglas also has a negative block. Lincoln-Douglas debate's modification of this "negative block" is what we refer to as the negative constructive. In the above section on "The Difference Between the Negative Case and Constructive," we saw that the negative constructive consisted of the negative case and the first negative rebuttal. This consideration is important here in that time must be devoted accordingly.

The first four to four and one-half minutes of the negative constructive should be devoted to the negative case. If the affirmative case looks difficult to beat, limit the negative case to four minutes. Again, do not sacrifice arguments. Instead, limit the extensiveness of the evidence presented in support of each argument. If the affirmative case is simplistic and appears easy to beat, you can afford to spend more time on your negative case.

It is imperative that you begin your negative constructive with your negative case. This ensures that you give your case primary importance in the round. Beginning with your case also allows you to begin the negative constructive with a persuasive, rapport-generating opening. Because of your familiarity with the case, beginning with the negative case also gives you momentum going into the speech.

The final two and one-half to three minutes should be devoted to the first negative rebuttal. It is imperative that you attack the affirmative case. Where possible, you should use the techniques of cross applying and filtering (see Chapter 15) to save time. As is illustrated in Chapter 23, you must use your preparation time to have organized and supported attacks against the affirmative case. The attacks must be efficient and organized. Deliver your attack, choose specific words to explain the attack, and then proceed to the next argument. A strong, efficient attack, at this point, can win the round.

Again, the final 15 to 30 seconds should be devoted to the delivery of a persuasive conclusion. Remember, sell yourself as a person as much as you sell your case as a negative philosophy.

Definition Standards

One of the best ways to save time in the negative case is to agree with the affirmative definitions and proceed to the negative case. You can do this only when the affirmative has presented definitions that are unbiased and fair to the negative philosophy. If the affirmative presents biased definitions, redefine the definitions according to your standards. There are two requirements the negative must meet in redefining the definitions. First, the negative must show that the affirmative's definitions are biased; and, second, the negative must show why the negative definitions are superior. Chapter 11 explains the standards warranting negative counter-definitions.

When affirmative definitions are acceptable, skip the negative definitions by stating, "The terms of the resolution are acceptable as defined by the affirmative." This not only saves time, but it also sends a strong message to the opponent and judge that the negative feels confident about winning the round by debating the resolution's intent and does not need to manipulate the words in the resolution.

Extensiveness of the Value

In some rare instances, both the affirmative and the negative will choose the same value to support. In these situations, the negative should still make the effort to state a value. Doing so confirms that the negative is not dependent upon the affirmative for debating the resolution. The negative wants to clash with the affirmative in the rebuttal speeches. For the initial case, however, negative integrity is the goal. If a switch in the resolution's wording were to occur, the negative case should be able to be substituted for the affirmative case.

As a negative debater, lure the affirmative into debating the negative case, instead of merely defending the affirmative case. Making a conscious point to list the negative value, even when it the same as the affirmative's, accomplishes this. Obviously, a sizable portion of the negative case will be devoted to supporting the negative value. Portions of this section of the negative case should still be read in an effort to maintain negative integrity. A large amount of time should not be devoted to this section, however, since the affirmative will not disagree with arguments that support a value that is the same. Instead, devote more time to your claim that the negative achieves the value in question better by negating the resolution.

Extensiveness of the Negative Criteria

The negative is not always forced to redefine the criteria of the round. If the criteria presented by the affirmative is equally advantageous to the negative, it is wise to accept the criteria and proceed with the round.

If you had planned on using cost benefit analysis as a criterion, and the affirmative presents cost benefit analysis, you should grant the criteria as being acceptable for evaluating the round, and proceed with the case. Occasionally, you can make the affirmative think that you are going to hit the criteria later in the round, even though you have every intention of granting the criteria to the opponent. Address the issue of criteria in your case, but do so lightly. Then, during your opponent's cross-examination, make a comment that you would like to see more support upholding the merits of your opponent's criteria. Occasionally, your opponent will slip into this trap and spend a portion of the first rebuttal upholding a criteria you plan on using anyway. In your second negative rebuttal, begin by granting the criteria, and then move straight to showing why the negative value is a better choice using the affirmative criteria.

Suggested Activities

1. Write an affirmative case for the current resolution or one given in the text. Prepare an outline copy of the case.

2. Write an essay describing the important elements and unique features of the negative case.

Unit III
REFUTATION AND REBUTTAL
IN LINCOLN-DOUGLAS

Unit III explains the second primary element in Lincoln-Douglas debate. Whereas Unit II focused on the presentation element–constructives, Unit III illustrates the proper way to address and refute an argument or contention.

Chapter 14 helps develop the skills that are characteristic of a general rebuttal speech. The concepts of analysis, support, and refutation are of particular importance. Chapter 15 illustrates the specific skills that are a part of the first and second affirmative rebuttals. Particular attention is given to the balance of defending and rebuilding the affirmative case, and attacking and refuting the negative case.

Chapter 16 addresses the negative rebuttals. The first rebuttal is defined as the refutation to the affirmative case presented in the negative constructive. This chapter highlights the strategy of attacking the first affirmative speech. The chapter also addresses the second negative rebuttal with regard to its strategies and responsibilities.

Chapter 17 is the final chapter in Unit III. The elements of fallacies, misapplied arguments, and tests of evidence are addressed. Chapter 17 is particularly useful for debaters who have experienced at least one tournament.

Unit III is one of the most critical segments of this book. In a matter of a few pages, it address one of the two main components to successful Lincoln-Douglas debate: deliberation and refutation. In situations where the entire Unit cannot be read prior to a tournament, Chapter 14 provides the necessary "foundation" of rebuttal skills needed. The remaining chapters are no less important and should be reviewed when time permits.

Chapter 14
Rebuttal Strategies

Learning Objectives

Chapter 14 explains rebuttals. Rebuttals are speeches that follow the affirmative and negative constructives. There are four speeches devoted to rebuttals: the first affirmative rebuttal, the first negative rebuttal within the constructive, the second negative rebuttal, and the second affirmative rebuttal. Chapters 15 and 16 are devoted to explaining the different duties of each of these speeches.

This chapter explains what should be included in a rebuttal. Furthermore, this chapter introduces the strategies to use in responding to opponents' initial arguments and defending your initial arguments from attacks. Both of these elements are critical to a successful rebuttal.

After completing this chapter you should be able to:

1. **Understand the importance of defending the case and extending with new logic or evidence in rebuttals.**

2. **Explain the difference between new arguments and new evidence, logic or analysis in rebuttals.**

3. **List the most important rebuttal skills.**

4. **Understand the time constraints in rebuttals.**

5. **Explain the strategies for a successful rebuttal.**

New Terms

Rebuttal

Extending

Cross application

Forecast

Filtering

Signposting

Mobile cards

Road mapping

Red herring argument

Introduction

The rebuttal is your opportunity to respond to attacks on your case and damage your opponent's case. While most debaters understand this concept, they don't always take full advantage of it. Most debaters assume that extension and attacks are the key to good rebuttals but do not feel there is any ordered pattern to rebuttals. In actuality, there should be as much structure in a rebuttal as there is in a constructive.

The *rebuttal* is defined as the portion of the debate designed to give the debater an opportunity to rebuild a case and attack the opponent's case. There are several concepts you must grasp to succeed in each individual rebuttal, but for now, we will concentrate on the principles that apply to all rebuttal speeches. Each rebuttal has its own special needs and requirements. In Chapters 15 and 16, each of the four rebuttals in the round is considered individually.

Qualities of a Great Rebuttal

Extending Arguments

Increasing or *extending* is defined as providing new logic, analysis, or evidence to further a point. The point can be in defense of your case or an attack on your opponent's case. A great debater creates new analysis to show why old arguments are weak. This should be important to you for two reasons. First, if you aspire to be a great debater, recognize that you will have to offer new logic, analysis, or evidence to defend your case or attack the opponent. Second, recognize that any argument can be beaten if an opponent has enough time to think about it. Thus, if you allow your opponent to attack using the same argument throughout the entire round, you can count on your argument being beaten. Keep the opponent off-balance by providing new support for your arguments. This new support can diffuse the attacks your opponent might be considering. New support and extended analysis are critical to maintaining control of the round.

Provide New Support and Analysis.

By the time you have reached the rebuttal speech, you should recognize that your opponent has already attacked what you presented in your first constructive. Because your opponent has already addressed your arguments, it makes little sense to repeat the same arguments in the same fashion. Instead, provide new support and analysis in hopes of reviving and strengthening your argument. Your opponent will probably not attack every argument presented, in which case, it is fine to use original supporting evidence. For the arguments that have been attacked, however, provide extension evidence to give each argument new support.

Have Fresh Attacks

Your original attacks should inflict some damage on the opponent's case. Once that damage is inflicted, those same attacks will not cause any more damage; they have done what they can do. As a result, you must find new evidence, analysis, and support to launch new attacks on your opponent's case in your second rebuttal. Simply reviewing what has already been said is a waste of time. Remind the judge of the effective attacks made on your opponent's case, but devote the majority of the rebuttal to introducing fresh attacks with fresh support.

The following section lists some of the skills you can develop to keep from merely repeating constructives. Mastering these skills will either get a losing debater back into the round, or allow a winning debater to "close the sale."

New Arguments Versus New Logic, Evidence, and Analysis

Note that this section advocates the use of new logic, analysis, or evidence. It does not advocate the use of new arguments. Presenting new arguments in the rebuttals generally is **not** accepted by most judges since the new arguments cannot be fairly refuted by the opponent, who has insufficient time to offer a response. Consider, for example, the situation in which an affirmative debater offers a new argument in the last affirmative rebuttal. How can the negative respond when he or she has no speeches left? Similarly, if the negative presents a host of new arguments in the second negative rebuttal, how can the affirmative be expected to respond to seven minutes of new arguments (the time given to the negative's second rebuttal) when he or she has only three minutes to speak?

So what are we talking about when we advocate new logic, analysis, and evidence? Logic, analysis, and evidence serve to illustrate the relative worth of the arguments throughout the round. Introducing new support for the arguments is fair even in the final rebuttals, since your opponent has had the whole round to offer attacks or defenses for these arguments.

Rebuttal Skills

Avoid Play-By-Play

To present new and effective support and attacks, do not repeat what you've already said. There are several traps that invite debaters to slip into this mode of repetition. The first is nervousness. When a debater becomes nervous or anxious, or simply does not know what to say, it is common to re-read the affirmative and negative cases. Practice rounds are the solution to reducing this problem and can help a debater feel more comfortable on stage. If you do get nervous, take extra preparation time before speaking, since this will allow you to collect yourself.

Also, avoid the use of some handicapping phrases that entice you to create a "replay" of the constructives. "The affirmative said this, but I said this," is one of the more common phrases that can severely handicap your ability to present an effective rebuttal. It is better to give a response such as the following: "The affirmative presented the claim that individual rights are superior to social protection. In response, I would like you to consider this thought . . ." While you are covering each point, you also are providing some fresh support and analysis.

Give Precedence to Your Case

Except in extenuating circumstances, the rebuttal should begin with the case support. This ensures that you enter the rebuttal with confidence. Discussing your philosophy also ensures that you will maintain the proper orientation (affirmative or negative) through the rebuttal. A negative that begins by discussing the affirmative philosophy can often slip into giving affirmative arguments by mistake. As surprising as it sounds, it does happen, especially after debating a number of rounds. Finally, beginning with your case allows for the possibility that your opponent will deliver a rebuttal that is a carbon copy of yours. This is advantageous because it places your case in the spotlight of both rebuttals, and it facilitates the possibility that your opponent will run out of speech time and not finish his or her own case.

After presenting your case it is also important that you deal with your opponent's philosophy. It is good to begin with your case, but staying on your case for an extended amount of time does not help you. Debate is a dialectic event; you must attack as well as defend. It is a common mistake for a debater to deliver what he or she thinks is a great rebuttal only to discover that time has expired and he or she has not touched the opponent's contentions. You must attack your opponent's case, and you must leave enough time to attack his or her case with substantial support.

Cover Both Cases

Dropping a point, argument, or case, means you lose it. It is like a football in a football game. Even if you knock a football out of your opponent's hand, it is not yours until you pick it up. There is a basic premise in debate that goes something like this: "If you fail to acknowledge or respond to a point, then it is assumed that you agree." You must tell the judge at each opportunity that you have in your favor your own arguments and the ones your opponent has dropped. In addition, it is important that if an opponent knocks an argument out of your hands, you pick it up again to keep it as your own.

If your opponent presents an argument and you fail to respond, your opponent must assume that you agree with it, or you would have offered some argumentation. Your opponent cannot read your mind, anticipate what argument you might make later in the round, and respond to that argument. For instance, if your opponent made a contention in the negative constructive, and you did not respond to it in your affirmative rebuttal, there is no way to anticipate what you will say in your last rebuttal. Thus, it is unfair to bring the argument back up in the last affirmative rebuttal. This works in reverse, however. If an opponent drops one of your contentions, you cannot be expected to defend it later. Thus, you should point out that your opponent has dropped an argument, and you should tell the judge you have no other recourse but to assume that failure to address the argument is symbolic of agreement with the contention.

If your opponent drops an argument, you should begin your rebuttal with: "My opponent failed to argue my case, and we can only assume there is agreement. Therefore, I ask that you accept the affirmative case." If you're the negative, your case here is even more important, since you have no time to attack affirmative arguments presented in the second affirmative rebuttal.

It is also wise, however, to quickly point out the content of the arguments your opponent dropped. Do not drop the case yourself simply because your opponent has dropped the case. Point out what has been dropped, and justify why it is important.

Watch Your Time

If there is a timekeeper in the room, be alert to time signals. It is a good idea to ask the timekeeper to give you your time in the way you prefer, either up or down. If you want to know the time left in the speech, instruct the timekeeper to keep time "down." If you want to know the amount of time you have used in the speech, tell him or her that you would like your time kept "up." It is also a good idea to ask to see 30 and 15 second cards. You can also ask the timekeeper to give you a 30-second warning orally. This ensures that you know when to wind down the rebuttal and present your personal conclusion. Finally, and most importantly, it is important to budget the depth of your attacks and defense based upon the time left in the round. To make certain you respond to all arguments, it is sometimes necessary to briefly touch on less important arguments.

Cross Apply Arguments

The use of time in rebuttals is extremely important. There will be situations in which you must conserve time to squeeze all that you have to say in to the available rebuttal time. On some occasions, an argument you use to support your case is similar to an argument you choose to attack an opponent's case, allowing you to cross apply the two arguments.

The process of *cross applying* is best accomplished by telling the judge, "If you take time to compare the affirmative and negative cases, you see that the affirmative's second contention and the negative's first contention are identical in that they both discuss the validity of the social contract. The following card (or analysis) discusses both the affirmative and the negative points on social contract validity." You must alert the judge first of the similarities of two points (the affirmative's and the negative's contention), and then of your intention to address both points simultaneously. The premise is to group similar affirmative and negative contentions, and proceed with the extension argument. It is critical that the judge know which of the arguments you are linking.

Cross applications should be planned prior to the beginning of the rebuttal speech. It takes only seconds of preparation time to assess which arguments of your case are the same as those in your opponent's case. Such preparation prevents the judge from getting the impression that you ran out of time and grouped everything together.

Cross applying can be dangerous if done incorrectly. A common mistake is to link arguments which are different in content. Most of the negative arguments, in some way, will be similar to the affirmative's. This does not necessarily mean that two arguments are the same, however, and you should use extreme caution in cross applying arguments.

Filter

Evaluate an argument based upon its relative importance. The arguments that win rounds are typically not easily won. Identify the important issues and devote time accordingly. This is where filtering comes into play. *Filtering* is the process of evaluating arguments as to their importance to the round's decision and eliminating discussion on those arguments that are not important. Filtering has another component. Arguments that are identified as not important in the round should be grouped and addressed as one argument. In this way, many unimportant subpoints are addressed in one discussion and are easily beaten quickly. This frees up rebuttal time for the really important issues of the round. The decision as to what should be grouped and what deserves individual attacks should be made prior to the initiation of the rebuttal.

Note that this filtration process should be used with caution. Filtering and grouping can become addictive. Over-grouping can cause misinterpretation of the opponent's case, and this misinterpretation can cost you the round. Assuming that an argument is unimportant, when in reality it is vital to the opposition's philosophy, is one of the greatest mistakes a debater can make.

Filtering also allows you to deal efficiently with dropped arguments. If your opponent drops or grants an argument, point it out. Remind the judge of your original argument and its impact. After picking up a dropped argument, do not waste time extending on it. You have already won it. It is tempting to spend too much time in winnable arguments. Those are the comfortable arguments for a debater, but they can spell a loss if overemphasized to the exclusion of others.

The tendency to focus on winnable arguments has sparked a new facet to Lincoln-Douglas, the *red herring argument*. It is common for a brilliant debater to place small, unimportant subpoints in a case for the purpose of being "beaten." A lesser opponent will go after these subpoints because they are easily beaten, and then stay on these subpoints throughout the round. Meanwhile, the brilliant debater grants the opponent these subpoints, and then illustrates their relative lack of importance. The result of the round boils down to one debater manipulating another debater into wasting valuable speech time on unimportant issues. As ridiculous as it sounds, it occurs time and time again. The victims of this strategy never figure out they were victimized, and they are condemned to believe they have been wrongly "voted against" because "they won that argument!" Little do they know that the "one argument" didn't even matter!

Use Preparation Time Wisely

The preparation period is the time to decide which arguments should be cross applied and which arguments should be filtered. Making these decisions during your rebuttal speech is not wise, as you will be left with a confused jumble of non-essential and misapplied arguments. In Chapter 20, the use of preparation time is addressed in relation to successful rebuttals.

Use Analogies

As is addressed in Chapter 26, the use of analogies can save time in explaining complicated topics. Since there are limits in the amount of time to explain arguments/attacks, the analogy can be a vital tool to making rebuttals more "economical." By using analogies, you will be able to fit more explanation of the same number of arguments into the time provided.

Have Mobile Cards

In many situations, a debater dominates constructives but flounders in rebuttals, costing him or her the round because of a lack of documented support and organizational skills. Great constructives use high power analysis founded on logic and backed up with effective documented support. Great rebuttals are no different. Good organization skills will allow you to apply logic and evidence to your rebuttal.

In many situations the case structure is the problem. While having evidence cards printed or pasted to a copy of the constructive is helpful in delivering the constructive speech, it is not good organization for the rebuttal speech. Trying to re-read one piece of evidence off a page of the affirmative case and another card of a different page of the case, is not efficient for the rebuttal. Papers begin to get lost, out of order, or out of place, and as a consequence, the rebuttal gets disorganized. If this happens while speaking, and you are forced to juggle five or six pages, your appearance suffers greatly. For this reason make a permanent copy of the constructive case in outline form. Make copies of each piece of evidence used to support the case, and paste these evidence pieces to note cards. You may still paste copies of your supporting evidence to the constructive, but having copies of that same evidence on note cards will allow you to use this evidence in the rebuttals without being hampered by cluttered pages. After the constructive is delivered, "store" the constructive in the back of your briefcase, and use the evidence that was copied onto note cards if you need to re-read it in rebuttals. The outline can give an idea of what arguments are listed at what place in the constructive, and the cards can be easily rearranged in the order needed for delivering an effective rebuttal speech. Creating a "mobile" case, via the case outline and supporting evidence cards, provides convenience and organization in rebuttals.

Road Map and Signpost

As you begin the rebuttal, tell the judge exactly what you plan to say in the speech. This short prelude is called a *road map or forecast* because it gives the judge directions on where you intend go in the speech. This is helpful so the judge can catch everything you have to say. Randomly presenting arguments as they come to mind is not persuasive and can be annoying. In most situations, the judge eventually catches up, but may miss many of your most important arguments.

Plan your speech beforehand, and then follow that plan. As you continue into the speech, inform the judge as to where you are on your road map. This is called *signposting*. For instance, when you are about to begin discussion of your second contention, you should alert the judge by saying: "If you would now direct your attention to the second affirmative contention, I would like to offer the following additional support . . ." Signposting allows the judge to follow all of the grouping and cross applying. It also allows the judge to follow what you have to say in the rebuttal. Remember, the only arguments that are important in the round are those that the judge catches. The more the judge can note, the better the chance you have of winning the round.

It is important that as you signpost and road map (forecast) you do not sacrifice fluency or persuasiveness. In normal conversation, it is not typical to hear a subpoint before every topic, so you need to disguise signposting to be persuasive.

Forecasting should not begin prior to the initiation of the speech; this is offensive to many judges. A good way to disguise forecasting is as follows: "I would initially like to discuss the benefits found in the affirmative philosophy, and then expose some of the harms found in the negative case. To begin with, let's consider the first contention of the affirmative case." In this manner, the road map is never seen, but you relay its intention to the judge. It equally is important that you maintain this disguise into the signposting of each individual argument. For example, "Let's now turn to the negative's second argument supporting the contention dealing with the social contract," is far more effective than saying, "Go to the negative's second contention, the second subpoint under there." The small amount of time that is invested in this method of disguising the signposting is time well spent.

End on a Good Note

In the last rebuttal it is always advisable to take a "step away from the debate" approach during the last 15 to 30 seconds. The debate was initiated with a personal opening, and it should end in the same way. If you remember, the rationale for a personal opening was to establish rapport with the judge. The final seconds of your last rebuttal should do the same. Coming away from the podium, setting the case and all cards down, and personally talking with the judge will get more ballots than trying to get that last argument crammed into the rebuttal. It will further the rapport you initiated with the judge in the constructive.

If you began the round with an analogy or relied upon an analogy through the course of the round, the last part of the rebuttal is a good place to come to the conclusion of the analogy. A final summary statement of the resolution's conflict and how your stance on the resolution provided the best value according to the round's criteria is also a good way to end the round. For example: "As you consider which choice to make to solve this resolution, I urge you to consider the affirmative. Affirming the resolution will preserve the necessary importance of . . . As has been demonstrated, this is vital when we consider the criteria for judging today's round, which is . . . I once again urge you to please vote affirmative, not only to decide this round, but also to preserve the value of . . . in society. Thank you." Stating that there is no ballot other than affirmative/negative is fine at times, but is sometimes perceived as arrogant. For this reason, it is a good idea to avoid ending a sincere rebuttal with an arrogant statement.

Suggested Activities

1. Practice giving 30-second persuasive endings to the affirmative second rebuttal.

2. Write an essay on the responsibilities of the affirmative second rebuttal.

3. After a classmate delivers a first affirmative constructive, have the class brainstorm all of the possible arguments that could be used against the case. Discuss how those arguments can be grouped and cross applied for more efficient time allocation.

Chapter 15
The Affirmative Rebuttals

Learning Objectives

Chapter 15 explains the first and second affirmative rebuttals. The first affirmative rebuttal is the first opportunity the affirmative has to rebuild a case and launch attacks on the negative case. This chapter describes how to proceed through the affirmative rebuttals as well as how to strategize on attacking the negative case.

After completing this chapter you should be able to:

1. **Explain the first and second affirmative rebuttal responsibilities.**

2. **Explain the importance of attacking the negative value and criteria and how to do it.**

3. **Describe how to attack negative definitions.**

4. **Explain the importance of the four methods for comparing affirmative and negative value criteria.**

5. **Define the rebuttal circle.**

6. **Understand how to allocate time and organize arguments.**

7. **List the top ten ways to attack an opponent.**

8. **Understand the importance of a persuasive conclusion.**

New Terms

First Affirmative Rebuttal
The Big Three Issues

Second Affirmative Rebuttal
The Rebuttal Circle

Introduction

This chapter introduces first and second affirmative rebuttal responsibilities. In this chapter, you will **not** look at each responsibility of the rebuttal, since you should be familiar with these responsibilities from reading Chapter 14.

The First Affirmative Rebuttal

First Rebuttal Responsibilities

The affirmative's responsibilities in the *first rebuttal* include attacking the negative value criteria, definitions, and case points. In cases where the affirmative value is the same as the negative value, it is not necessary to attack the negative's value. In most cases, however, the negative value is different, and must be attacked by the affirmative.

It is not always necessary, however, to attack the negative criteria. Sometimes the negative criteria is the same as the affirmative criteria; other times the negative criteria is different, but works equally well for the affirmative value. In other situations, however, the negative criteria may discriminate against the affirmative value. In these situations you should attack the negative's criteria. Refer to Chapter 5 for a discussion of criteria.

If the negative redefines the definitions, he or she must justify these new definitions. If your opponent does try to overturn your definitions, you should explain why your definitions are critical to your case and/or why your opponent's arguments are invalid. Chapter 11 should help you in making that argument.

Attacking the negative case points is a complex process for the first affirmative rebuttal. You have only four minutes, so it is important to organize your rebuttal and be concise to conserve time. Specific strategies are discussed in the next section.

It is often tempting for debaters to attack the first thing the opponent says in the round. Do not get caught by this temptation and waste valuable speech time on the opponent's introduction (which merely is for rapport building). If your opponent was successful in establishing rapport with the judge, there is nothing you can do about it now, and, most likely, it won't end up on the judge's flow sheet.

First Rebuttal Strategies

1. Assess the Entire Negative Case. In the first rebuttal select the five or six most important negative points. Go after these points! Analyze the negative contentions by addressing the *Big Three Issues* in the round. They are:

> a. How does the negative show that his or her value is reached at a high degree?

b. What are the merits of the negative's value?

c. What is the validity of the negative's criteria?

The negative case attempts to show that the negative's value is achieved to a high degree by negating the resolution. Demonstrate that the negative's value is not greatly achieved by negating the resolution. The second question attempts to show that the negative's value is important to humankind or to a particular society. Show that the negative's value is not, or is less, significant to society or humankind. The third issue to attack is the negative's criteria. You have two strategies here. First, show that the negative's criteria is not a strong criteria for evaluating the values in the round (see Chapter 5). Second, show that the negative's criteria does not facilitate choosing the negative's value. There will be other arguments about the specifics of the topic, and you should attack these where possible. The above three issues, however, are the most critical in the round.

2. Select Short Evidence Cards. Your most important goal of the rebuttal is that you make all your necessary attacks. Instead of reading one or two pieces of evidence to support a few of the arguments, it is better to present five succinct pieces of supporting evidence to validate your claims and hit all of the arguments. Direct evidence is best. You can elaborate more in the second affirmative rebuttal.

3. Group Similar Arguments. Since you have limited time in the first affirmative rebuttal, it is important to conserve time by grouping similar arguments and addressing the whole group with one affirmative argument. If you group arguments that do not have the same meaning, you may miss some vital points. Do not become addicted to grouping. Some subpoints will be so critical to the success of the negative case that if you group those subpoints into one argument, you may miss out on fully addressing some subpoint meanings and lose those subpoints.

4. Cross Apply. Another method for saving time is the cross application of arguments in the affirmative case to those in the negative case. If one of the contentions in your affirmative case is equivalent to the argument you would ordinarily present against a negative argument, you should ask the judge to recall the logic and support you offered for that contention in your affirmative case. In this way, you can draw upon the logic, support, and explanation that was presented in your affirmative case to attack the negative contentions. Once again, use extreme caution, since what you cross apply may not always fit the contention in your affirmative case. A misapplied argument is sometimes worse than no argument at all.

5. Practice Word Economy. Probably the best way to save time in the first affirmative rebuttal is to practice word economy. Develop the ability to present complex thoughts in short, direct sentences. While many believe flowery, elaborate speech is the way to persuade a judge, the best method of persuasion is often direct, to-the-point analysis of the issues. This is especially true in the rebuttals where time considerations limit the amount of flowery speech you can deliver. Practice the essence of word economy: say what you mean; mean what you say.

6. Keep Moving. It is important that you keep moving in the rebuttal. This means that you cannot dwell on one argument for too long. You may not be totally pleased with the detail you offer each argument, but remember that you have another rebuttal to offer more detailed argumentation when necessary. It is common to see debaters become enthralled with one argument and stay on that argument for the full four minutes. Do not do this! Attack the Big Three issues in the negative case, and then move on to other sections.

Organizing the First Affirmative Rebuttal

Prior to making the Big Three attacks, begin the rebuttal with a review of the affirmative case to ensure that you have enough time to make your case. If the debate comes down to debating one case over the other, you want your case to be the one being discussed. Beginning with the affirmative case gives preference to your side.

Beginning with the affirmative case has its merits, but it also requires a great deal of discipline. Budget your time effectively to cover the negative case within this rebuttal. You cannot defer the negative case until your next rebuttal because the negative would have no attacks to counter. This would make the debate unfair.

Begin the review of your case in the same way you introduced it. Rebuild the value; then the criteria; then the definitions, if necessary; and then the case points. If you don't have much time, drop all subpoints or minor contentions that are not critical to the round's outcome. Typically, this means that you will have to drop everything that does not answer the Big Three Issues in the round. Do not drop things unless absolutely necessary.

The way you budget your time is critical to your performance in the first affirmative rebuttal. Always allow at least one and one-half of the four minutes for reconstructing your case. Do not spend more than two and one-half minutes on the negative case attack, unless you do not need the full one and one-half minutes to rebuild the affirmative. Remember, your affirmative case began prima facie, and you want it to end that way.

The order of your attacks in the first affirmative rebuttal should follow this pattern:
- Attack the Negative Value
- Attack the Negative Criteria
- Attack the Negative Definitions (if necessary)
- Attack the Negative Case Points (The Big Three Issues)

The Second Affirmative Rebuttal

Second Rebuttal Responsibilities

The advantage of speaking last in the debate depends upon how the last rebuttal is used. You only have three minutes to cover a number of issues, and this time moves very quickly. If you are conscious of what you must get done and plan ahead in your organization, you will have no trouble covering the essential issues outlined in this section. There may be several arguments, contentions, thoughts, responses, etc. to cover in the last rebuttal, but realize there is only so much that can be said in three minutes without sacrificing persuasiveness.

The *second affirmative rebuttal* has to extend and summarize the issues raised in the first affirmative rebuttal. This requires comparisons of affirmative and negative values, criteria, definitions, and case points.

If affirmative and negative values are similar, explain why the affirmative enhances the values most. If the affirmative and negative criteria differ, you have two responsibilities. First, recap the round's argumentation over the criteria and provide additional support. Logically explain why your criteria is better capable of evaluating the values in the round. Second, show, according to criteria, that your value is the better of the two values.

Definition disputes should end with the first affirmative rebuttal. If definitions come up again in the second rebuttal, show that the affirmative definitions are fair, and that the negative has not fulfilled the responsibility of providing standards for justifying the re-definitions.

In the cases where the affirmative and negative values differ, take the 45 to 60 seconds of the rebuttal to make comparisons of the values in the round. If there are any case contentions that uphold the merits of the two values, incorporate those contentions into this discussion.

In comparing values, address four primary questions. First, answer why your value is more beneficial than your opponent's value. In and of itself, why is "life" better than "individual rights?" Second, answer why affirming the resolution realizes the value. Will your resolution of "life" be realized if the judge votes affirmative? Third, answer why affirming the resolution gains "purity and high degree of the value." By voting affirmative, will the judge give society all of the merits of the value of "life" without causing any negative side effects, such as totalitarianism? What are the disadvantages to voting for your value? Are they significant? Fourth, explain why your value is really achieved. Does a vote to affirm genetic engineering ensure the value of life? Provide detailed logic, analysis, and evidence to uphold your value and defeat your opponent's value. Answer these questions in the first minute of your rebuttal. Keep in mind that most of your case is devoted to answering question number three. If you did not have to debate the criteria, use that time for further extension on the values in the round.

Keep in mind that most of your case is devoted to answering question number three. If you did not have to debate the criteria, use that time for further extension on the values in the round.

During your preparation time, take a sheet of paper, and make a list of what negative arguments correlate with your affirmative arguments. Make an overview of the most important affirmative arguments, and identify related negative arguments. It is important to state that this is how the affirmative and negative cases will be covered. It is generally easier to begin at the beginning of the affirmative case and proceed downward. Keep in mind that you will have already addressed some case contentions in your evaluation of the affirmative and negative values and criteria.

Begin by addressing the first affirmative case point and whatever related negative contention applies. In addressing each point, use what is called the *rebuttal circle.* This is defined in the following four steps:

1. Do not restate your argument and your opponent's response.
2. State your argument, and provide additional logic, analysis, or evidence to uphold the contention.
3. Discuss your opponent's response.
4. Tell the judge why this response is not valid because of the logic, analysis, or evidence you just presented.

Proceed in this fashion point-by-point until you have completed the affirmative case. Then go to the negative case and address any points that were not discussed while addressing your case. Do not ignore any contention. You will be pressed for time, but if you proceed systematically and efficiently you will have more than enough time to address four or five issues in the case. Since you will have already covered the values at the beginning of the rebuttal, you can save time by referring any contentions related to the value or criteria to your prior discussion.

Finish your case comparison by showing how the case contentions combine to create a pure and beneficial value with no side effects that the judge can uphold by voting for the affirmative. You have only a minute and a half (at best) to compare both cases, and it is critical that you discuss them both at the same time. Word efficiency is a critical part of a successful second affirmative rebuttal.

Set aside the last 15 to 30 seconds of the rebuttal to step away from the round and talk **with** the judge to revive the rapport established in the introduction. Put down all cards, briefs, cases, flow sheets, etc. Step away from the podium, and review the round in your own words. Focus on how your value is superior to your opponent's value (by way of your criteria), and how affirming the resolution creates the "pure" value. Remember, the judge ultimately evaluates your performance in the round. It is far more important that you appear persuasive than it is for you to have won the last argument.

Second Rebuttal Strategies

1. Plan Ahead. You should know what you are going to say while you are still in the preparation period. Nothing can substitute for planning ahead. Notice the importance of prior planning in the ability to cross apply arguments from the affirmative to the negative case.

2. Use Word Efficiency. Learn to say complicated thoughts in simple, short sentences. This comes with practice.

3. Use Effective Filtration. While addressing the negative and affirmative cases, it is especially important to filter through the arguments. Spend time only on what is important in the round. Ask yourself how each argument applies to the values in the round. If an argument effects the quality or achievement of your value, discuss it. If the argument is less significant, combine it with another contention.

4. Use Effective Grouping. You must be able to group similar subpoints under one contention. Understand that some important arguments will arise in the round that are not "officially" listed as contentions by either your opponent or yourself. You must still address these issues as major parts of the round.

5. Use Effective Cross Application. The ability to apply negative arguments to your case contentions can be the difference in the round. Cross application allows you to "kill two birds with one stone," and, thus, free up more second rebuttal time for different arguments.

6. Be Conscious of Time Allocation. Time allocation should resemble the following:

15-30 Seconds	Criteria Comparison
45-60 Seconds	Value Comparison
60-90 Seconds	Case Comparison
15-30 Seconds	Concluding Remarks

7. Be Persuasive. While rushed for time, you must not appear rushed for time. Maintain composure, and end the rebuttal with a pleasant, persuasive discussion of the round. Remember, the way you present an argument is far more important than the argument itself.

The Top Ten Ways to Attack an Opponent

There are an infinite number of ways to attack an opponent's case. The ten best ways to refute an opponent's claims are written as rhetorical questions to get you thinking about flaws in the negative case and attack. These questions apply to both the first and second affirmative rebuttals.

1. Does this argument apply to only one society only? The resolution is not limited to the United States or any one specific society unless specifically stated. Therefore, it must be evaluated in terms of all humankind. An opponent's argument that deals only with the U.S. or any one selected society doesn't apply to the round's discussion.

2. Does this argument apply to only one time frame? The resolution is not limited by any one time frame. We are not concerned just with today; we are equally concerned with tomorrow and all time periods in which the conflict in the resolution exists. If your opponent's argument makes sense only within the context of one time frame, it doesn't apply to the discussion of the resolution.

3. Is there a contradiction within the case? Sometimes your opponent will make a series of unbeatable claims. Each, by itself, is unbeatable. Together, however, there may be a contradiction that cancels each of them out. For instance, a case may have one point that claims that the quality of life is far greater than the value of life itself. A later contention, however, may claim that the opposite is true. Study the case carefully. If a case is too good to be true, it usually isn't true. Look for contradictions.

4. Does this argument assume that something is inherently "good?" It is common to see contentions that assume that the result created is inherently "good," or the result prevented is inherently "bad." Your opponent cannot say that a value is worthy just because it ensures the preservation of democracy. This argument assumes that democracy is inherently good, and socialism is inherently bad. This is not enough. Your opponent must show why democracy is good, or why socialism is bad.

5. Is this argument realistic? Is it plausible to assume that because a Native American Art Museum in New York is shut down, we will experience a global thermonuclear holocaust? An argument must be realistic to be believable, and believable to be persuasive. Be critical of your opponent's claims about cause and effect.

6. Is your opponent's argument supported by a source? While evidence is not critical to a Lincoln-Douglas debate round, it is no secret that both debaters are not experts on the topic. To avoid a conversation between two amateurs, the advise of experts is necessary to validate anything that seems outrageous or controversial. Does your opponent have the expert evidence to support the claims?

7. Is the evidence from a credible source? Who are the negative's sources? What qualifications make the source capable of making judgments? The burden of proof requires your opponent to show the qualifications of sources. If source authority cannot be shown, challenge the source as potentially biased or unqualified.

8. Are there any impacts to this argument? What are the consequences of your opponent's argument? Will society feel any impacts from this occurrence? If your opponent makes the claim that some shift in social norms will occur, he or she must show how this is important. We cannot be left to assume that a "shift in social norms" will cause disaster in the human race. This burden of proof is left to your opponent, and you must ensure that it is fulfilled.

9. Is more harm than good produced? An argument may appear to produce a number of positive benefits for society, but what about the harms it produces? A war may ensure the values of freedom and liberty, but what about the death and suffering it causes? Challenge your opponent to face the harms caused by an argument as well as its benefits.

10. Can your side of the resolution do it better? Occasionally, ask yourself whether your side of the resolution might be able to produce more of the benefits your opponent is claiming. Negating the resolution might save some lives, but if affirming the resolution saves more lives, the affirmative position is stronger. With every argument, value, and criterion, check to see if your side of the resolution can achieve better benefits than your opponent's. The quickest way to victory is to take an opponent's contention and claim it as your own.

Suggested Activities

1. Bring extension evidence for each of the main case points to class and explain how it would apply.

2. Practice words economy by condensing the thrust of your affirmative case into as few words as possible. Concentrate on vivid words with impact.

3. Write a short essay discussing the responsibilities and the time considerations of the first affirmative rebuttal.

Chapter 16
The Negative Rebuttals

Learning Objectives

Chapter 16 discusses the first and second negative rebuttals. The first negative rebuttal is the portion of the negative constructive (the first negative speech) in which the negative debater refutes the affirmative case. The second negative rebuttal is what is referred to as the negative. It is the second speech the negative has in the debate.

After completing this chapter you should be able to:

1. **Explain the responsibilities of the first and second negative rebuttals.**

2. **Determine when to attack affirmative definitions.**

3. **Explain the strategies for attacking the affirmative values, criteria, and case.**

4. **Understand how to rebuild and extend the negative case while attacking the affirmative case.**

5. **Understand the organizational and time allocation structures of the negative rebuttals.**

New Terms

First Negative Rebuttal
Second Negative Rebuttal
Drop

The First Negative Rebuttal

This section discusses the *first negative rebuttal* portion of the negative constructive, not the speech that has traditionally been called the negative rebuttal. In this book, that speech is called the *second negative rebuttal*.

First Rebuttal Responsibilities

The first responsibility of the negative rebuttal is to attack the affirmative value. There are times when the affirmative value is the same as the negative value, and the only discrepancy is over who better achieves that value. In those cases it is not necessary to attack the affirmative's value. In most cases, however, the affirmative value is different, and, thus, should be attacked.

Several attack strategies can be employed against the affirmative value. The common goal of each strategy is to reduce the importance of the value in the round. Ten specific strategies are given later in this chapter.

It is not always necessary to attack the affirmative criteria. Sometimes the criteria is the same as the negative criteria, and other times the affirmative criteria, while it is different, works equally well for the negative value. In these situations, an attack on the affirmative criteria is not necessary.

In other situations, the affirmative criteria may be discriminatory against the negative value. In these situations, attack the criteria. Refer to Chapter 5 for a discussion of criteria.

It is not necessary to attack the affirmative's opening. Your goal is to build rapport with the judge, not to advance the affirmative case. You should, however, use the first negative rebuttal to attack the affirmative definitions if your case redefined terms.

The major responsibility of the rebuttal is to attack the case points. This is a complex process. At best, you have only three minutes of the total seven minutes for rebuttal. Thus, it is important to organize your rebuttal and conserve time. Word efficiency is a critical part of a successful first negative rebuttal.

First Rebuttal Strategies

1. Assess the affirmative case in its entirety. There are several strategies that fulfill the rebuttal responsibilities. Begin by asking, "What portions of the affirmative case are the strongest points? What contentions and subpoints can be grouped together?" These questions and others should dominate your pre-speech analysis. In this rebuttal, select the five or six most important affirmative points. Go after these points. The Big

Three Issues in the round are:
1. How does the affirmative show that its value is reached at a high degree?
2. What are the merits of the affirmative's value?
3. What is the validity of the affirmative's criteria?

Most of the affirmative case will probably focus on the first question. The affirmative will attempt to show that the affirmative's value is fully realized by affirming the resolution. Demonstrate that the affirmative's value is not greatly achieved by affirming the resolution.

The second question will not dominate as much of the affirmative's case, but it is nonetheless important to apply it. Show that the affirmative's value is less significant or insignificant to society or humankind.

The third issue to attack is the affirmative's criteria. You have two responsibilities here. First, show that the affirmative's criteria is not a strong criteria for evaluating the values in the round (see Chapter 5). Second, show that the affirmative's value does not meet the affirmative's criteria. If the affirmative has a criteria of cost benefit analysis, argue that the costs of the affirmative value are greater than the benefits. If the affirmative has a criteria of utilitarianism, argue that the affirmative value does not create the greatest good, or it does not create good for the "greatest number." In this way, you attack the criteria and the value at the same time.

2. Select short evidence cards. Your greatest goal in the rebuttal is to make all necessary attacks on the affirmative. The amount of support is not that critical as long as there is some support. Instead of reading one or two pieces of evidence to support two out of five arguments made in the rebuttal, it is better to read one succinct piece of supporting evidence against each claim. It also helps to use cards from the same source, if possible. This eliminates the need to give the source listing several times. The more direct the evidence, the better. More elaborate evidence can be brought up in the second negative rebuttal.

3. Group similar arguments. Since you have limited time in the first negative rebuttal, it is important to save time grouping similar arguments together and address that group with one negative argument. It is important that all of the contentions grouped are similar arguments that have basically the same meaning. If you group arguments that do not have the same meaning, you will lose these arguments. Understand that the whole affirmative case cannot be grouped into one argument. There will be marked similarity among subpoints. Thus it is acceptable to group those arguments under their main contention and make a negative attack against that one contention. Grouping more than one main contention, however, is generally not done effectively. The simple fact that the affirmative has organized these thoughts into separate contentions should be an indication that they are not similar arguments. Do not become addicted to grouping. If time allows, address each pertinent issue in the round, regardless of whether it is a subpoint, an example, or a contention. Your primary responsibility, however, is attacking the Big Three Issues. To do this, group remaining subpoints into main themes and make your attacks from there.

4. Cross apply. Another method for saving time is the cross application of arguments in the negative case to those in the affirmative case. If one of the contentions in your negative case is equivalent to the argument ordinarily presented against an affirmative argument, point this out to the judge and ask him or her to recall the logic and support offered in your negative case. Once again, use extreme caution, since what is cross applied may not always fit the contention in your negative case. A misapplied argument is sometimes worse than no argument at all.

5. Practice word economy. Probably the best thing you can do to save time in the first negative rebuttal is to practice word economy. Develop the ability to present complex thoughts in short, direct sentences. While many believe flowery, elaborate speech is the way to persuade a judge, the best method of persuasion is often direct, to-the-point analysis of the issues. This is easily said, but it takes practice to speak concisely, clearly and directly

6. Keep moving. Don't dwell on one argument for too long. You may not be totally pleased with the detail offered each argument, but remember that you are using three minutes to attack six minutes of affirmative constructive. You can give more detail in the second negative rebuttal. Attack the big three issues in the affirmative case, and then move on. Carefully watch the timekeeper as you proceed through the round. Remember that you will want to save the last fifteen seconds for your personable ending.

7. The top ten ways to attack an opponent. There are ten basic ways to refute an opponent's claims in a round. Refer to Chapter 15 for a full description of these methods of attack.

The Second Negative Rebuttal

The second negative rebuttal is what is traditionally referred to as "the negative rebuttal." This six-minute speech is one of the most difficult in a Lincoln-Douglas round. This is the negative's last opportunity to refute the affirmative case and defend the negative case, and you must use your time wisely.

Second Rebuttal Responsibilities

Since both debaters face common issues, many of the responsibilities in the second negative rebuttal are the same as those in the second affirmative rebuttal. As a consequence, some of the following information is similar to what was presented in Chapter 15. The order of these responsibilities as well as the manner in which you carry out these responsibilities is different from the second affirmative rebuttal.

Criteria. Begin by comparing and contrasting negative and affirmative criteria. It is not always necessary to make an elaborate argument for the merits of the negative criteria. Sometimes the negative criteria is the same as the affirmative criteria, and other times the affirmative criteria, while different, work equally well for the negative value. In the first affirmative rebuttal, it is common for the affirmative to skip the negative criteria entirely. If an opponent has failed to address your criteria, point this out to the judge. Provide a brief description of your criteria and its relative worth. This may include a brief analysis or even a piece of supporting evidence.

In other situations, the affirmative criteria may discriminate against the negative value. You have two primary responsibilities in comparing the criteria in the round. First, you should recap the round's argumentation over the criteria. How did the affirmative attack the criteria? You must respond to those arguments. Then you should provide additional support for the criteria. In doing so, provide a logical assessment of why your criteria is better capable of evaluating the values in the round. Second, show that by using your criteria, your value is the best of the two values in the round. The bottom line is that you must attack your opponent's criteria if it discriminates against the negative value, and you must attack it during the first 30 seconds of the second negative rebuttal.

Values. The most important concept in Lincoln-Douglas debate is the value. As a result, it is imperative that your value is intact after the round is finished. You must make your value strong enough so that it can survive the upcoming second affirmative rebuttal. It is not enough to merely respond to the attacks. You also must anticipate what your opponent will say against your value in the second affirmative rebuttal and formulate responses.

At this point in the speech, rebuild and extend the negative value, and also make comparisons to the affirmative value. In addressing the values in the round, answer four primary questions. First, answer why the negative value, even outside the context of the debate, is beneficial. Second, answer why negating the resolution achieves the value. Third, answer why negating the resolution gains a "purity and high degree of the value." Will the judge, by voting negative, give society all of the merits of the value without also causing harmful side-effects? What are the disadvantages of voting for your value? Are they significant? Fourth, answer whether your value is really achieved or not. Provide detailed logic, analysis, and evidence to support your value and defeat your opponent's value.

The comparison of the affirmative and negative values should be made within a minute and thirty seconds. Keep in mind that most of your case will be devoted to answering question number three (the degree and purity of your value). If you did not have to debate the criteria, use that time for further extension on the values in the round. If you did have to use the first 30 to 45 seconds for a comparison of criteria in the round, you should have used a total of two and one-half to three minutes of your rebuttal up to this point.

Definitions. The first negative's rebuttal goal should be to end all definition controversies. If, however, definition battles continue into the second rebuttals, do not ignore them. Address the issue briefly with a 10 to 15-second overview. Show that the negative definitions are fair and have been justified with the appropriate standards for re-definition. Then move on! Do not spend more than 15 seconds here.

Case. The next three minutes of the rebuttal should be devoted exclusively to the cases, both affirmative and negative. As you address the negative case, incorporate affirmative arguments that are similar to address both simultaneously. Your preparation time is vital to your ability to do this, since your "cross references" to the affirmative case should be made prior to the beginning of the rebuttal. You should not be making a negative argument and then looking down the affirmative flow to see which arguments are similar. Make all cross references during prep time.

To make this simultaneous comparison of negative and affirmative contentions, begin by addressing the first negative case point and whatever related affirmative contention applies. In addressing each point, use what is called the rebuttal circle. This is defined in the following four steps:

1. Do not restate your argument and your opponent's response.
2. State your argument, and provide additional logic, analysis, or evidence to uphold the contention.
3. Discuss your opponent's response.
4. Tell the judge why this response is not valid because of the logic, analysis, or evidence just presented.

Some points of your case will have been covered in your support of the negative value during the first two minutes of the rebuttal. Address these sections, then refer the judge to your initial discussion.

After completing your case, go down the affirmative case, point by point. As you come to a contention, either address the contention with new evidence, logic, or analysis, or refer the judge to prior support you presented. Some of the affirmative case will have been covered in the initial comparison of the values and criteria, and still another section will have been discussed in reference to the negative case. The sections that have not been attacked by these two avenues, however, should be attacked here.

The total amount of time spent on this part of the rebuttal should not exceed two and one-half to three minutes. After this section of the rebuttal is completed, you should have 30 seconds remaining.

Conclusion. While it is tempting to use all three minutes of the rebuttal for addressing issues, lay aside the last 15 to 30 seconds of the rebuttal to step forward and talk with the judge (instead of *at* the judge). Put down all cards, briefs, cases, flowsheets, etc. Step away from the podium, and review the round in your own words. You should especially focus on how your value is superior to your opponent's value (by way of your criteria), and how negating the resolution creates the "pure" value. The goal of this discussion is to revive the judge-debater rapport established in the case opening. Remember, the judge will ultimately evaluate your performance in the round. It is far more important that you appear persuasive than it is for you to have won the last argument. Thirty seconds of time invested here will return innumerable rewards.

Second Negative Rebuttal Strategies

The negative has an advantage of having the longest rebuttal in the round. The negative has six minutes in which to respond to four minutes of the affirmative's first rebuttal. If done properly, the negative can give the affirmative a "knock out punch." The affirmative has only three minutes to respond to all that is addressed in the second negative rebuttal. If you are conscious of what must get done and plan ahead in your organization, you will be able to introduce enough analysis and argumentation to prevent the affirmative from addressing it all. There may be a great deal of "extensiveness" to offer to each argument in the rebuttal, but realize that it will be the number of well founded arguments, not the extensiveness of a few, that will defeat the affirmative. Provide detailed discussion to the most important issues and light discussion and support to the less significant issues. The goal is to introduce enough issues to prevent the affirmative from addressing them all. To help accomplish this goal, this section enumerates several qualities that can help formulate a successful second rebuttal. The most important qualities to incorporate in the last rebuttal are:

1. Make Note of Affirmative "Drops." It is unfair to the negative for the affirmative to *drop* or not address a contention, value, criteria, or argument, and then pick it up again in the second affirmative rebuttal. The negative has no way of responding to these arguments, since there is not another negative speech. The penalty for dropping an argument in the first affirmative rebuttal is to lose that argument. If an affirmative has dropped one of your contentions, values, criteria, etc., he or she should lose it. The negative must point out that the affirmative has dropped the argument. If the negative does not point it out, then it is assumed that the negative also has dropped the argument, in which case, the argument, value, etc. is dropped from the round entirely. The bottom line is this: point out to the judge what your opponent has dropped in the first affirmative rebuttal.

2. Stay Time Conscious. Your time allocation should resemble the following:

30	Seconds	Criteria Comparison
2	Minutes	Value Comparison
3	Minutes	Case Comparison
15-30	Seconds	Concluding Remarks

3. Effective Extensions. Extend the negative arguments and responses to the affirmative case. Your goal in the second negative rebuttal is to introduce enough well-developed arguments that the affirmative cannot respond to them all in the three minutes he or she has in the second affirmative rebuttal. Extension is vital to winning the round for the negative.

The following strategies that are explained on pages 126-127 should also be employed in the second negative rebuttal: **Good Prior Planning, Word Efficiency, Effective Filtration, Effective Grouping, Effective Cross Application, and Effective Persuasiveness.**

Suggested Activities

1. Have one student read an affirmative case, and have three students prepare a negative speech in response. Have the class listen to all three, but have the negative speakers out of the room for the other negative speeches. Brainstorm as a class which speaker was more effective and why, and which arguments were more effective and why.

2. Practice 30-second final persuasive speeches.

3. Write an essay over the methods of comparing and contrasting the affirmative and negative values.

Chapter 17
Argument Fallacies and Tests of Evidence

Learning Objectives

Chapter 17 explains the common fallacies in arguments presented in Lincoln-Douglas debates. As debaters become more experienced, they begin to recognize the flaws in opponent's arguments. Debaters should also listen to evidence carefully and determine if it is valid. This chapter explains how to sharpen your ability to detect faulty logic and evidence.

After completing this chapter you should be able to:

1. **Understand the importance of analyzing opponents' arguments and evidence.**

2. **List and explain the five common logical fallacies.**

3. **Explain how the common debate fallacies occur in Lincoln-Douglas.**

4. **Understand how to detect weaknesses in opponents' evidence.**

5. **List and explain commonly misused debate arguments.**

New Terms

Fallacy
Fallacy busting
Misused argument
Ad hominem argument

Introduction

Ideally, debate is a search for truth through logical analysis. Realistically, truth is difficult to define. What is logical may not be real or true. If you watch detective or murder mystery television shows or movies, you know that the logical clues don't always lead to the real criminal.

A debater's search for truth is more realistically a search for what makes the most sense in a given round. For a judge, the better set of arguments is the one which withstands logical tests and tests of evidence. Your responsibility is to reveal weaknesses in an opponent's thinking and to avoid them in your own. To do this, you must familiarize yourself with common *fallacies* or flaws in your opponent's reasoning, and weaknesses in evidence.

Common Fallacies

The process of proving flaws in your opponent's arguments is called *fallacy busting*. The following section is designed to highlight some of the most commonly used fallacies. It is important to become familiar with the following *misused arguments* so that you can beat them when your opponent uses them against you. It is also important that you avoid using them yourself.

There are several categories of fallacies. Five of them common to debate arguments are: appeals to tradition, hasty generalizations, appeals to popular opinion, ad hominem arguments, and begging the question.

Appeals to Tradition

An appeal to tradition is an argument that claims something is preferable because it always has been so, or something is not preferable because it never has been so. In debate rounds such appeals often take the form of references to the Constitution or to the Supreme Court's philosophy on a given issue. The faulty logic in this argument is that the Supreme Court continually reassesses the ordering of values. As society changes, the order of values changes as well. Arguing that we should continue to do or believe something because of a long-standing tradition, in and of itself, is not justification to accept the claim.

The other problem with arguments based on the Constitution or the Supreme Court is that these arguments assume United States traditions are applicable worldwide. Unless the topic is specific to the U.S., our traditions are not the best guide for society as a whole.

Hasty Generalization

This is a conclusion based on incomplete evidence. Debaters make hasty generalizations for one of two reasons: lack of research to argue against a new or different argument or an assumption based on a belief something is good or preferable because it is a value. This is one of the most common fallacies in debate, and, therefore, warrants considerable discussion.

An argument based on the belief that democracy is the best form of government is an example of a potentially unsupported argument. The logic behind this argument rests in the "value" of protecting democracy. This fallacy is surprisingly common, because most debaters have grown up with the idea that democracy is indeed the best form of government and certainly an idea worth protecting. The problem with this idea is that it focuses entirely on impressions cast by childhood teachings and not upon present comparison of all social governments. It may be true that democracy is the best government, but that must be proven by the opponent. Do not let an opponent assume that democracy is valid just because it is democracy. The institution of democracy has many problems, and just because it is called "democracy" does not necessarily make it the best form of government. For example, if democracy is so perfect, why would a few lobbyists control many of the national policy decisions that result in thousands of homeless, a threatened environment, and underfunded education? This is not to say that democracy is not worth protecting. It simply means that a debater must prove that democracy is valuable in order for it to be judged as such in a debate.

In addition, there is nothing exclusive about most resolutions in respect to the United States. Selecting to affirm or negate a resolution based on what it does to democracy may not be a valid reason given that non-democratic countries are also affected by the position the resolution presents.

Other debaters may argue that a form of government, such as a parliamentary form, is preferable to preserving certain values such as economic, military, and social stability. In this particular argument, the debater could claim that because the Japanese have found great success in the parliamentary form of government, it is reasonable to assume that all others who try that form will enjoy equal success. It is easy to convince a judge that because something has worked in one society, it will be equally successful in others. This conclusion is not necessarily true.

Appeals to Popular Opinion.

This is also referred to as the bandwagon fallacy. This fallacy exists when an argument is made based on how many people believe in or do something. Popular support does not necessarily prove a value is superior. Consider the roots of Lincoln-Douglas debate and the slavery versus states rights issues. There certainly was popular opinion in the South in support of states rights, but that did not justify protecting the value over human rights.

Any debater relying on public opinion polls to support a position is potentially guilty of committing this fallacy. The popular opinion cannot stand alone as proof. It is essential also to demonstrate the impacts of upholding a particular value.

Ad Hominem Arguments

This Latin term means "against the man." An *ad hominem argument* is made against a person instead of against the person's ideas. If a debater quotes a particular philosopher who upholds a value, an opponent might argue that the value should not be decided based on that person's support, because he or she is not as highly respected as other philosophers. Other philosophers might be more famous, but that does not mean that the lesser-known philosopher does not have a valid point. It is important that the idea be attacked on its merits and not on the personality or fame of the person putting forth the idea.

Begging the Question

This is a form of circular reasoning. The claim and the reason for making the claim are the same. For instance, a debater might argue that something is the moral and correct thing to do because it is moral and correct. The morality and correctness are left unproven.

As with some of the other fallacies discussed, the basis for this one is rooted in our culture and our beliefs that there is a single right or moral way of doing things. "It's the American way," becomes the justification. Again, we cannot assume that an argument based on our system and culture is relevant to a broader view of the world that Lincoln-Douglas topics typically ask debaters to analyze.

Commonly Misused Debate Arguments

In addition to the above fallacies, there are several arguments that are misused frequently. All of them are arguments with which you should be familiar.

If Not A, Then B

It is common to encounter debaters who believe that if the resolution states that A is greater than B, the negative must only prove that B is equal to A in importance. However, the negative has an equal responsibility to have and support a case that illustrates why the resolution should not be affirmed, and why the value supported by the negative is superior to that supported by the affirmative. The negative must prove both that A should not be valued above B, and that B should be valued above A.

The mere existence of the resolution implies a conflict between the two objects of evaluation—A and B. If A and B could co-exist harmoniously and equally, there would be no need for a resolution as there would be no social conflict. Furthermore, the existence of a resolution implies that when the objects of the evaluation come into conflict, there must be a decision. For instance, when a police officer stands on a suspect's porch, he or she must decide whether to enter and invade privacy to protect society from drug sales or to leave the porch and validate that the right to privacy is more important than the protection of society. A police officer cannot remain on the porch forever—not entering and not leaving. He or she must make a choice.

Totally Defend Your Value

A commonly misused argument is the idea that if a resolution states, "Resolved: A should be valued over B," the affirmative is locked into attacking B and defending A. The word "totally" is important in that many debaters assume that if the affirmative does not totally defend A, he or she will lose the round. On occasion, this locks debaters into missing their most important responsibility in the round. The most important affirmative responsibility is not to maintain the "perfect goodness" in the affirmative value, A, or ultimate badness in the negative value B, but rather to illustrate that A should be placed above B. It is entirely possible that the affirmative will support the merits of both A and B, but he or she will support the merits of A more than B. This is all that an affirmative must accomplish to win the round. Negative attacks against value A mean nothing if the affirmative establishes that value A is still a higher priority than value B. This works both ways. The negative needs to prove only that value B should be valued over value A, not that value A is always bad and B is always good.

Time Frame Limitations

It is worth reiterating that while Lincoln-Douglas resolutions are not limited to the most convenient time or place, they should be addressed in the appropriate time frame. The values in Lincoln-Douglas are pervasive to every human and every society. In addition, these resolutions include all time frames in which the resolution dilemma exists. Both debaters should rely upon evidential support that is applicable to the resolution. Furthermore, the affirmative or the negative cannot chose one time frame and attempt to resolve the resolution only then. For example, the affirmative cannot choose only the early 1940s to discuss national security's preeminence over individual rights. By the same token, the negative cannot choose only times of peace in negating the resolution.

Tests of Evidence

Evidence is an essential part of Lincoln-Douglas debate. Opinions, facts, and statistics can all bolster a debater's case. However, evidence must meet strict tests to assist a debater in proving a point. The following are common tests to apply to your own and your opponents' evidence.

Is Evidence In Context?

Occasionally a piece of documented evidence is presented in a round to validate a certain claim, such as, "The individual's inability to know prevented him or her from enjoying a full and happy life." If your opponent read that card documenting a case study, and then applied that card to a "censorship of the media" argument, he or she would be unbeatable. If the full context of the card were known, however, its meaning might change considerably. For instance, if the card referred to withholding adoption information from a child, and not the media's withholding of information from the general public, the card would have a different meaning altogether.

It is also common to encounter debaters who support their cases with evidence that has nothing to do with contentions. Pay close attention to what the card is supposed to support (its "slug"), and what the evidence piece actually states. It is common for a debater to state a contention point, or slug, and then read a piece of evidence that has nothing or very little to do with that contention. In most cases, the judge and the opponent are too busy writing the slug to listen adequately to the evidence. Pay close attention to the evidence that is read. If you are unsure about the relation of a card to its slug, ask to **see** the card in the cross-examination period.

Finally watch for pieces of evidence that sound "diced." Occasionally a debater will find it advantageous to eliminate certain parts of a piece of evidence and replace these with ellipses (". . .") to make what used to be a negative card sound affirmative. A favorite cut is to eliminate critical portions of the card, and read only those portions that support the debater's claim. For example, a debater supporting smokers' rights might read the following card (non-read portions are in parentheses): "(Even though some believe that)...smoking is not harmful...(this is not true)." With any piece of evidence, the elimination or insertion of a "not" will change the evidence's meaning entirely. You can see that these two cuts change the meaning of the card altogether. Remember, if a card appears too good to be true, it probably is. Ask to see it if it sounds suspicious.

Is the Source Qualified?

A source must be qualified on the topic at hand. It is important to know who your sources are and why they are qualified to reach their conclusions. Competence is the formal name given for this test. A competent person is one who is knowledgeable on the topic and is well-known as an expert. Just because a person is an expert on one topic does not make that person an expert on a field outside his or her scope of experience.

In addition to being competent, it is important that a source be unbiased. You need to know on what basis the individual reached a conclusion, and whether or not an outside interest influenced the person's conclusion. For instance, a member of Congress who receives large contributions from the National Rifle Association is likely to claim that individual freedoms are jeopardized by a waiting period for handgun purchases. Does the individual really believe that? Is sufficient evidence provided by the Congress member to prove a loss of freedom? These are the types of questions you should ask about sources.

Relevance

Evidence must relate to the issue under discussion. Evidence on the right to privacy that refers to cases of search and seizure does not necessarily apply to a topic dealing with pornography. A debater must prove that the relationship exists.

Sufficiency

This test is not as important in Lincoln-Douglas as it is in cross-examination debate or extemporaneous speaking since logical analysis is more important than evidence. However, a debater must still demonstrate that the degree of proof provided is sufficient to support the point. There should be sufficient examples to prove that a value is achieved or jeopardized.

Placing qualitative importance upon certain ideas without extensive support within the round is also a violation of the sufficiency test. Some concepts, such as "life," are assumed to be good by most people. In certain cases, however, these ideals may not be valued as all that important. Out of habit it is easy to refer to freedom, liberty, individuality, life, etc. as inherently good. It is true that in many cases these concepts are inherently good, but in many other cases, they are not. As as rule, make sure that evidence firmly establishes a value's importance. Do not rely upon an assumption that these are automatically "valuable," because a good judge will not assume anything.

Recency

On topics dealing with contemporary issues, such as health care or the environment, evidence should be as current as possible. In addition, expert testimony from philosophers or other credible individuals should relate to the context in which the issue is discussed.

For instance, Thomas Jefferson was capable of commenting on many areas of philosophy, but he is not an expert on twentieth century immigration problems. How could Jefferson have known the U.S. would be faced with such a dilemma? The immigration problem in the eighteenth century was getting people to come to the U.S., not to stay out of the U.S. Strangely, a respected source such as Thomas Jefferson is almost never refuted by debaters even when his comments are not applicable to current social dilemmas. It is true that many noted philosophers are credible, but it is not necessarily true that these individuals are experts in social dilemmas in the 20th century. Any 18th century individual who is used to comment on 20th century social issues may be out of touch with the essence of the social dilemma.

While the date of evidence used in Lincoln-Douglas debate does not make it any better or worse, the evidence used to support analysis within a round should be taken from the time period in which the resolution conflict exists. Resolutions that involve concepts, ideas, actions, or technology that is relatively new to humankind is better addressed by more modern philosophers and evidence. This does not mean that evidence has to be "right off the press" but it does mean that any documentation used in supporting analysis should be within the proper time context. Some value conflicts have been around since the beginning of humankind, and almost any philosopher has domain in commenting on the topic. The rights of the individual versus the rights of the society, for example, was a social dilemma in Jefferson's era and today. Quoting Jefferson as saying, "America must seek to acquire more land and entice more immigration into the country," is taken out of context and should not be allowed.

Suggested Activities

1. Write an essay discussing the different types of fallacies. Use examples to illustrate each type.

2. Listen and identify fallacies in a tape of an L-D round.

Unit IV
THE MECHANICS
OF LINCOLN-DOUGLAS DEBATE

Unit IV is designed to explain the fundamental skills that are necessary for the constructives and the rebuttals. This unit particularly is devoted to the verbal communication of the debater in a Lincoln-Douglas round.

Chapter 18 addresses the fundamental skills of delivery and persuasive techniques. This chapter focuses on multiple areas of delivery, particularly on the strategies the debater can use to improve his or her appearance on the "debate stage."

Chapter 19 is designed to develop successful cross-examination skills. This chapter focuses primarily on the ways in which the debater can use the cross- examination period to his or her greatest benefit in gaining momentum in the round.

Chapter 20 focuses on the proper use of preparation time. This chapter is concerned with the debater's responsibilities for each potential preparation time slot. This chapter nicely ties with Unit III, since it outlines the primary issues that should be prepared for, and subsequently acted upon, in the rebuttal speeches.

The final chapter is Chapter 21. This chapter illustrates the different methods of recording the argumentation in the round by introducing the concept of "flowing." Two different methods are illustrated in this chapter, as are several tips for developing both speed and precision in recording the round's events.

While all of these chapters are important. Chapters 18 and 21 should be read in situations where limited time is available to the debater prior to a tournament. Chapters 19 and 22 can be addressed at a later time but are still vitally important to the developing debater.

Chapter 18
Effective Delivery
and Persuasion Techniques

Learning Objectives

This chapter teaches the basics of delivery. Unlike cross-examination team debate, the success of Lincoln-Douglas is as much dependent upon a persuasive style of speech as it is upon what is said. This chapter illustrates the fundamental skills that are a part of persuasive speech.

After completing this chapter you should be able to:

1. **Understand why delivery is important in Lincoln-Douglas debate.**

2. **Understand the considerations in developing an appropriate rate of delivery.**

3. **Understand the importance of transitions, vocal tone, and harmonics.**

4. **Identify common nervous behaviors and know how to eliminate them.**

5. **Understand the importance of body language, appropriate dress, and good eye contact.**

New Terms

Delivery

Transitions

Fluency

Auditory

Eye Contact

Introduction

Public speaking is a means of communicating a speaker's thoughts to an audience. Persuasive speaking is the process of presenting information in a manner which leads an audience to accept and act upon the speaker's information. In Lincoln-Douglas, the primary goal is persuasive speaking. The speaker must present ideas in a fashion that is understandable and pleasing to the audience. Understanding the message is obviously critical. A message that makes the audience feel at ease and projects the image that the speaker is at ease is also important. Why? A speaker who appears comfortable also appears confident, and a confident speaker is a persuasive speaker.

It is also important that the speaker gain and maintain audience attention. This, like the projection of confidence, is also a function of delivery. In essence, the process of involving the audience in the speech is the ultimate goal of delivery.

In respect to Lincoln-Douglas, however, the most important goal is to appear as the better debater in the round. You should note that while the case, criteria, and value are all critical elements upon which the judge will make his or her decision, the final decision rests upon the way in which the debater presents thse elements. At the bottom of every Lincoln-Douglas ballot is a statement the judge must complete:

"In my opinion, the better debating was done by the _____."

The important concept here is that while the substance of the debate is important, it is ultimately **you**, the debater, who is judged. The way in which you present your ideas is as, if not more, important than what you actually say. This chapter is designed to help develop the skills that can make you a better presenter and communicator as well as a better debater.

The Four Divisions of Delivery

The components of a successful *delivery* are almost endless, since small, subtle elements may contribute to the "pleasing nature" of a presentation. These components, as they relate to Lincoln-Douglas debate, however, can be divided into four categories. These categories include the rate of delivery, the degree of fluency and successful progression from one thought to the next, the tone and harmonics of the voice, and the speaker's physical appearance. Each of these components is critical to the Lincoln-Douglas debater's success.

Rate of Delivery

The rate of speaking is one of the primary factors that determines a debater's image in the judge's mind. A delivery that is too fast can intimidate, anger, or otherwise isolate the judge, and it won't persuade the judge. On the contrary, a delivery that is too slow creates an atmosphere of boredom, and the debater will again risk losing the judge's attention. So what is the appropriate rate at which a debater should progress?

The appropriate rate is the rate at which you feel most comfortable. For most individuals, this is the rate of normal conversation. Strive for a "normal" tone, and you will be the most persuasive. If you lose the audiences' attention, you are probably progressing too slowly. If, on the other hand, your speeches are interrupted by many "uhs," "ums," and "ands," you are probably speaking too fast.

The best way to judge your speed is to try it out. Through practice rounds (and by reading ballots from tournaments), you should be able to garner enough feedback as to whether you are going too rapidly and losing your audience or going too slowly and boring the audience. Tape record or video tape practice to get a better sense of your rate.

The ultimate goal in the presentation is to create a feeling of familiarity and comfort for the judge, and this begins with a speed of delivery that is natural to him or her. Easier said than done, right? Naturally, you will not know the speed of delivery the judge prefers until the round begins. You should begin your presentation at your preferred speed, and continue with this speed through the first speech of the round. As you progress, however, watch the judge's reactions. If you are receiving signals that the judge is lost (a frown, a confused face, etc.) you should slow the pace down. If, on the other hand, the judge's attention begins to wander, you might consider speeding up your pace a bit. You should never increase your pace much past your "best speed." Monitor the judge's reactions and adapt accordingly.

Fluency and Thought Progression

Once you have established your chosen rate, you must develop the "glue" that holds your delivery together: the fluency of *transitions*. Transitions are the words, phrases, or sentences that allow you to connect one thought to another. The effective use of transitions provides for the element of fluency. It is important that you can link separate thoughts together into one comprehensive presentation, since this is what wins rounds.

Fluency has its genesis in familiarity. The more comfortable you are with the material, the better your fluency will become. For example, compare your ability to fluently present the alphabet versus the "Gettysburg Address." The more the material is second nature to you, the more fluent your presentation will become. The more the progression of one thought leads to the next, the more persuasive your presentation will be.

A related element to familiarity is confidence. The more you are confident in your ability to present a persuasive speech, the more persuasive and fluent your speeches will become. Self-confidence arises from two sources. First, you must convince yourself that you are capable of performing this event. If you can read this book and follow its message, you are capable of presenting a persuasive speech. Second, you must build your confidence through practice rounds. Even if you are without the opportunity to engage in practice rounds, you can still practice "imaginary" rounds while you are home alone. If you do have the opportunity for practice rounds, engage in the activity of "debating yourself" while you are alone. It will not make you crazy to practice your speeches while alone. If you start losing the debates with yourself, then you should seek professional advice! In addition to practicing constructives, you should also practice speaking in rebuttals (make up arguments from a fictitious opponent, and try to beat them), since fluency is equally important in rebuttals.

Vocal Characteristics

A persuasive debater must present a case in a familiar and comfortable fashion so that the judge is "trusting" of what the debater has to say and not distracted by obnoxious elements of the debater's presentation. Vocal characteristics are fundamental to many debaters' inability to "put their judge at ease." Typically, one of three main elements is responsible for this problem.

The first problem is the most distracting but also the easiest to correct: the use of improper grammar and/or slang terms. Words such as "wash" and "can't," when pronounced incorrectly, can destroy a debater's persuasiveness of delivery. It may seem trivial, but one word that is pronounced incorrectly can sufficiently distract a judge. Equally troublesome is the substitution of slang terms for otherwise correct words. For example, "awesome" is a good word, but not as substitution for the term "beneficial." (Consider: "Individual rights is beneficial for our society," and "Individual rights is an awesome thing for our society.") The quickest solution to this problem is to engage in practice rounds with your coach (or an English teacher) as the judge. Ask this individual to focus not on the content of the round but instead upon your diction. Take the critiques from these individuals seriously, and make an honest effort to correct problems. If you don't have this opportunity, record yourself on audio or videotape, and listen to your diction. Problems soon will be obvious.

The second fundamental problem many debaters experience is local accents. This is not a problem if you debate only at local tournaments. If you debate nationally, it might be. There is absolutely nothing wrong with a local accent, but some judges may not get past an unusual accent to hear what you are saying. To solve this problem, you must recognize which words bare the "blunt" of your accent. That is, you should isolate the words or syllables that most noticeably demonstrate your accent, by using audio tape. Also, you should begin to note how other "persuasive" individuals speak. For example, watching network news anchors will provide you with the "neutral accent" that is characteristic of persuasive speaking.

There is the possibility that you may naturally possess unflattering vocal characteristics (squeaky, whining, or nasal sounds). Work with a drama teacher or someone who can give you voice and diction training.

Finally, there is the importance of varying tone to maintain the judge's interest in your presentation. For example, a monotone (all the same tone with no variation) simply is boring. As a consequence, attempt to vary the tone of your voice, especially at critically important times, through changes in pitch, inflection and emphasis. When you are presenting a particularly important point, the tone and volume of your voice should rise slightly to illustrate its importance. Also note that strategically placed pauses can be as effective as speaking. Pauses occurring immediately before and after a contention can accent this argument's importance. Develop this skill through practice.

Physical Appearance

The final element of a successful delivery is the debater's physical appearance. While the first three elements all affect the judge's impression of you via *auditory* signals (what the judge hears), this element affects the judge's impression of you by way of visual cues.

Nervousness. It is natural to be nervous when beginning a debate round. What you should try to control, however, is the appearance of nervousness. One of the best ways to eliminate nervousness of any kind is through practice rounds! It is important, however, that as you practice you recognize any nervous habits you exhibit. Twisting a ring, playing with your hair, tugging at your blouse or tie, pacing or shifting your weight, playing with change or keys in your pocket, and rolling your weight back and forth on the sides of your feet are all forms of nervousness. The best way to determine if you are exhibiting nervous behaviors is to ask your coach to watch your presentations and comment on any distracting behaviors. If possible, you also should take advantage of videotaping your practice debate rounds, since this will give you direct feedback as to what is distracting in your performance. At home, you should practice presenting your constructive speeches (or mythical rebuttal speeches) in front of a mirror, since this allows you to see your nervous behaviors immediately as they occur. Recognize any nervous behaviors you exhibit, and make a conscious effort to correct or eliminate them.

Stage Presence. Your presence in a debate round is as important to the judge's conception of you as an actor's presence on a stage is to the audience. For this reason, your spatial and physical placement and movement is critical to your delivery.

The first element of stage presence is where you stand before the judge. Locate yourself in the middle of the judge's focal path, immediately in front of him or her, when possible. Obviously, if the judge chooses to sit to the extreme side of the room, you will not want to stand against that wall. You should stay as close to the middle of the room as possible and still be in the judge's primary visual field. It is also important to maintain a comfortable distance from the judge. You should be close enough to the judge to maintain his or her attention, but not so close as to make the judge uneasy.

The temptation to hide behind desks, podiums, or tables should also be avoided. The more objects between you and your judge, the less your judge will feel the urgency to pay attention to your speech. Furthermore, gestures illustrating certain points will be hidden from the judge's view, and thus, a large portion of your communication ability will be handicapped. It is to your advantage, therefore, to stand away from these "blocking" objects.

The second element of stage presence is the temporal component, defined as the "timing of movements on stage." As we discussed in the section on "nervousness," uncontrolled pacing distracts from a presentation. Remaining in the same place throughout the speech is, however, equally harmful to a delivery. If you do not move throughout the speech, you risk losing the judge's attention. For this reason, deliver the introduction in the middle front of the room. After finishing the opening, take a step or two back while the "less important" aspects of the speech (i.e., definitions, preview, etc.) are presented. From this position, begin the speech. As you get to the second important contention in the speech, take three or four small, casual steps to the front and left of your present position. From this position, develop the second contention. As you reach the third contention, take three to four steps to the right of your present position. Following the third contention, take a couple of steps back, lay down your evidence and case, and come front and center (the position where you presented your introduction) to present the conclusion.

It is not so critical that you follow the above protocol exactly. It is important that you move while presenting your speech to maintain the judge's attention and that this movement be controlled, planned and purposeful, and correlate with natural "breaks" in the speech.

Appearance. Your first impression is the most significant one you make. As a consequence, dress in a manner that is conservative and acceptable. What you should understand, however, is that many of the judges will be older, and their opinions will generally favor a clean cut, well dressed young man or woman.

Avoid wearing distracting clothes, make-up, jewelry, or other accessories. For example, large earrings, wild ties, large class rings, "gaudy" necklaces, hats, "slick or shiny" suits, etc., are all examples of accessories that can distract the judge from what you have to say. Any article of clothing that restricts movement is also dangerous in that your full attention may be drawn away from the purpose of the round. If you have a question about appropriate dress, consult your debate coach.

Gestures. In addition to the spoken word, there are many physical forms of communication used to illustrate the importance of a message. Gestures are the means by which you use body language to communicate added emphasis. The use of the arms and hands allows you to illustrate the importance of a topic. Once the important point has been made, "return" the gesture to your side. Gestures are much like the movement around the stage. It is critical that they be used sparingly to ensure their effectiveness. If the judge comes to recognize that a gesture correlates with an important point, the extension of a gesture will have increasing power in influencing the judge. Gestures used non-sparingly will have little or no impact on the judge.

The use of facial expression is also an important mechanism for illustrating the importance of a contention. For example, raising the eyebrows can show surprise or concern. Feelings of sincerity can be generated by this gesture, and other facial gestures hold the same power if used thriftily.

Eye Contact. The final element of effective delivery is *eye contact*. Eye contact allows you to impart a feeling of sincerity with respect to what you are saying. Furthermore, eye contact ensures that you maintain the judge's attention. If you decide to bypass eye contact, it will be easy for the judge to "tune out" your message with little remorse. Effective eye contact can make a judge feel the weight of his or her obligation to listen.

In addition, effective eye contact ensures that you will be in touch with any signals the judge may be sending, such as head nods, frowns, looks of confusion, etc. Eye contact is the critical component for success.

Suggested Activities

1. Pick evidence at random and read orally.

2. Take an old flowsheet and deliver a first negative constructive without using evidence.

3. Video tape your next practice round and write a critique of your performance.

Chapter 19
Cross-Examination Skills

Learning Objectives

Chapter 19 teaches how to use the cross-examination periods. A three-minute cross-examination period immediately follows each constructive speech. This is the time the opposing debater asks questions of the debater who has just finished speaking. This chapter illustrates some key concepts about the cross-examination period as well as provides a list of dos and don'ts. The cross-examination period is the only time during the debate in which both debaters are on stage for direct comparison. Thus, it offers strategic possibilities.

After completing this chapter you should be able to:

1. Understand how cross-examination can be abused.

2. List the strategies for a successful cross-examination period.

3. Explain why it is important to control the period.

4. Understand the need for questions and how to prepare prior to the round.

New Terms

Clarification
Cross-examination traps

Introduction

Although there is conflict throughout the round, the cross-examination periods represent the time of the greatest direct conflict. What is said in the cross-examination periods rarely is recorded by the judge, but the manner in which you conduct yourself can influence a judge's ballot. This section underscores the importance of the cross-examination periods and establishes a strategy for conducting cross-examination. In preparing for and participating in cross-exam periods, control and momentum are the keys.

Abuse of Cross-Examination Periods

Before discussing cross-examination strategies, it is important to look at the way Lincoln-Douglas debaters can abuse these periods. Frequently, debaters lose rounds because they misuse the cross-examination periods. Below are three common abuses:

The Rest Period Philosophy

The first mistake made, especially by beginning debaters, is to use the cross-examination period as a "time out" to "rest." The debater who ignores the importance of the cross-examination period is simply "sitting out of the game" while the opponent passes him or her by. Every second in the round is a second that is being evaluated by the judge. If you allow your opponent to control the six minutes of cross-examination, you allow your opponent six more minutes to persuade the judge of his or her position and the opportunity to establish an invincible momentum. It is your job to continue to persuade the judge even during the cross-examination periods.

The Clarification Philosophy

On occasion, *clarification* is necessary. If your opponent does not provide a clear presentation of his or her ideas, it is crucial to ask for clarification. It is impossible to debate the issues without understanding them. It is important, however, to draw the line between "necessary" and "excessive." For example, asking your opponent to "briefly go over all of the case" is inexcusable, and shows, at best, you did not understand anything that was said, and, at worst, that you do not know how to respond to anything that was said. Clarification should be used in extreme moderation.

The Argumentative Philosophy

Many debaters subscribe to the philosophy that debating is the same as arguing. This is not the case. Debating involves deliberation of ideas; arguing is a confrontation between people. In Lincoln-Douglas debate, you are debating against your opponent's ideas, not your opponent. As a consequence, personal attacks on your opponent do not help to win rounds. In many cases, Lincoln-Douglas debaters use the cross-examination periods to "bicker" with the opponent:

> Debater One- "On your first point... You really don't believe that, do you?"
>
> Debater Two- "Yes, I do."
>
> Debater One- "Oh, come on, you can't really believe that? Where do you get that opinion? Well , let's go on. Your second point, now you can't honestly say you believe this one?"
>
> Debater Two- "Uh, yes... I can."
>
> Debater One- "You can? Oh, I don't believe it! You are impossible. I can't believe you! No further questions."

The questioner and the judge gain little, as far as ideas are concerned, from this type of exchange.

Strategies to Successful Cross-Examination

Understanding the previous pitfalls helps you establish a successful strategy to control the round's momentum. The following suggestions for strategy development should help you optimize the cross-examination time.

Argument Selection

The mark of a good debater is the ability to determine which arguments must be further clarified. Failure to understand the opponent's arguments is a result of either not understanding the topic or poor note taking skills. Using cross-examination time to ask an opponent to repeat or explain an argument does not develop your position. Work on listening and taking notes to reduce the need for easy questions. Certain arguments are going to be unbeatable without some preparation on your part between speeches.

In addition to avoiding questions which ask only for repetition or explanation, also avoid questions on complex arguments. Opponents have the advantage since they fully understand their arguments. You will be familiar with many of your opponent's arguments. These are the arguments you should select for cross-examination. Remember, the key to a successful cross-examination period is momentum. A series of questions focusing on issues you understand better than the opponent does makes it appear as if you control the round. If you ask questions about issues your opponent understands better than you do, your opponent appears to be in control. Consider the following scenario:

Debater One- "You say that the individual's right to privacy is essential in that if it falls, all other rights will fall. Is that correct?"

Debater Two- "Yes, that is correct."

Debater One-"Let's go to your second point."

This exchange establishes the credibility of Debater Two's argument, because Debater One obviously has no reply to the argument. The momentum swings to Debater Two. Debater One must work that much harder to regain the round's momentum.

Control Time Allocation

All of the speeches in Lincoln-Douglas debate are given specific time limits to ensure fairness. The notable exception to this rule is the cross-examination time. It is possible that one debater could control the collective six minutes of the two cross-examination periods. Imagine debating an opponent who had six more minutes to speak than you did! It would be almost impossible to win. Your goal is to create that "unfairness" by speaking more than your opponent during the cross-examination periods. You want to occupy as much of both cross-examination periods as is possible. The more you talk, the better your chance of planting your arguments in the judge's mind and of establishing momentum in the round.

The quickest way to establish domination is to prevent the opponent from doing the same. If you prevent your opponent from controlling the cross-examination time, you will have gained this advantage. Do this by asking questions that can be answered in yes/no or short answer format. Yes/no responses are generally not persuasive, and thus, by forcing your opponent to respond with a yes or no answer, you not only control quantity of time, but also quality. Questions that begin with, "Would you please explain. . ." are not advisable, since a good debater turns such a question into a three-minute extension of the case.

It is critical that you are careful in how you phrase a yes or no question. Some questions cannot be answered in a yes/no format, and you should not persist in badgering your opponent into answering with just a yes or no or else you might annoy the judge. For example, a debater who persists with the following: "Yes or no . . . I said, yes or no. No explanation is needed, just say yes or no . . . yes or no, that's all I want . . . Yes or no," will probably not score big points with the judge. Suppose someone asks you the question, "Have you stopped beating your siblings yet? Yes or no?" How would you respond? You would want to explain that the question assumes you beat them in the first place.

Remember your own your cross-examination period. If you allow your opponent to ask questions in both cross-examination periods, you subsequently allow your opponent to gain ownership of the round. Occasionally, it is necessary to simply say, "Remember, I asked you first," when an opponent attempts to turn the table. If an opponent does not understand the question and asks what was meant by the question, it is perfectly fine to respond to the request and ask your question in different words. By no means, however, should you answer a question your opponent asks in response to your question. In your cross-examination, you should be the only debater asking questions about the round. Keep in mind that when a debater asks a question in response to your own, it is usually because he or she does not have an answer to your question. Don't let table-turning relieve the debater of answering. Invite your opponent into answering with a yes or no, but never insist that he or she answer only with a yes or no.

It is also to your advantage to control your opponent's cross-examination period. When you are being questioned, give long and elaborate answers. This controls the balance of time in the round. There are three benefits to this action: it gives added persuasiveness to your answer, it allows for a control of time, and it prevents your opponent from asking many questions.

Once again, take precautions. If an opponent cuts you off in the middle of an answer, be polite and stop the reply. Do not persist in giving an answer after your opponent has moved on. On the other hand, make sure that you persist long enough to give a complete and persuasive answer. If you feel you are being limited by your opponent's "break in," simply and politely state, "If you would like me to fully explain your question, I will be happy to do so, but I cannot give your question justice unless you allow me to complete my reply. The answer to this question is not yes or no." Once again, there is a limitation at which you have to decide if you must persist in your answer in order to maintain momentum, or if you should stop your reply and maintain the image of politeness.

Calling for Evidence

On occasion you will want to see a piece of evidence an opponent has read to review either its source, context, or exact wording. Whenever this situation arises, do not allow the opponent to re-read the card by asking, "Would you please re-read that card under your first subpoint?" If you suspect that your opponent is using the card out of its context, ask to see the card. If your opponent has read the card out of context, it is probable that he or she will read it out of context the second time as well. In addition, if you are preparing an argument against the card, it is to your advantage to be able to study the exact wording instead of hearing your opponent's interpretation of the card. Nothing is gained by hearing a piece of evidence a second time. It eats up valuable cross-examination time which could have otherwise been used for other crucial questions. Finally, if the judge by chance did not hear the argument the first time, he or she will most certainly catch it the second time.

Proper Demeanor

Avoid arguing against your opponent rather than against the opponent's arguments. Look straight ahead during both cross-examination periods and never at the opponent as this creates the impression that you are bickering. This stance also helps avoid visual distractions. Looking straight ahead creates a professional image, and makes you appear more persuasive because you maintain eye contact with the judge.

Because the cross-examination period is a direct comparison between debaters, it affords the opportunity to make "huge leaps" in rapport building. You should show enough aggressiveness to appear in control of the round, but you should also maintain a certain degree of politeness and professionalism, since this creates a comfortable rapport with the judge. Be determined in questioning, but also be calm and composed in the process.

As impressive as your ideas and thoughts may be, you still may not own the momentum of the round after cross-examination periods. Your appearance is almost as important as what you say. A debater cannot expect to portray an image of control if he or she appears visually dominated by the opponent. You should stand slightly in front of your opponent (even a matter of inches can have a huge effect in terms of visual magnitude). This creates an image that makes you appear "larger" and more masterful. It is also advisable to stand to the side of the podium, as this will occasionally entice your opponent into standing behind the podium. Never stand behind the podium as this creates a subconscious barrier between you and the judge. Be conscious of how you visually appear to the judge, and you'll have an advantage.

At times, it will be critical to interrupt your opponent. If an opponent attempts to eat up your cross-examination time, it is important to use a high degree of tact in interrupting him or her. It is critical to be polite when you interrupt. Begin with a polite, normal tone, "Thank you, that is enough." Then proceed to a slightly louder voice, "That's all I need on that question. Thank you." Finally, if your opponent persists in rambling, smile and say, "Thank you. Can we proceed to the next question?" If this persists, make eye contact with the judge, and then repeat your last statement. Usually, this will be sufficient. It is critical that you say all of these statements with little emotion.

Set Up Arguments

Cross-examination questions are best used to set up your later arguments. When you attempt to establish your negative case or your first affirmative rebuttal, the cross-examination period is essential in preparing the needed groundwork. If you can get your opponent to agree to conclusions that establish your points in the negative constructive or first affirmative rebuttal, it is easy to claim that those are valid arguments when presenting them in their respective speeches. For example, if you can get your opponent to agree to the value of freedom, and you can get him or her to admit that democracy is the best way to achieve the value of freedom, then there is no need to spend two minutes of your next speech trying to convince your judge that democracy is the best value. You only need to say that your opponent agreed to such a conclusion in the cross-examination period. Then you are on your way to winning the round.

You need to be creative to *trap* an opponent. Just as you should anticipate cross-examination questions, you should also anticipate cross-examination responses. You need to know what an opponent will or will not agree with. The best way to trap an opponent is to disguise trap questions. To set a trap, ask a series of yes/no questions that the opponent must agree or disagree with.

Once you have trapped an opponent into a certain conclusion, do not fall victim to the temptation of "letting the cat out of the bag too early." Stop short of the logical conclusion question. Keeping the trap until the next speech prevents an opponent from responding to it immediately. If an opponent has to wait until the next speech to escape the trap, he or she will usually either forget it altogether, or be preoccupied with it for the rest of your speech, either way hurting his or her persuasiveness. Finally, the judge will wait in anticipation wondering, "What was that question in cross-examination for?" This anticipation serves to make the springing of the trap that much more meaningful when exposed in rebuttals.

Incorporate Analogies

Analogies are powerful tools in intellectual discussions. They are also quite dangerous when used improperly. As a consequence, exercise great caution in using analogies, and even more caution when they are being used against you. Analogies are best used as a way of securing agreement. You want to avoid agreeing to something you will regret later.

When an opponent uses an analogy against you during a cross-examination period, attempt to get your opponent to reveal the meaning of the analogy during the cross-examination period. This affords the opportunity of responding to the analogy early before it gets out of hand. The longer an opponent refers to an analogy, and the longer the judge listens to it, the more persuasive it becomes. You do not want an opponent's analogy to make it into the rebuttal speeches because this forces everyone in the round (including yourself) to listen to its meaning for at least the duration of that speech. The implications of the analogy should be out in the open during the cross-examination time. Refer to Chapter 26 to better understand the use of analogies in cross-examination.

Plan Ahead

Lincoln-Douglas debaters hear the same arguments again and again from round to round. Produce questions that apply in each round where a topic is debated and that set traps for the opponent later in the round. Your ability to anticipate is greatly advantageous.

In addition to your own pre-planned questions, take note of good questions your opponents ask you. If a question is difficult for you to answer, write the question down. In later rounds when you are defending that same position, use the question against your new opponent. If it worked against you, you will most likely find it effective against another opponent. If an opponent adequately responds to the question, you will then know how to answer the question if it is ever asked of you again.

A good set of pre-planned affirmative questions also forces consideration of questions you might be asked while negative. In addition, if you ever find yourself lost in a cross-examination period, or without anything to ask, the pre-planned list gives you a "road map" to follow as you proceed. In essence, it ensures you will have a set course for the cross-examination, and you will not drift off on a number of different, inconsequential tangents.

Conclusion

The strategy points explained above are the key ingredients to winning debate rounds in the cross-examination periods. They are also your insurance that you will not be beaten in the cross-examination periods. The above advice will make you good at cross-examination performance. It will not, however, make you great. As with all debate advice, the best way to be a great cross-examining debater is to practice. You will learn how to trap an opponent and respond to his or her traps only by experiencing actual cross-examination in practice debate rounds. The above advice combined with practice will make a debater invincible in the face of the most qualified debaters.

Suggested Activities

1. Present a case and have the entire class cross-examine it without time limits.

2. Using the current resolution or one listed in the book, write a list of pre-planned questions to ask the opponent.

Chapter 20
Using Your Preparation Time

Learning Objectives

Chapter 20 is designed to teach the use of preparation time. Preparation time is the three minutes between speeches used to prepare for the next speech. This chapter should familiarize you with preparation time and give guidelines for its use.

After completing this chapter you should be able to:

1. **Budget preparation time.**

2. **Understand the importance of using all of the preparation time.**

3. **Discuss the responsibilities for each preparation time period.**

4. **Explain the responsibilities of each preparation time opportunity.**

New Terms

Preparation time
Composure

Introduction

Preparation time or prep time is designed to allow the debater to regroup and organize his or her thoughts prior to presenting the next speech. As a consequence, Lincoln-Douglas debaters are expected to make their "unplanned rebuttal speeches" appear well planned and organized. As might be expected, however, this task is difficult. Debaters generally have difficulty making rebuttal speeches as fluent, organized, and persuasive as their constructive speeches. This difficulty stems largely from the inappropriate use of prep time. This section discusses the keys to using prep time successfully.

Budgeting Preparation Time

Debaters have three minutes of prep time to use at their discretion throughout the round. Prep time is recorded cumulatively. Thus, if you choose to use 45 seconds before the constructive speech, you will have two minutes and 15 seconds remaining for the rest of the round. The next time you call for prep time, the clock will begin at two minutes and 15 seconds, and the time will continue decreasing until you begin speaking or until it has expired. Once prep time is used up, any further time taken for preparation comes out of the next speech time. As a result, it is important that you use prep time wisely.

Affirmative Strategies

It is advisable to spend one to two minutes of preparation time prior to the first rebuttal, and the remainder before the second rebuttal. This division of time better allows the affirmative to prepare a speech that rebuilds the affirmative case and forces the negative to extend.

Regardless of how much prep time remains prior to the second rebuttal, use it all. This allows you to gain the necessary composure to complete the round in a confident manner.

Negative Strategies

The intent of prep time in the negative is the same as in the affirmative. You must gain a sense of *composure* as well as prepare a speech that is organized, fluent, persuasive, and comprehensive. Properly divide prep time and use it completely to ensure that you can accomplish these goals.

There are two main needs for prep time if you are the negative. Since approximately four minutes of the negative constructive is prepared ahead, you need less preparation time before this speech. The negative rebuttal is six minutes long and must be planned to a large degree during prep time. As a general rule, use one minute before the constructive and two minutes before the rebuttal.

The following chart summarizes time allocation recommendations:

Lincoln-Douglas Debate
Affirmative Constructive – 6 minutes
Negative Cross-Examination – 3 minutes
Negative Preparation Time – 1 minute
Negative Constructive (case and rebuttal) – 7 minutes
Affirmative Cross-Examination – 3 minutes
Affirmative Preparation Time – 2 minutes maximum
Affirmative Rebuttal – 4 minutes
Negative Preparation time – 2 minutes
Negative Rebuttal – 6 minutes
Affirmative Preparation Time – 2 minutes
Affirmative Rebuttal – 3 minutes

Use all prep time to prevent a flustered, disorganized rebuttal. This allows you to find that one last piece of evidence, or formulate that last important thought that could shift the entire course of the round.

How To Use Prep Time

This section provides a good "goal sheet" of things that need to be covered in the prep period and before the round begins.

Affirmative Prep Times

Pre-Round Preparation. Before the round, concentrate on the affirmative opening. This opening should be the most fluent portion of the round, and it should set the tone of persuasiveness. Prepare cards and/or briefs that might be useful against your opposition, but do not spend a great deal of time thinking about the negative; concentrate on the affirmative.

First Rebuttal Prep Time. First, list all arguments granted or forgotten by the negative case. This is the first thing you should read in the affirmative rebuttal. Second, assess damage done to your value and criteria. You must rebuild your value and criteria immediately. This is essential. Use prep time to prepare adequate supporting arguments for your criteria and value. Third, find arguments to counter negative attacks on the affirmative case. Fourth, prepare arguments against the negative value and criteria . Ask yourself what you can do to counter this value and diminish its importance. Fifth, find extension evidence, and develop logical attacks on the negative case. Here, you want to assess the negative case weaknesses and attack case structure. Your final responsibility is to relax and gain composure. Focus your mind on what has to be covered, and organize your thoughts.

Second Rebuttal Prep Time. First, note all of the affirmative arguments the negative has missed or dropped throughout the round. Be prepared to point these out. This prep period should be used to organize your thoughts concerning these arguments. Second, prepare logic and evidence to rebuild the importance of your value and criteria. Plan your presentation on the value and criteria to be short and to the point but still comprehensive enough to win the argument. Third, prepare to attack the negative value and criteria. Fourth, prepare to reestablish the affirmative case. Fifth, prepare to attack the negative case, point by point. Finally, prepare a closing statement about 20 seconds long. Point out the main conflict of the resolution, the reason affirming the resolution enhances your value, and why this value is most important when you consider the criteria for judging the round.

Negative Prep Times

Pre-Round Preparation. Prior to the start of the round, anticipate what can be expected. With every resolution there are some affirmative contentions that will appear in virtually every round. Prior to the affirmative constructive, lay out some of the cards/briefs that might address these common arguments. Have these prepared for the first negative rebuttal. Finally, prepare to be attentive to the affirmative case. Although you want to be fully into the negative philosophy, record as much of the affirmative case as possible to help you later on in the round.

First Negative Prep Time. First, prepare attacks on affirmative definitions if needed. Second, prepare attacks on the affirmative's value and criteria. Remember, it may not be needed if the value or the criteria is the same as yours. Make the decision in the prep period. Third, prepare a point-by-point attack of the affirmative case. There should be at least some point of logic for each point. Locate evidence to support logic wherever possible. Fourth, review opening comments to the negative constructive. Attempt to be more persuasive than the affirmative from the start of the round. Persuasion begins with a well-rehearsed opening to your constructive. Also, prepare the closing to the negative constructive. Fifth, relax. Gain composure, and establish self-confidence.

Second Negative Rebuttal Prep Time. First, list all negative arguments the affirmative dropped and/or forgot to pick up in the first affirmative rebuttal. Second, assess the damage done to your value and criteria. Prepare arguments to rebuild/support your value and criteria. Since you are preparing for your last speech, you also will want to prepare arguments that compare your value and criteria to the affirmative's value and criteria. While you have already addressed the negative and affirmative value/criteria, now is the time to directly compare the two. Third, prepare attacks on the affirmative case. Prepare to extend the attacks on the affirmative case made in the first negative rebuttal portion of the negative constructive. Fourth, locate new extension evidence for the negative case. Fifth, prepare a closing statement of about 20 seconds. Finally, relax. Use all remaining time to gain self-confidence and composure.

Conclusion

It is a good idea to always carry a stopwatch in your briefcase. When you get to a round, lay the watch out on the desk beside you so that it is in full view of everyone in the room. This ensures that the timekeeper knows that you are also keeping your own prep time. This also gives you a good idea of where you stand in terms of remaining prep time. In addition, it is a good idea to ask the timekeeper to call out prep time in 30 second intervals. This ensures you are constantly reminded of what time remains. While preparation time is important, you should also prepare as you listen to your opponent. Have evidence and briefs at your fingertips, and locate them as you listen. Write a few words opposite the negatives arguments on your flow sheet to remind you of what you want to say. Take advantage of every minute available to organize your ideas and material and you will present a confident, persuasive speech.

Suggested Activities

1. Write an essay discussing prep time responsibility.

2. Debate an entire round without using any evidence for rebuttals. Use your prep time solely for organization and argument development.

Chapter 21
Developing the Art of Flowing

Learning Objectives

This chapter teaches how to record what is said in a Lincoln-Douglas round. Lincoln-Douglas is based not only upon the persuasive characteristic of the constructive case presentations, but also upon the refutation and analysis characteristic of the rebuttals. You need a reasonably good idea of what your opponent has said to challenge his or her position. This chapter introduces the art of flowing, which enables you to record the round's events.

After completing this chapter you should be able to:

1. **Set up a flowsheet.**

2. **Explain the two methods of flowing and their advantages and disadvantages.**

3. **List the standard abbreviations used for Lincoln-Douglas flowsheets.**

4. **Develop symbols for the current resolution.**

5. **Appreciate the importance of practicing flowing.**

New Terms

Flow
Flowsheet
Horizontal method
Vertical method
Symbols

Introduction

To be a great debater, you must be able to respond to your opponent's case. In addition, you must be able to defend your case against your opponent's attacks. Debate is a dynamic event. You must deliver, and you must respond.

The primary skill that allows a debater to attack and respond is the ability to *flow*. In essence, a debater must be able to record what is said and where it is applied. If you cannot accomplish this goal, it will be difficult to present effective rebuttals in an organized form. While it is true that not all judges will flow a round (write down every argument presented in the round), all judges will evaluate the debaters based upon organization within their speeches. Mastering the ability to flow or to record the arguments presented in the round gives a debater an advantage in the organization of rebuttals.

Flowing is an art. You must ultimately develop your own style of flowing. A successful method for one debater may be confusing and inefficient for another. As a consequence, it is helpful to experiment with different methods and find a style of your own. The suggestions in this chapter will enable you to visualize possible ways to flow.

Flow Sheet Set-up

Regardless of what style you chose, your first decision is the initial set-up of the *flowsheet*. There are two basic options for arranging the flowsheet: the horizontal and the vertical. Each of these methods has advantages and disadvantages. To enable you to take better notes, a legal pad or art pad is recommended.

The Horizontal Method

The *horizontal method* is advantageous in that it gives you more space to record the round. By establishing the affirmative case on one sheet and the negative on another, the debate can be recorded as it proceeds. Each constructive argument is recorded as it is presented. Subsequent attacks against these arguments are recorded just to the right of the constructive arguments. Rebuttal responses to these attacks are recorded directly to the right of the attacks. Further attacks (if applicable) are then recorded to the right of the responses. In this method, the round "flows" from one argument to another, hence the name "flowsheet." An illustration that demonstrates the flow of one argument in a round follows:

HORIZONTAL METHOD (No Abbreviations)

Affirmative Constructive	Negative Constructive Responses	First Affirmative Rebuttal Responses	Negative Rebuttal Responses
II. A. Free Press Provides for Verification of Judicial System	Verification is a disguise used by the media to influence the outcome of the trial. Judicial System is hurt.	Trials may be intimidated by the press, but at least they are protected from tyranny on the part of judicial officials. The indiv. is assured a fair trial because of the press.	Harms proposed by the Affirmative are prevented by other means. Tyranny is not prevalent with the press. The press causes unnecessary bias in trials, all of which could be avoided.

The point of the previous diagram is to give you a perspective of how an argument can be traced through a round. Obviously, it is difficult to write down every word in complete sentences while in the middle of a "heated round." For illustration purposes, however, this serves well. The procedure for eliminating the "wordiness" of the previous descriptions by the use of symbols is described later. Notice the way in which the argument proceeds from one speech to another. The ability to see the way in which an argument proceeds from its initial presentation to its conclusion allows you to understand the argument's integrity throughout the round. The affirmative, using the previous flowsheet, can trace how the negative has responded to the argument and can decide how to respond in the last rebuttal to preserve the initial argument on "judicial verification." Without the flowsheet, it is virtually impossible to remember the way the argument progressed.

The flowsheet ensures that you do not forget to make an argument in response to your opponent's attacks, and it ensures that you can spot the instances when an opponent misses one of your arguments. This is one of the major advantages of the horizontal method.

The horizontal style has another advantage in its ability to provide the debater with a review of the whole round's progress. Following is an illustration that demonstrates the advantage of the horizontal method. The page for the affirmative case is shown. A separate page would have the negative case in the first column, the first affirmative rebuttal in the second, the second negative rebuttal in the third, and the second affirmative rebuttal in the fourth. This display, with all of its abbreviations and symbols, may seem a bit confusing for now, but concentrate on the advantage of seeing the whole round with ease.

The essential disadvantage to this method is the negative image it creates for the debater. For many judges, the sight of a debater holding a legal pad in a horizontal direction is distracting. In most cases this drawback is not harmful enough to outweigh the advantages you receive by being organized and on top of the round. The other disadvantage is that most students are not used to taking notes in a horizontal method. Not being familiar with this method can cause considerable problems. The way to avoid this disadvantage is to practice using the horizontal method. Like many things in Lincoln-Douglas, this is a powerful tool if you invest the time to master the skill.

HORIZONTAL METHOD (With Abbreviations)

Affirmative case	Negative Const. Responses	Aff. Responses	Neg Rebuttal
V=Q of L C+CBA	Life >than Q of L CBA fine	People die for Q of L	Instict to surv. Not be a hero
I. Ind RTP=Soc. . Obligat	Soc obligat to protect rest of soc. members	Soc. protects all by sticking to Soc Contrc Viola. of RTP=revolt	RTP not essent. Indiv willing to sacfic. RTP
A. Soc+Legally Respo	Legal? What law–not U.S. spec.		Dropped Legal
B. RTP in Soc Cont.	Soc. Cont. requires Indiv to sacrifice RTP for security	Soc Cont. insures RTP Inailiable R.; violat=	People willing to sac. RTP; to protect security under Soc Contr
C. RTP enh;ances rights	Rights granted by soc.; full meaning of rights no good w/out soc. existance	no soc. at all R. granted by higher being. Inailiable R.s exist w/out soc.	Can't apprec. Rs w/out Soc. No F. Speech w/out
II. Ind RTP secures Soc	Soc. Sec. Indiv.	Ind. makes soc. not vice-v.	Soc. Sec. essenc of Indiv
A. RTP=Self functi indiv	Indiv. could not exist w/out soc. Self functic. indiv no longer exists. Must live w/others to apprec. rights	Indiv. could exist. Documented– Soc need Indiv.; Must have RTP to apprec. Individuality	Indiv. needs Soc or essence of being
B. RTP upholds state of Soc	State of soc. upheld by many things. No RTP will not destroy soc. Look at WWII precedent	War time sacrif. is when soc almost dies	Pull INC argum. Aff misses here

The Vertical Method

The second option in flowing styles is the *vertical method.* The vertical method uses the same logic the horizontal method uses: one attack gets set alongside its corresponding argument. The difference is the separation of constructives and rebuttals.

The advantage of this style is the comfort it affords to most debaters because they are familiar with writing "down a sheet" instead of across it, and, therefore, they're already used to taking notes this way. Finally, there is an advantage in rebuttal appearance. The debater appears as a persuasive public speaker by the manner in which he or she holds the legal pad.

There are disadvantages to the vertical style. The most prominent disadvantage is the cluttering effect. To make comprehensive and organized rebuttal presentations, it is important that all information presented in the round be recorded. It is still important, however, to place attack arguments against the corresponding constructive arguments. Logically, there are two alternatives to accomplishing both of these objectives: the flow notations have to be made smaller and more vertically elongated, or the constructives and rebuttal speeches have to be split.

The following examples illustrate the "Constructive/Rebuttal Split" option. The second option, condensing the information via smaller writing, should be obvious.

With this system, the constructive and rebuttal arguments are on separate pages. This method requires four sheets of paper: two for the affirmative case arguments and two for the negative. As you can see, you gain a familiar and pleasing style while you sacrifice some organization and readability as a result of having to refer to four pages instead of two. It is important to experiment with different methods in finding a personal style of your own.

It is also advantageous to experiment in modifications of the two major styles. The essential ingredients that should be included in all modifications are the following:

1. A comprehensive record of the major points said in the round.

2. Side-by-side listing of alternating affirmative and negative arguments.

3. A pleasing, but effective appearance to make the flow very readable.

4. Organization that you can follow and understand.

"Constructive/Rebuttal Split" Option	
Affirmative case	**Negative Const. Responses**
V=Q of L C+CBA	Life > than Q of L CBA fine
I. Ind RTP = Soc. Oblig.	Soc. oblig. to protect rest of soc. members
A. Soc = Legally Resp.	Legal? what law – not U.S. spec.
B. RTP in Soc. Cont.	Soc. Cont. requires Indiv. to sacrifice RTP for security
C. RTP enchnces rts.	Rights granted by soc.; full meaning of rights no good w/out soc. existance
II. Ind RTP secures Soc.	Soc. Sec. Indiv.
A. RTP = Self func. indiv.	Indiv. could not exist w/out soc. Self func. indiv no longer exists. Must live w/ others to apprec. rights
B. RTP upholds state of Soc.	State of soc. upheld by many things. No RTP will not destroy soc. Look at WWII precedent

"Constructive/Rebuttal Split" Option Condensed

Affirmative Rebuttal	Negative Rebuttal
People die for Q of L	Instict to surv. Not be a hero
Soc. protects all by sticking to Soc Cont. Viola. of RTP = revolt	RTP not essent. Indiv willing to sac. RTP
	Dropped Legal
Soc Cont. ensures RTP Inalien. Rts.; violat = no soc. at all	People willing to sac. RTP; to protect security under Soc. Contr.
R. granted by higher being. Inalien. Rts. exist w/out soc.	Can't apprec. Rs w/out Soc. No F. Speech w/out Soc. given langua.
Indiv. makes soc. not vice-V.	Soc. Sec. essenc. of Indiv.
Indiv. could exist	

The Abbreviation of Arguments

In addition to developing your own style, it is imperative to learn to abbreviate long words, phrases, and sentences into short symbols and similar representations. As you can tell from the previous illustrations, it would be virtually impossible to record every word that was said in a debate round. It is possible (and necessary), however, to record the main concept of each argument presented in a round by using *symbols.*

You will soon learn that the use of symbols becomes increasingly easy with practice. If you make it a habit to translate the spoken word into your own shorthand, and then re-translate it into the spoken word, the practice of symbol usage becomes second nature.

The development of symbols is easy if you employ some basic rules of common sense. In the illustration showing the flowsheet of an entire debate, you will notice the use of many varieties of symbols. These varieties can be grouped into categories. Some of these categories are listed below:

Types of Symbols

The first type of symbols are the standard abbreviations of Lincoln-Douglas. This category includes things that are found in virtually every Lincoln-Douglas round. Examples include:

V =	Values
C =	Criteria
I, II, III, etc. =	points one, two, three, etc.
def. =	definitions

The second category is symbols for values and criteria. This category includes symbols representing re-occurring values and forms of criteria.

Q of L	= Quality of Life
L	= Life
Indiv.	= Individualism
Lib.	= Liberty
Saf.	= Safety
Sec.	= Security
Prog.	= Progress
CBA	= Cost Benefit Analysis
Util.	= Utilitarianism
Futur.	= Futurism
Deont.	= Deontology

The third category is for common terms. This category includes symbols for terms that occur consistently.

Soc.	= Society
Indiv.	=Individual
Demo.	=Democracy
Social.	=Socialism
Comun.	=Communism
"Captil.	=Capitalism
Soc. Conrct	=Social Contract
RT	=Right to (whatever)
RTP	=Right to Privacy,
RTK	= Right to Know, etc.
spec.	=specified
w/out	=with out
@	=at
w/	=with
$	= dollars, funding, cost, etc.
#	= numbers, amounts, many, etc.
%	= percentages

The fourth category is for terms of comparison. This category has a few terms that stand for comparisons.

=	is "equal to", or "causes", or "provides for", etc.
≠	will be equivalent to "not equal to", "does not cause", "does not provide for", etc.
Ø	= "no, nothing"
↑	= "increase", "enhancement", or "more of"
↓	= "decrease", "diminishment", "less of", etc.
>	= greater than
<	= less than

An arrow coming from one object to another = "will cause"

The final category is symbols specific to the arguments being debated. This category includes words that are not specific to one resolution, but are used over and over again from one resolution to the next, making symbol use practical.

N. S.	= National Security
I.	= Individuality
E.	= Environment
D.R.	= Development of natural resources
GE	= Genetic Engineering
CD	= Civil Disobedience

6th	= Sixth Amendment (Fair Trial)
RFT	= Right to a fair trial
C	= Censorship
P	= Privacy, Pornography, etc. (no link intended here!)

It is important to establish what each symbol means far in advance of each tournament. This ensures that you are comfortable with the symbols during the round. It is a good idea to practice using symbols in your preparation for the tournament. It is also important that the argument-specific category not carry over into future topics, since each resolution should have its own set of symbols. As you can see with the symbol "P," the meaning can be privacy or pornography. The same is true with "C," censorship or criteria. It it advantageous to use symbols, but excessive use can become confusing and detrimental to the initial cause.

Practice

Flowing is nothing more than effective communication between two parts of your brain—the writing part and the speaking part. When you take notes on what is said, you are using the writing part of your brain. When you begin to deliver your rebuttal speech, you then make use of the speaking part of your brain. You expand upon what the writing part of your brain has recorded on the paper. The goal of flowing is to increase the lines of communication between these two parts of your brain. The more these two parts of your brain learn to work together and understand each other's signals, the more effective you become.

Practice rounds are the best place to practice flowing, but there are several great flowing opportunities that take place outside of debate rounds. Any public speaker that is attempting to convey an organized message provides you with a good opportunity. When sitting in church, flow the minister's sermons. When watching the news on TV, flow the presentations. If you have an exceptional teacher, flow lectures. Flowing is nothing more than note-taking refined to debate standards. There are endless opportunities to practice for the debater serious about improving flowing skills.

Conclusion

Of all the skills debate has to offer, there are five skills that will carry over into the remainder of your life:

1. The ability to research.
2. The ability to speak in front of people and be persuasive.
3. The ability to understand public policy and social decisions.

4. The ability to organize thoughts and ideas into coherent form.
5. The ability to effectively record what another has to say to you (i.e., the ability to take notes).

The fifth skill is a great advantage in college or in any situation in which you must efficiently record what is being said. It is advantageous (both in terms of debate and your future) to begin to develop this skill now. You'll be glad you did!

Suggested Activities

1. Watch a video tape of a round and practice flowing it.

2. Compare the flowsheets in the previous exercise and discuss what information should have been written doen.

3. Try both methods of flowing to see which is most comfortable.

Unit V
ADVANCED LINCOLN-DOUGLAS
DEBATE STRATEGIES

This unit gives the experienced debater, who might have reached a "plateau," the opportunity to overcome that obstacle by understanding some of the more subtle elements that go into determining the victor of a Lincoln-Douglas debate round. Unit V is not excessively difficult, which makes it accessible for students who have at least some practical experience in Lincoln-Douglas debate. It is extremely helpful, and almost necessary, that the students studying this section have had some experiences, since portions of the chapters make reference to "in round" debate scenarios.

Chapter 22 addresses the number of different debater "types" a student of Lincoln-Douglas can expect to encounter at tournaments. This chapter allows the student to "identify" personal styles according to his or her strengths and weaknesses. This chapter's discussion leads into Chapter 23, which makes use of the debater's strengths in developing a "game plan," or strategy, for competing with individuals who have different debate styles.

Chapter 24 is of fundamental importance to the advanced debater. This chapter deals with the principle of judge adaptation. Students can study different judge characteristics to make educated guesses about a judge's voting philosophy, and this information, in turn is used to direct the presentation within the round. This chapter provides additional projects students can undertake in gathering and storing information about the judges they see regularly, thereby giving them the opportunity to adapt to that judge the second time around.

Chapter 25 explains the process of speaking extemporaneously, or only with notes, after limited preparation. Since much of Lincoln-Douglas debate requires an extemporaneous style, this chapter is important in improving delivery skills. Chapter 26 discusses the use of analogies as a means of communicating complex ideas. Chapter 27 contains additional advice for improving debate skills. These suggestions come from the author's personal experiences as a debater and a coach.

This unit, as evidenced by its title, is not critical to the debater who does not have a great deal of time to learn about the event of Lincoln-Douglas debate prior to a tournament. For the advanced debater, however, Unit V is a refreshing change of pace that can further the career of even the most successful of debaters.

Chapter 22
Understanding Debate Styles

Learning Objectives

Chapter 22 discusses different styles debaters employ. As you increase your Lincoln-Douglas experience, you will recognize that while each of your opponents is unique, each uses one of five different debate styles. This chapter introduces those five styles and describes the characteristics of each. The following chapter on adaptation refers to these five styles.

After completing this chapter you should be able to:

1. Explain the Lincoln-Douglas spectrum.

2. Classify and explain the five debate styles.

3. Explain the style that best suits you and why.

New Terms

Lincoln-Douglas spectrum
Philosophical

Introduction

Chapters 7 and 8 illustrate the importance of being familiar with both theories of Lincoln-Douglas debate. In the next chapter we develop a "game plan" for attacking opponents. Developing this game plan requires you to be familiar with each of the five styles. These styles can be viewed as a debate spectrum. Since your game-plan will consist of getting opponents to debate "your" style of debate, you need to know your style and understand your opponent's style. Understanding the debate spectrum is the first step in understanding the strengths and weaknesses of each of the debater's styles.

The Lincoln-Douglas Debate Spectrum

In Chapters 7 and 8 you were introduced to two different theories of Lincoln-Douglas. These theories are important because they make up the two ends of the *Lincoln-Douglas spectrum*, although neither one is entirely correct by itself.

If you are not familiar with the concept of a "spectrum," consider the nature of color. On one side of the color spectrum is white, the presence of all colors. On the other side of the spectrum is the black, the absence of any color. In between these two extremes are all the different colors. As you approach one of the ends, you will find that the colors begin to take on the character of that end. As you approach the black end, for example, the colors are darker. As you approach the white end, the colors are lighter.

The same is true of the Lincoln-Douglas spectrum. On one side of the debate spectrum is the oratorical theory of Lincoln-Douglas. On the other side of the spectrum is the debate theory of Lincoln-Douglas. Combinations of the two are between these two extremes. As you approach one end, you find that the debate style takes on the characteristics of that end. For example, as you go towards the oratorical theory end of the spectrum, the debate style takes on those characteristics.

The important thing to note about the Lincoln-Douglas spectrum is that it does not try to explain which theory is the correct theory. Too many people have wasted time trying to determine which of the two theories is the correct way to approach Lincoln-Douglas. The truth is that there is no one correct answer. Each debater should try to find his or her place on the debate spectrum. You should debate in your own style and not be worried about whether the "experts" say it is the right or wrong way to debate. You will be successful as long as you determine and follow your own style.

For the purposes of this discussion, the oratorical theory is on the left end of the spectrum, and the debate theory is on the right end of the spectrum. This placement, however, is completely arbitrary. As a consequence of this placement, debater Type A is far to the left and represents the oratorical theory. Debater Type E is far to the right and represents the debate theory. Debater Type C falls exactly in the middle.

You may wonder why it is important to consider the debate spectrum. Understanding your place on the debate spectrum is the first step to understanding how you debate best. It also is essential to developing a game plan to get your opponent to debate your style.

Debate Styles

It is important to understand that there are an infinite number of points on that line where your style may fall. As a result, your style is inherently unique. Each of the styles has its advantages and disadvantages; thus, it is not "bad" to be one or another debater type. Directly below is a graphic of the Lincoln-Douglas spectrum followed by an explanation of each style.

| A | B | C | D | E |

Oratorical Theory			**Debate Theory**	
Slow rate			Rapid rate	
Philosophical			Significant evidence	
Logic			Pragmatic	
Little substructure			Structured speech	
Abstract			Concrete	

Style A: Oratorical Theory Style

Notice the mark on the spectrum representing Style A. This debater, almost without exception, embodies the characteristics of the left side of the spectrum. The rate of delivery is slow, and is packed with *philosophical* arguments that rely entirely on the foundation of logic. Any supporting evidence in this style is from noted philosophers such as Kant, Locke, Jefferson, etc., and not from recent surveys or statistics. The organization of the case consists of one to three main contentions with no subpoints. This debater is characterized by the abstract.

This debater has an advantage in establishing judge/audience rapport, and is generally well practiced at speaking "with" instead of "at" the audience. Many debaters of this style speak in lofty, elaborate, and often nebulous language, making many of the ideas presented seem far removed from reality. This is an impressive style, but, ironically, is less persuasive. Many debaters of this style try to support philosophical arguments they do not fully understand. Their ability to present great constructives is notorious, but their inability to fully understand the complicated nature of many of their arguments leads to destructive rebuttals. In addition, while many of the ideas may seem philosophically correct, they seldom appear "real" because they are so lofty and abstract. With little "modern" supporting evidence, this debater often has trouble when asked to explain the value implication today.

Style B: Leaning Toward Oratorical Theory Style

Notice the position of point B on the spectrum. The type B debater has similar tendencies to the type A debater. Both use logic as the primary mechanism of persuasion. The evidence in this style is still philosophical, but it is a more modern philosophy. Debater B likes to expand on the grand philosophers and theorists with some modern evidence. The use of evidence here is sometimes factual and sometimes philosophical. This allows this debater to adapt to judges who are farther to the right on the spectrum. The speaking style is slow, but faster than the type A debater. While the type A debater often "hypnotizes" an audience with eloquent speech, the type B debater impresses the audience with a combination of lofty speech and a direct analysis of the resolution.

It is more difficult to develop the type B style, but it is much more effective and useful in a variety of situations once it is achieved. The type B style is adaptive, and, thus, effective.

Style C: A Mixture of Oratorical Theory and Debate Styles

The type C debater is located directly in the middle of the spectrum. This type of debater typically shifts his or her style depending upon the resolution being debated. If the resolution deals with a pragmatic topic, such as genetic engineering, he or she leans more to the right of the spectrum with modern evidence. If, however, the resolution deals with abstract concepts, such as freedom and liberty, he or she leans to the left of the spectrum by using philosophical evidence.

Since Lincoln-Douglas resolutions change frequently, this debater has the ability to address both pragmatic and philosophical topics with success. At different times during the round, this debater also has the ability to speak with different "voices." If there is a time in the round where he or she must be particularly "impressive," such as a case opening or a conclusion, he or she may speak slowly and flowery. If, on the other hand, this debater needs to fit a number of arguments in a small amount of speech time, he or she can speak quickly and directly .

The disadvantage to this style is that the debater never becomes especially proficient at any one style. If the type C debater attempted to debate a type A debater in a philosophical round, the type C debater would probably lose. Because the type C debater does not specialize in any one style, he or she does not become an expert at any one style. As a consequence, the type C debater has an advantage over all other debater types when the round becomes "mixed" between the pragmatic and the philosophical, but he or she will be at a disadvantage when debating any round that is purely philosophical or pragmatic.

Style D: Leaning Toward Debate Theory

Just as debater type B was similar to debater type A, except less extreme, debater type D is similar to type E, but less extreme. The type D debater relies upon the speed associated with the right side of the spectrum as well as the more modern, pragmatic evidence for support of contentions. In addition, the type D debater also relies upon more structure to organize the increased evidence he or she offers in the round.

The rate at which the type D debater proceeds, although still fast, is slower than the type E debater. The Type D debater speaks more slowly to be more persuasive. The rate is still much faster than would be found in normal conversation, but it is still realistic. The advantage of this rate is that it allows the debater to present more information without sounding abnormal or leaving the judge behind.

The type D debater depends on modern evidence but occasionally relies upon philosophical thought (i.e., Jefferson, Locke, Kant, etc.) to evaluate the evidence presented in a round. While the type E debater is more apt to continue an evidence war, the type D debater draws upon such noted philosophers as Plato, Aristotle, etc. to explain why his or her evidence is superior to his or her opponent's. This ability, while effective, is difficult to master, and, thus, there are far fewer type D debaters than there are type E debaters.

Finally, the degree of structure the type D debater offers the debate is not as extensive as the structure offered by the type E debater. In this philosophy the organization contains two to three main contentions with anywhere from two to four subpoints under these. Double subpoints are almost never seen.

The structure decreases as the round progresses. As a consequence, this debater organizes the beginning case into subpoints for initial understanding, and then, as the round progresses, reduces the subpoints into their main contentions for maximum persuasion. The ending rebuttal for this philosophy usually focuses on the two or three main contentions, and the subpoints are reduced to reasons for supporting each contention.

The type D debater must combine the philosophical evidence with the pragmatic, the initial intricate structure of case with the reduced structure of the rebuttals, and the high degree of speed with a slower, persuasive rate of delivery.

Style E: Debate Theory Style

This style requires a philosophy that is radically different from that of debater A. While debater A relies on a slow rate of delivery, debater E relies on a fast paced delivery. So fast, in fact, that the type E debater can present massive amounts of information within short speeches. When the judge takes a good flow sheet, this debater is tough to beat. He or she can deliver large amounts of information in a small amount of time.

The type E debater can respond to a large amount of evidence presented by an opponent. This debater can finish strong and often pull off a win in the last rebuttal speech. A favorite strategy of a type E debater is to trick an opponent into a game of speed, pitting his or her speed against the opponent's.

The type E debater does sacrifice persuasive speaking. Speech at the speed of light is not what a judge is used to hearing. As a consequence, it is not persuasive. A type A, B, C, or D debater will be successful against the type E debater if he or she holds to his or her own style. The only way a type E debater will be successful is if he or she can bring a debater of a different style into his or her field of play.

In addition to speed, the type E debater relies on pragmatic evidence to support issues. While the type A debater relies upon the philosophical theorists for evidence support, the type E debater relies upon the most recent evidence available. For this reason, the evidence of the type E debater generally comes from periodicals and recent reports. This makes resolutions of modern ethics this debater's specialty. Resolutions discussing the abstract, such as liberty, freedom, equality, etc., are dominated by type A and B debaters who rely on philosophy. While resolutions dealing with modern ethics, especially ethics in relation to technological advances (i.e., genetic engineering), are the domain of the type D and E debaters who rely on the modern evidence for support. This does not mean that type E debaters cannot succeed in resolutions dealing with abstract values. In resolutions that are more philosophical in nature, however, the type E debater must try that much harder to make up for lost ground.

Finally, the type E debater structures a speech much more than the type A debater. This is necessary to organize the massive amounts of information presented. This high degree of structure usually includes three to four main contentions with occasional subpoints under each. Occasionally, these subpoints even stretch to include double subpoints. As you might guess, there is a danger of over-structuring the speech, making the presentation less persuasive to the judge. The structure also interferes with fluency, since this debater constantly interrupts ideas to label points.

Conclusion

Now that you are familiar with the styles of debate and can identify your own style, you are ready to be introduced to "game planning." Contrary to popular belief, much of what happens in Lincoln-Douglas is decided far in advance of the round. The manner in which the round proceeds is determined by two people: you and your opponent. While you cannot control what your opponent does, you can predict his or her actions by the way in which you organize yourself. The next chapter explains how to develop a game plan.

Suggested Activities

1. Write an essay explaining which type of debater you are.

2. Write an essay on the qualities of each debate type.

3. Watch a video of a debate round and discuss as a class what type each debater is.

Chapter 23
Developing a Game Plan

Learning Objectives

Chapter 23 teaches how to develop a game plan. The game plan is the strategy you develop to present your speeches according to your style. It also helps you determine how to adapt to your opponent's style.

After completing this chapter you should be able to:

1. **Explain the concept of a game plan.**

2. **Explain the four major components of a game plan.**

New Term

Game plan

Introduction

The development of a *game plan* depends upon four main components: (1) the rate at which you proceed; (2) the amount of structure you
incorporate into your speeches; (3) the overall content of the debate; and
(4) the degree of "opponent rapport" to be maintained throughout the
round. To successfully develop a game plan, have a solid understanding of
each of these components.

The Rate of Delivery

The rate at which you present your case is a major factor in how the
round proceeds. You should select your rate of speed based upon your skill
as well as your opponent's. If your ability to speak faster and still be
persuasive is greater than your opponent's ability to do the same, you
should develop your game plan to allow you to speak rapidly. This does not
mean that you should speak uncontrollably fast, as this will destroy your
persuasiveness. It does mean, however, that you should push your
opponent into having to cover more material than he or she can handle.
Your initial constructive should include considerable structure and content, since this forces your opponent to speak at a higher speed to keep up
with the round. When you face a style A or B debater (see Chapter 22), you
should employ this strategy.

If your ability to speak rapidly and still be persuasive is less than
your opponent's, you should adapt your game plan to slow down the rate
of the round. You do not want to get into a speed war with your opponent.
You should try to speak more eloquently and with more detail. Try to entice
your opponent into speaking at a slower speed than he or she would
normally speak. Do this by selecting the important arguments and
stressing them to the judge. Group arguments to make it clear to the judge
that quality, not quantity, is important. It is important to remember that
rate refers to the rate at which you can speak and still maintain persuasiveness.

The Structure of Arguments

Your speech's structure can also influence the round's outcome.
An opponent who is on the left side of the speaking spectrum (oratorical
theory) will respond with eagerness when only two or three contentions
with no subpoints are given. On the contrary, providing multiple contentions and subpoints to a debate theory debater is an equally poor choice.

If you identify yourself as left of your opponent on the debate
spectrum, you should reduce your structure in an effort to entice your
opponent to debate a round with little structure. As you approach cross-
examination, group your opponent's subpoints into main contentions, and
make your attacks from there. This early reduction in structure allows
breathing room as the round progresses.

If you can identify yourself as right of your opponent on the debate spectrum, you should maintain an extensive structure in your case. During all possible scenarios, you should maintain this subpoint structure and invite your opponent to do the same. Since you are further right on the spectrum, this should be to your advantage.

The Debate Content

The content of a debate round can be controlled to a degree by what is discussed and what is emphasized. Some issues will arise for which you are unprepared. It is possible to circumvent some difficult issues. Do not anticipate difficult issues and attempt to defeat them before the opponent argues them. Also, avoid trying to deny an argument that cannot be denied. For instance, on a topic claiming that genetic engineering's advantages outweigh its disadvantages, it is unwise to deny that individuals could abuse the technology to create a super race.

It is also possible to deal with a difficult issue by minimizing its importance. Compare it to an issue on which you are strong.

Aggressiveness

The degree of aggression involved in a debate round can often be planned far in advance of the round. Too much aggression is distracting to the judge, leads to bickering, and destroys rapport. Lost rapport can result in a loss, even if you win the round on arguments. On the other hand, being too polite can create an impression of being timid and not confident in what you have to say. This can result in decreased persuasiveness.

To determine the appropriate level of aggression or politeness, it is imperative that you analyze your opponent, and how your opponent performs in the round. An opponent who appears to be more aggressive than you warrants a defensive aggressiveness. You should attempt to be more aggressive than normal in hopes of sparking excessive aggressiveness in your opponent. The key to this strategy is to entice aggression to a brink point, and then back off, leaving your opponent with a shadow of excessive aggressiveness.

On the contrary, an opponent who appears to be less aggressive warrants a different consideration. It is important to protect yourself from being too aggressive. Once again, you are searching to be as aggressive as possible without going over the brink. You should take advantage of your opponent's weaknesses, but be careful not to appear rude or overbearing in your attacks.

Politeness can often be as much of a weapon as is aggressiveness. Responding to overly aggressive attacks with politeness can sometimes highlight the rudeness in your opponent's responses. This technique often destroys your opponent's rapport with the judge and leaves you in the driver's seat for the rest of the round.

Conclusion

How you relate with your opponent, in terms of rate, structure, content, or aggressiveness, has a substantial impact on how the judge perceives your performance. To be successful in Lincoln-Douglas debate, it takes more than just winning the arguments. It takes a certain degree of strategy to evoke certain responses from your opponent, and a certain confidence in your debate style. How you capitalize on the dynamics between you and your opponent strongly influences the judge's evaluation of your overall performance.

Suggested Activities

1. In an essay discuss the three game plan components.

2. Match each student with another student and have each write a game plan as if they were preparing to debate one another.

Chapter 24
Judge Adaptation

Chapter 24 teaches a little-known and appreciated topic in Lincoln-Douglas: judge adaptation. Just as each debater has a preferred style, each judge also has a preferred way he or she likes to see debate performed. Successful debaters recognize this preference and adapt to it. This chapter helps you become familiar with the principles of judge adaptation, and provides you with some strategy points for successful adaptation.

After completing this chapter you should be able to:

1. **Explain the ways in which a debater can classify a judge's preferred debate style.**

2. **Make adjustments in your style to suit the judge's reactions.**

New Terms

Judge Adaptation
Lay judge
Politics

Introduction

Although the winner of a Lincoln-Douglas round is determined largely by skill, there is a subjective element that factors into the final result of each round: what kind of debater the judge favors. Adapting to the judge, therefore, is critical to ensuring your chances of victory.

Although a great debater displays personal integrity and pride, he or she also knows when to set some of this pride aside in order to adapt to the judge's preference. This is not to say that great debaters have to sacrifice their personalities and ideals, but judge adaptation is an important part of being successful in Lincoln-Douglas debate. Debate success, as in all speaking events, is related to the degree to which you can speak with the audience. If you can establish audience rapport, you will be successful in persuading the audience. *Judge adaptation* is nothing more than determining what motivates the judge and speaking with him or her about that motivation. You do not change your position or your value. You merely find a way to relate it to the judge's motivations.

Although you will encounter an infinite number of judging preferences, there are some general categories that allow for better prediction of preferences. It is important to understand that there are no set rules or characteristics that enable you to determine what a judge is thinking. Some of the advice presented here is based on generalization. There are exceptions to all of the assumptions. Age, occupation, and appearance can give you some clues to a judge's political philosophy or style preferences. However, nonverbal feedback is the best guide to determining a judge's reactions to what you say and how you say it.

Lay Versus Experienced Judges

The most crucial characteristic to evaluate in adapting to a judge is whether or not the judge has debate knowledge. Judges with no debate or judging experience are known as *lay judges*. These judges are often fairly easy to detect. They usually have their judges' instructions nearby, ask procedural questions, and take few, if any, notes.

When encountering a lay judge, remember to keep the rate of delivery slower, to explain thoroughly, to make connections between your arguments and your opponent's, and to make fewer arguments. Do not assume that because a judge has no actual debate or judging experience that the judge is not knowledgeable about the topic. Attorneys and other professionals are often recruited as lay judges. These individuals are capable of understanding complex arguments but usually prefer a persuasive, natural speaking style.

Experienced judges may know about debate, but they do not share the same attitudes about theory, style, or political philosophy. As a result, do not assume too much. Other factors, explained later, must also be considered.

Conservative Versus Liberal Philosophies

Because much of what a Lincoln-Douglas debater says is related to "political" topics, it is important that you realize a judge may not share your political orientation. A conservative judge accepts some arguments as valid, while a liberal judge considers the opposite arguments as legitimate. Whether the judge knows it or not, his or her personal beliefs influence the way he or she perceives and accepts or rejects your arguments. Although the ideal judge is a "blank slate" upon entering the round, you cannot assume that any judge is ideal.

Few judges will vote against an outstanding debater just because he or she happened to support a political philosophy that was in opposition to his or her own. Some judges, however, will allow this political bias to enter into decision-making. Even judges who will not vote against you because of their political opinions are still more apt to believe arguments that fit their own philosophy. After all, judges are only human.

How do you determine this difference in political philosophy? The following factors provide some guidance, but they are not foolproof. No two individuals reach a political philosophy through the same route. Two individuals of the same age who were raised in different economic, racial, and social settings may have opposite philosophies. Age is not the key factor—life experience is. Thus, you should not jump to conclusions based on one characteristic alone.

For purposes of discussion, this chapter assumes your judge fits one of the following categories: volunteer community judges who may have little or considerable judging experience, former debaters, college students, teachers, or coaches.

Determining Philosophy

The first consideration in determining the judge's political philosophy is age. It is a good, although not always accurate, generalization to assume that older judges (over 60) are more conservative. Older judges tend to be established in a social system that is working well for them. As a result, these individuals tend to advocate little change in the social system. In addition, there is a nice sense of security in knowing that the way things are today is the way they are going to be tomorrow. This opposition to dramatic change is representative of a conservative philosophy toward change, not necessarily toward a liberal or conservative policy.

The two main sources of "older judges" are individuals from the community and debate coaches from other schools. The first of these categories goes nicely with the above stereotype, as they are older, well established "pillars" of the community. Keep in mind, however, that many of the 1960s radicals are now more than 50 years old and maintain some of their liberal views.

Teachers and debate coaches, on the other hand, are more likely to be liberal in regard to change, since the present society does not exactly favor their economic goals or needs. In addition, teachers, including college professors at college sponsored tournaments, generally advocate free and creative thinking.

On the other hand, there are some judges who are liberal because of their age. College students and younger judges are generally in the process of breaking into the social system. Their youth allows them to dream and see visions that are not ordinary. These individuals often find it beneficial to advocate social change to allow the fulfillment of these dreams and their placement into the social system. As a consequence, college students and younger judges are more often liberal in their attitude toward change. College campuses have always been more liberal in relation to "accepting new ideas" when compared to the rest of society.

It is important to note that not all college students are liberal in their views toward change. In the 1980s, college students were far more conservative than their counterparts in the 1960s and '70s. The college a student attends can be an indicator of political philosophy, as some campuses are known for either liberal or conservative leanings. Find out as much as you can from your coach or teammates about your college judges.

A key to knowing who your likely judges are and what philosophies they hold is to ask debaters who attended the tournament in the past and your coach. When you learn your judge's name, if it is on the schedule, ask your coach or other debaters if they know anything about the judge. Some tournaments ask judges to write a judging philosophy. If these are available, take advantage of them.

Adapting to a Philosophy

The first rule of responding to a judge's political philosophy is to begin the round as you ordinarily would. Prior to the round, however, you should make a guess as to the political philosophy of the judge. Making this guess is difficult, and you should use the above general guidelines to assist you in predicting with what the judge will agree. Once you have made your guess, test the judge as you present some sample arguments. Present your first constructive normally, but pay close attention to the way the judge reacts to your argumentation. If he or she agrees to statements that are more conservative (i.e., if he or she shows signs of agreement such as nodding his or her head, or does **not** show overt signs of disagreement) you should operate on the assumption that he or she is more conservative than liberal (or vice versa).

It is important that you do not go to either conservative or liberal extremes in this process. Your best bet is always to stay close to the middle of the road. In some situations, however, it is necessary to take a political stand on an argument in the round, and this process can assist you in choosing how to present it. If you know something about the judge, adapt your arguments and analogies to the judge's needs and experience as either an established professional or a student. For instance, present change as a positive to protect an older judge's values.

Style Preferences

The age of a judge can also provide you with clues as to how you should present your case. The older the judge, the more likely it is that he or she will appreciate more persuasion and more realistic arguments. It is better to stick to the main issues of the resolution and work on persuasively presenting these issues, instead of trying to present large quantities of information at a high speed. The debater who works to "persuade" via logic, examples, and slow, persuasive speech will better convince most older judges.

The older judge will, in most cases, be wiser, and thus, will know the wisdom in not accepting "blind assumptions." You should explain all arguments, especially the ones that are more complex. Assuming that an older judge will understand and believe a "blind" argument is not a good idea.

If a judge appears to be of college age, it is a good bet that he or she is probably a past contestant. Therefore, you can expect that the judge has a good grasp of the "event" of Lincoln-Douglas. He or she probably has enough understanding of the event that you can move a little faster in your presentation and assume that the judge understands the meaning of some of the "stock" issues of Lincoln-Douglas.

You can also assume that he or she has an understanding of Lincoln-Douglas rules. For example, when a negative presents his or her own definitions without providing "alternate definition standards," you can point out the responsibility of the negative in relation to Lincoln-Douglas rules. It is important that you still explain the "unfairness" in such an action, but it is reasonable to push the issue more than you would with an inexperienced judge. It is also reasonable to structure your argument more, and spend more time attacking the opponent's case. This allows for more direct clash, which past debaters seem to appreciate once they become judges. Use similar strategies with debate coaches.

Keep in mind that the above guidelines are not infallible. These guidelines are established on the assumption that the younger judge has had experience with the event of Lincoln-Douglas debate. There is the possibility that a past prose contestant may get stuck in a Lincoln-Douglas round between prose rounds. Evaluate your judge as you progress through the round. If a judge takes notes and keeps up with your arguments, style, speed, and structure, you should continue your pattern. You can only assume that your initial assessment of the judge was correct. If, on the other hand, the judge seems to be confused, lost, or otherwise distressed, change your pattern and assume that your initial assessment of "past contestant" was incorrect. In this case, apply lay judge standards.

Remember Repeat Judges

Over the course of the year many debate coaches will judge you or your teammates. It is to your advantage to get to know these coaches and the other judges they consistently bring with them. Knowing these coaches is the first step to them knowing you. Having a good reputation with coaches works to your advantage in the long run.

It is beneficial to become familiar with the styles these individuals like to see in Lincoln-Douglas. The preferred styles of Lincoln-Douglas debate judges range along an infinite spectrum. As a consequence, the more you know what other coaches like, the better you will be able to adapt to that style. As a result, your chances of winning the round will increase. Knowing that a judge likes a slower, more persuasive, philosophical approach will allow you to adjust accordingly and give that individual what he or she wants to see.

You should also note what certain debaters are presenting as case arguments throughout a tournament. As you debate certain individuals, note what arguments are prevalent in their cases, and note their school. If you have a judge in a later round who is from the same school as a previous opponent, you should use some of the arguments from that previous opponent's case. Because many coaches will help debaters write their cases, the arguments a debater uses are often representative of what the coach (and now, your judge) finds believable. In addition, it is probable that the coach has heard a debater's case run in practice rounds prior to the tournament and is familiar with the argumentation and analysis in that case. Introducing these same arguments will not require the normal, extensive explanations required to convince the judge of their merit. Capitalizing on this familiarity can be advantageous.

Observe the Judge's Appearance

If all else fails, the way a judge dresses can indicate the way he or she will vote. A male judge with long hair in a pony tail and an earring in his ear is likely to be more liberal in his philosophy. On the other hand, a businessman dressed in a blue pinstripe suit is likely to be much more conservative. There are also several occupational clues you can investigate. A Catholic priest is not likely to buy into an argument concerning world distribution of birth control.

On the other hand, some arguments will be especially persuasive to other occupations. Look for occupational dress, as this can be a powerful clue in your adaptation. For example, an individual who comes to the round dressed in a car mechanic's uniform is more likely to relate to analogies concerning cars versus analogies of foreign trade. Some arguments will be insulting to certain occupations, as well.

The "equipment" a judge brings to a round can be an indication of the style he or she prefers. A judge who appears with a number of different colored pens and flow pads is probably a "flow judge." This individual probably is used to the increased speed that is characteristic of "flow" debate. In this situation, it is fine to proceed with a faster, more structured presentation. On the other hand, the judge who comes to the round with only a pen and notepad or no notes will probably be persuaded by a slower, more persuasive presentation.

The most important thing about judge adaptation is that you realize that adaptation is not an end, but a process. Adaptation skills come from being able to recognize and adjust to clues in the environment. Just as a linebacker in football can sometimes anticipate where a ball carrier is going by the way in which he lines up, so can a debater predict the manner in which a judge will evaluate the round by subtle clues in the environment. Judge adaptation is an acquired skill by way of practice. Judge adaptation is simply learning what environmental clues signal the presence of certain judging philosophies. This learning is dependent on experience, but is even more dependent on your desire to keep learning. A debater who stops learning is like a shark that stops swimming: he or she dies. You should capitalize on the experience of your coach, experienced debaters on the team, or debaters from other schools. The only way you will be able to find out information about certain judges is to ask questions. You can learn a great deal about judges from carefully reading ballots after tournaments. Even if you do not agree with what a judge has to say (or the way in which he or she voted), read the ballot carefully and try to determine why the judge voted a certain way.

It is to your advantage to keep a "little black book" on all individuals who judge your rounds. Each time you get a certain judge, make an entry in the book that describes his or her preferred style, pet peeves, political orientation (conservative/liberal), preferred speed, etc. You can gain this information from your ballots. If the judge voted against you, record the reasons why. If he or she voted for you, note the good things you did to earn the ballot. Also, call upon the information your coach and teammates have to offer about different judges. Any information you record in this book will help you the next time you have these individuals as judges.

One final note on judge adaptation: it is always better to lose a round and save your professional character than to upset a judge. One round is hardly worth the loss of many subsequent rounds that judge may decide in the future. You should not make any rude comments, inside or outside of the round, concerning your judge, opponent, or anyone for that matter. Keep in mind that inside of the round and out you are establishing an image. Preserve that image with integrity, and protect it after it is well established. Judge adaptation is giving the judge what you think he or she will accept as reasonable and persuasive. This does not mean that you should sacrifice your beliefs. Doing so is insulting and annoying to the judge, and it greatly destroys your professional image. Be honest and polite, and be yourself.

Understand Debate Politics

Politics is the playing of favorites to advance certain schools and/or individuals over others. If you have a choice in the matter, avoid school politics in Lincoln-Douglas debate. Anything that you do to aid one school (i.e., giving a debater from that school evidence to beat a debater from another rival school) will upset the second school. The vengeance the second school will have towards you will be remembered far past the gratitude from the first school. This vengeance will undoubtedly come back to haunt you. If you choose to trade evidence, make it your policy that your evidence is open to anyone who asks. In this way, there is no special treatment given, and thus no special vengeance incurred. If it is necessary to trade evidence with only one school, do it through the mail after the tournament (and keep the trade quiet).

While you should not participate in school politics, there is an advantage to being familiar with the political scene of other schools. Knowing which schools are politically against each other can be beneficial in that you know who to avoid "upsetting" while in a tournament environment. It is unwise to ever talk about another school and/or its coach and contestants. It is literal suicide to insult one school in front of another school that is allied with the school you are talking against. Be familiar with the politics, but do not get involved.

Suggested Activities

1. Participate in a class discussion about judging styles.

2. Watch the video of a debate round and write a ballot giving a decision and reasons for it.

Chapter 25
The Value
of Extemporaneous Speaking

Learning Objectives

Chapter 25 explains how extemporaneous speaking can contribute to your success as a Lincoln-Douglas debater. While extemporaneous speaking is an event in its own right, it is useful to the Lincoln-Douglas debater in developing critical "delivery" skills. This chapter explores the way in which extemporaneous speaking can facilitate the development of "champion" presentations and thinking clearly on your feet. By participating in both extemporaneous speaking and Lincoln-Douglas, you can enhance your success in the latter and your overall enjoyment of forensics.

After completing this chapter you should be able to:

1. **Explain the qualities of extemporaneous speaking and how these qualities benefit the Lincoln-Douglas debater.**

2. **List the nine steps in developing extemp skills.**

New Term

Extemporaneous speaking

Introduction

Extemporaneous speaking (extemp), although not the focus of this book, plays a vital part in a Lincoln-Douglas debater's success. You must master several important skills to be a successful debater, one of which is the ability to speak extemporaneously.

Extemporaneous Speaking Qualities

Tone of Voice

Extemp training helps produce a continuous and harmonic delivery. It is apparent that great songs really have nothing to do with the lyrics, but more with how they are sung. In other words, the singer is responsible for a song's success more than the song. In many situations, it will not be what is said that is important, but rather how it is said.

It is important to note that extemp literally forces the debater to slow down and talk with an audience, instead of talking at the audience. By using the pattern of extemp, an individual can be trained to talk in a manner that is much more consistent with everyday life. It is important to note that a judge will always respond more readily to a tone of voice he or she is used to hearing in the everyday world. It is difficult to believe that a judge's friends speak via a rapid string of subpoints or a lofty philosophical voice full of grand theories.

Persuasion begins by talking in a realistic and common manner, and with a tone that parallels what the judge is used to hearing. Extemp creates a pleasing voice quality by making the debater concentrate on what the judge finds pleasing, instead of what the "flow" finds pleasing. Once a debater recognizes and develops this important concept, his or her range in persuading debate judges is endless.

Fluency

Extemp breeds fluency. You should develop the ability to shift from one thought to the next in a natural manner. After practice, your transitions should become second nature. If debaters could be as fluent talking to their judges as they are in talking to their friends, they would be unbeatable. The quickest way to develop fluency is to practice speaking.

Extemp, by all measures, is not comfortable. You are asked to speak with some expertise on a topic after only 30 minutes of preparation. In addition, you are asked to develop some sort of answer to a question. In essence, you must take a stand and defend it.

Extemp speakers learn how to do all of this with limited preparation through research and practice. Extempers also understand that organization of ideas promotes fluency. Development of good organizational skills also improves your Lincoln-Douglas delivery skills.

Sharpening the Mind

Extemp also has the capability of developing sharp minds. Most debate rounds are not pre-arranged, and as a consequence, what is said or done in a debate round is uncertain. It is easy to see why people who can think on their feet usually win debate rounds. In other speaking events, a good memorization ability will generally equal success. In debate, however, most rounds are not won in the memorized portion of the round—the constructives—but are won in the rebuttals. It is in the rebuttals that a debater must be able to use what resources he or she has on file to formulate theories or thoughts that support a position. If, at a moment's notice, the debater can create thoughts that support his or her position and then successfully apply those thoughts against his or her opponent's claims, he or she will win the round. This is the essence of good rebuttals. This skill is also fundamental to extemporaneous speaking.

In extemp, an individual is given a challenge (the topic) which is similar to the challenge given to the debater during a round (the opponent's case). He or she is asked to use his or her resources (extemp files/evidence on hand) to create thoughts to respond to the challenge (the extemp topic/ the opponent's case). After creating these thoughts, he or she is asked to apply them directly to the challenge. Finally, he or she must defend these ideas when asked questions from the judge (or, in debate, from the opponent). In both cases, debate and extemp, you are asked to do all of this in a relatively short period of time. If you can successfully perform the skills necessary in an extemp round, you will also have the necessary tools to be a great (not good, but great) rebuttal speaker in Lincoln-Douglas.

Exposure to a Wide Range of Topics

Extemp exposes the debater to the big picture of United States and foreign societies in which all values ultimately fall. Lincoln-Douglas debate asks the debater to make value decisions that encompass not only the U.S. but all of humankind. In some situations, the key to developing a great case is knowing how the remainder of the United States and the remainder of the world value certain principles. This, as you might guess, also correlates to extemporaneous speaking. Extemp trains its contestants to expose themselves to a number of different societies' values. For example, an extemper may be asked to explain why men and women in the Middle East value dying in a holy war more than they value survival. Here, extempers are asked to "step into the shoes" of people quite different from themselves and recognize the vast difference in cultural values. Later, during a debate round, this same extemper/debater may be asked to defend a resolution such as, "Resolved: Society's rights are more important than individual rights." This debater has an advantage in that he or she has knowledge of a value system which places society's values much higher than the value of the individual. By relating the Middle East as an example, he or she can show, in many situations, that individuals actually make the choice to subordinate their ultimate individual right (life) for the good of society. Clearly, such an example could make the difference in the round. Keep in mind, however, that this individual might not have picked up this knowledge without the aid of extemp.

Good extempers are also trained in keeping their eyes and ears open at all times for information that might help them in an extemp round. This training is seldom found in Lincoln-Douglas debate. As Lincoln-Douglas debaters, it is easy to wait for the topic to be released before you do any research. In extemp, however, there is an infinite number of topics. Extemp forces its contestants to be constantly aware of information that could help them win a round. A serious extemper always is exposing him or herself to information about past history, present conditions, and future projections. All of this helps him or her win extemp rounds, and equally can help him or her win debate rounds. Extemp can entice the debater to become more socially, culturally, and politically aware of his or her surroundings.

Analogies

Extemp asks its participants to **explain** concepts to their judges. For an extemper to be successful, he or she must develop the art of "explanation." It is not enough for an extemper to make a claim and support it with a piece of evidence, as in debate. The extemper must speak **with** his or her judge and explain the concept in question. Extemp also gives the debater practice in taking complex ideas and putting them into simple, easily understood analogies. Analogies win debate rounds! There is no substitution for the familiar when it comes to being persuasive. If you can get a judge to see complex ideas in a simple, familiar analogy, you will be successful in the persuasion portion of your delivery. It is important to respect the power of the analogy (see Chapter 26). For now, you should recognize that the use of analogies to explain complicated concepts to the judge in a familiar way is a common skill developed by extempers and a skill needed greatly in Lincoln-Douglas debate.

You should recognize that extemp creates the ability to build analogies. Lets face it; extemp done poorly is boring. Creative extempers recognize this and use interesting jokes, anecdotes, movie plots, children's stories, cartoons, etc., to make topics such as the trade deficit as intriguing as UFOs. Regardless of how exciting we think Lincoln-Douglas debate is, many judges (especially those who have judged six or more rounds in a day) do not find it nearly as exciting. It becomes a great debater's job to make the mundane values (such as liberty, equality, freedom of speech, etc.) exciting and interesting. The debater who can make a boring value exciting, without a doubt, is more persuasive, and is remembered when the judge signs the ballot. It is important that the Lincoln-Douglas debater develop the same skills that the extemper develops. Analogies are one of the best ways to make any value more exciting.

Enhanced Reputation

Extemp, in addition, gives the debater a new reputation with his or her peers and judges involved in both debate and extemp judging. Most of the people judging debate will be the same people judging extemp. Thus, if you become well known as an excellent extemper (and well exposed to these judges), you soon will be recognized as an excellent debater.

In addition, the debater who is also an excellent extemper is not only familiar to the judge, but also respected for being diverse enough to handle two events instead of just one. For example, debaters who qualify for the NFL national tournament in both debate and extemp are given a black "Double Qualifier Ribbon," which can be intimidating to both opponents and judges alike. The reputation of excelling in both events usually precedes the debater, giving him or her an added advantage even before the round begins.

Development of Extemp Skills

Now that you know extemp is an invaluable tool for the developing debater, the question becomes: "How do I, as a serious debater, go about achieving all of the goals I want from extemp?"

The following is a successful plan for developing the extemp skills that are beneficial for a Lincoln-Douglas career. Use this plan to develop and fine tune your speaking and analysis skills.

Stage 1 – Goal Setting

Get a feel for the goals of extemp. Begin a personal notebook with the goals and how to achieve them through practice and participation. This notebook can be just a legal pad in a briefcase. Begin the notebook by writing the goals you wish to get from extemp on the front page. Specifically, list the following and keep track of your progress on each, via your coach's comments and ballot critiques:

> Tone of voice that is continuous and harmonic
> Fluency between thoughts
> Development of a sharp mind (quick responses)
> Development of analogies
> Exposure to many different value cultures
> Reputation

Stage 2 – Establish a Reference Point for Your Speech Progress

A good debater listens to criticisms made about his or her perfor-mance; a great debater makes and listens to his or her own criticisms. To do so, you must be able to see yourself. Videotape yourself if possible. If video is not available from your school, use an audio tape to record your initial performances. It is important that you establish a reference point by which to judge your progress, and prescribe things you wish to work on. You can't improve upon your weaknesses until you see and hear them.

Stage 3 – Establish Positive Influences for Creating Your Own Style

Establish some positive influences for creating style. Watch public speakers who exemplify the goals identified in stage one. By doing so, you develop a style that is a mixture of all you see as well as your own ideas. The goal here is not to replicate, but instead, to identify the different methods of public speech that prove to be persuasive. Identify the techniques you like and incorporate them into a style all your own. View video tapes of different public speakers. These may include John F. Kennedy, Ronald Reagan, and other past presidents; Martin Luther King, Jr.; and current speakers. Watch C-SPAN on cable television to get a wide range of speakers and topics. The list could include more local personalities such as older teammates, successful debaters/extempers from other schools, etc. The list here is infinite. Find good speakers, and then notice the things that make them effective. What persuades you is most likely to fit your style of persuasion. Remember, you are unique, and your style of speaking should reflect that uniqueness. Once these "favorite" characteristics are identified, you should record them in your notebook. These characteristics are the essence of your speaking style and will become the essence of your success if you stick to developing them.

Stage 4 – Establish Audience Rapport

It is important to make the judge feel at ease with your speech. A practiced debater makes his or her judge feel at home with what the debater has to say. Any number of activities can be used here. One enjoyable activity is a ghost story speech. The goal is to speak on something with which you feel entirely comfortable. Thus, you want to select something that can draw your audience into the speech. Of course, these dramatic methods of involvement (i.e., the ghost story) probably will not be used in later debate rounds. The development of a thought process that can generate creative ways of involving the audience, however, will be of importance later.

Stage 5 – Develop the Ability to Think on Your Feet

If you can respond well in a tight situation, the chances of winning a close round are high. Once again, choose a topic for your speech. The content at this point is unimportant. Perform your speech in front of classmates, friends, family, whoever, and instruct them to ask questions that are as difficult to answer as possible. The goal here is to be a good politician and address questions with confidence. Draw upon all the resources you have, i.e., personal analogies, statistics, facts, etc., and attempt to get out of a tough situation. The more hostile the audience, the better this exercise is for your development. Remember, your opponent in a debate round is not going to give you easy questions to answer.

Stage 6 – Establish Argument Sincerity

A sincere argument is the most persuasive, and that becomes the end goal in winning a debate round. Content begins to matter at this point. Select a topic you care about a great deal. Then deliver an extemp speech that draws upon as many sincere thoughts as possible. Following this speech, turn the table. Deliver a speech in the same sincere fashion, but on a topic that initially means little to you. Determine why or how this topic affects you and others. This begins to test your political ability. If you increasingly can become sincere about topics that are initially meaningless to you, you will have the persuasive ability to win Lincoln-Douglas rounds on just about any topic, affirmative or negative.

Stage 7 – Develop Your Creative Ability

By developing your creative ability, you will find ways to beat your opponent's arguments. Remember, impossible arguments are only impossible because someone hasn't looked at them in a creative fashion. The activity here is simple. Everyone in the class puts in five topics (if there are not five people in your class, or if you are working alone, have a friend draw up five topics. The quality of the topics is not crucial). These topics can be about anything. The sillier the topics are, the better the exercise. This is your chance to deliver speeches on topics that are entirely fun. The goal is to deliver a speech that relies entirely upon your creativity to make it work. Essentially, you are testing your ability to tie a foreign topic into something with which you are familiar. This skill may save you in a rebuttal when you are forced to deal with a round-deciding, never-seen-before argument presented by your opponent.

Stage 8 – Combine Spontaneity, Creativity, Sincerity, and Voice Tone

Piece the spontaneity, creativity, sincerity, and voice tone together by doing a real extemp topic. The real practice of extemp begins here. The activity here is simple: practice. Practice using all of the skills listed previously to perform persuasive speeches. While you practice, you may find it beneficial to perform your speeches in front of a mirror. In this way, you get the benefit of seeing your bodily movements, as well as practicing eye contact with yourself.

Conclusion

Hopefully, the described stages will help you develop your extemp skills, and, subsequently, your Lincoln-Douglas debate skills. If you approach the described system with a good attitude, you will gain some seldom taught speaking skills. No matter where you are in terms of speaking skill, the described program will further your ability to become persuasive and victorious.

Suggested Activities

1. Incorporate the strategy plan discussed in this chapter to develop extemp and debate skills.

2. Practice extemping over current events topics.

Chapter 26
Mastering the Analogy

Learning Objectives

Chapter 26 teaches you how to use analogies. Analogies are the debater's most powerful ally, since they allow him or her to communicate complex ideas via a familiar and simple construct. By using analogies, the debater can illustrate his or her point in a time efficient manner. This chapter familiarizes you with the fundamentals in developing analogies as well as the skills needed to prevent an analogy from being turned upon you.

After completing this chapter you should be able to:

1. **Understand the use and value of analogies.**

2. **Explain the considerations given to the use of analogies.**

3. **List and explain the seven methods of creating effective analogies.**

New Terms

Analogy
Anecdotes

Introduction

In Lincoln-Douglas debate it is a common occurrence for a debater to have to address extremely complicated topics in an effort to solve a resolution. Lincoln-Douglas debaters often spend hours upon hours mulling over articles, books, and topic analyses trying to understand what the resolution intends. At some point, most debaters get a good grasp on the meaning and implications of each side of the resolution. The individuals judging Lincoln-Douglas debate do not spent a vast amount of time preparing for each topic. As a result, a large gap in communication can develop between the debater and the judge.

It is the task of the successful Lincoln-Douglas debater to close this gap. He or she must relate to the judge the thoughts he or she has developed through multiple hours of research, but must do so in a way that the judge understands. The problem most debaters have in Lincoln-Douglas is that they assume that because they understand their arguments, their judges also understand the arguments. Debaters quickly forget that they have the benefit of hours of research time, which makes complicated arguments seem simple. This task is complicated because the debater has only 13 minutes to make a case for a value. This is no small task. Condensing "hours" of understanding into a debater's presentation of "minutes" is the most difficult job for Lincoln-Douglas debaters, however, it is what sets them apart.

Each debater has the same amount of time to overcome the problem of transferring his or her thoughts to the judge, thus, there is no advantage given to either debater. The individuals judging Lincoln-Douglas debate are all experienced. If they are not specifically experienced in debate, they are at least experienced in understanding ethical decisions because of their past experiences. The first of these equalizers maintains fairness, and the second provides an opportunity for great debaters to move ahead of the crowd.

The key to making the transition from the "debater's mind" to the "judge's mind" lies in the ability to draw upon the past experiences of the judge. If you can tap into the experience the judge has in past ethical decisions, you can then translate complicated thoughts on the resolution into a set of principles familiar to the judge. A tool for translating complicated thought into familiar form is the *analogy*. Creating analogies allows your judge to understand the complex thoughts you have on the resolution.

The Value of Analogies

Not only will an analogy provide your judge with a better grasp of an argument's meaning, it will also allow you to legitimize your argument by relating it to another well established fact. If, for example, you are trying to prove that our natural resources will not last forever, you can legitimize this claim by relating it to an analogy of a man or woman who keeps going to a cupboard for food until it is empty. In the analogy, you can claim that if the man or woman keeps withdrawing food from the cupboard without replenishing it, the cupboard eventually becomes empty, and the man or woman dies. By relating the food in the cupboard to the natural resources in the earth, you can then illustrate to the judge the real danger of over-developing our natural resources. This analogy legitimizes the argument that continual withdrawal of our natural resources without replenishment equals depletion and death.

Analogies are also beneficial in that the debater who uses analogies is often better remembered in the judge's mind after the round is complete. A judge who keeps thinking about an interesting analogy will ultimately think about who introduced it, and to what it was analogous (the original argument). In both situations, both you and your case are remembered after the last speech, which is critical to picking up a close ballot.

Analogies can also be beneficial in getting your opponent into admitting an argument. At times, you will be able to present your opponent with an analogy in the cross-examination period. By asking your opponent a question that relates to the analogy, you may be able to trap him or her into admitting your argument is correct. For instance, with the above analogy of the food pantry, you might be able to get an unsuspecting subject to admit that continual removal of food from a cupboard without replenishment will lead to barrenness and starvation. In your next speech, you can explain the analogy and show how your opponent has admitted that the depletion of natural resources without replenishment will lead to barrenness and death. In this way, you can muster the greatest form of argument defense: your opponent's support.

Cautions in Using Analogies

A word of caution should be offered to the discussion of analogies. Nothing will lose a round faster than mishandling an analogy, especially if it is your opponent's analogy. Whenever analogies are introduced into a round, be especially cautious as to what you say or to what you agree or disagree. Just as you can use an analogy to trick an opponent into admitting to an argument, so also your opponent can do the same to you. Analogies are designed to mask the real argument, and, thus, you must be especially careful of discussing an analogy with your opponent. In addition, you also should be careful with analogies you present in the round. If you present an analogy into a round, and your opponent finds a way to "flip" that analogy around so it works against you, you stand to lose the round. Always think your analogy through before introducing it into the round.

How to Create Analogies

Analogies are derived from relating an experience familiar to the judge to the argument you wish to present. Because of the nature of their design, the only way to become good at delivering analogies is to expose yourself to a number of different experiences. If you expose yourself to sports, literature, history, science, television, movies, etc., you will have more experiences upon which to draw in making analogies in rounds. Exposure to a number of fields and practice in designing and using analogies are the most important ways of developing great analogies. In addition, there are other ways of developing your mind to create successful analogies. Here are eight tips to developing great analogies:

1. Watch Movies

Movies are the great American pastime. The power of movies rests in the fact that they are seen by many individuals. Even if everyone does not see the actual movie, many see the previews or are familiar with the title. You can develop the ability to use movies as analogies by going to video stores and making a list of movie titles with which you are familiar. Even if you have not seen some movies, you can get a good idea of the plot by reading the description on the movie box. Invest an afternoon in a video store, and make a list of some popular (and classic) movie titles and their plots. You should then store that list among your debate files. If, for whatever reason you need an analogy to make a point, you can refer to the list for assistance. In using a movie as an analogy, give a quick plot summary to ensure your judge understands the analogy's basis. Read the plot summaries in newspaper reviews for ideas.

2. Learn of Friends' and Family's Stories

Strange as it may sound, the truth is often better than fiction. Knowing interesting stories about your friends and family can be a great source of analogies. Make a list of the best stories you have heard. No one will want to hear of your boring family stories, but humorous anecdotes can be very persuasive in a round. Family vacation stories are a great source of analogies!

3. Discover Literature

Many debate coaches are also trained as English teachers. If you are familiar with some of the classic pieces of literature, you will be able to offer these individuals an analogy that is very familiar. For judges who are not English teachers, story lines from popular pieces of literature can be effective tools in establishing an analogy. Even modern story lines, such as Tom Clancy's books, are good sources of analogies, since many people have either read them or heard about them from friends. Since you will not have time to read a great number of books during the debate season, you can still use this technique by asking friends, teachers, parents, etc. about books they may have read. Even reading *Cliff Notes* can give you some background to the story lines. As with the first two suggestions, you should record your favorite book titles and plots in a notebook for future reference.

4. Read Children's Books

Children's stories are great sources of analogies. Because they seem so out of place in a high school debate round, they make a lasting impression on the judge. Since most American children grow up with similar children's stories, these tales can be a great source of familiar analogies. Children's stories are also short and easy to read in a short amount of time, which will allow you to expose yourself to a number of different stories. Dr. Seuss, Richard Scary, and The Brothers Grimm are all great places to begin your analogy development.

5. Familiarize Yourself with History

History allows one generation to communicate with another. Even if you have nothing in common with an older judge, you will have history to draw upon. American and world history are both great sources of analogies, since both are relatively familiar to most judges. In addition, history is real, which makes the "legitimizing function" of the history analogy that much more meaningful. Once again, it is not necessary that you read every history book in your library to have a solid understanding of historic analogies. Asking teachers, parents, and others about historic events can be a great way of learning history in a relatively short time. History told by people such as Paul Harvey is a great source of analogies since each story packs a dramatic ending. The book, *Don't Know Much About History*, provides the essential elements to many historical events in a readable context.

6. Know Your Politics and Political Anecdotes

Political figures and their actions offer the funniest analogies you can find. In every book store you can find many books written specifically on the antics of political figures. Stories about presidents and other well known political figures are powerful because the names are highly recognizable. The unknown story about a political figure can be an effective way of capturing a judge's attention and making a point. For this reason, analogies spring forth from the political arena. You should make an investment in one of these books, or go to your local or school library and check out some of the many books on political *anecdotes*.

7. Hang Out with Little Kids

As strange as it may seem, "hanging out" with little kids can be a great way of practicing analogies. Analogies come from two sources:

sources you find (like those above) and your imagination (i.e., analogies you make up). As you associate with little kids, especially those who ask many questions, you will find yourself explaining complicated phenomenon by using analogies. When a child asks you how a car works, you may find yourself making an analogy to his or her tricycle without even knowing it. This is great training for your imagination, since you will be called upon repeatedly to explain things in terms that are familiar to the child. While your debate judges will not be children, this exercise is highly beneficial in developing the inner source of analogies: your imagination.

8. Read Political Cartoons and Comic Strips

There is a great deal of social commentary in these art forms. They often present analogies for you.

Suggested Activities

1. Write an analogy that might be used in a debate round. Have each class member share and then compile an analogy bank for future use.

2. Write an essay discussing the use of analogies in explaining complicated thoughts. Use as many examples as possible.

Chapter 27
Final Tips For the Successful Debater

Chapter 27 wraps up this textbook and provides you with some parting tips on Lincoln-Douglas. These new tips will be invaluable to you as you evolve into a successful Lincoln-Douglas debater.

After completing this chapter you should be able to:

1. Learn from your ballot and practice rounds.

2. Exhibit appropriate tournament behaviors.

3. Increase the breadth of your knowledge on value issues.

4. Improve the quality of your performance at each tournament.

New Term

Blocking out a case

Introduction

In addition to all that has been covered up until now, there are several extra tips. While nothing will make a great debater except practice and experience, the difference between two great debaters may be the result of the smallest item. Be aware of the following tips to aid you in your development.

As with the rest of this book, the following advice is applicable throughout your debate career. You will never outgrow the following suggestions. To learn how to advance past the status of a "good debater" into the ranks of the elite, you would do well to read the following twelve tips:

Final Twelve Tips

1. Increase Your Debate Quality

This sounds obvious, but most debaters settle into a lull of complacency. There are several levels of attained skill that tempt the debater from achieving his or her full potential. After becoming the best debater on your team, or the best debater in your area, or in your region, state, or district, you may be tempted to sit back and relax. Many debaters succumb to this temptation and don't reach their potential. This is not to say that every debater must become a national champion to be successful. You should honestly assess how far you can go, and then travel that distance. If winning a certain percentage of your rounds is your first goal, set a new level when the goal is achieved. If being state champion is your goal, do not settle for regional champion. Once you have achieved your goal, push yourself into attempting the next level. Who knows? You might win there as well.

There are so many ways a debater can increase his or her debate quality. Going to as many tournaments and debating as many rounds as possible is the best way to improve your debate quality. Do not be afraid to go to tournaments that have "high caliber" competition. Sometimes losing can be the best way to improve your skill, because it can teach you how to improve. Practice rounds are also a good method of learning how to improve.

At each tournament, make the most of what that tournament has to offer you. After being eliminated, go watch those who are still competing. Study what those debaters do to get into the final rounds. Even if you do not like the debaters, they are obviously doing something you are not, since they are in the final rounds. Watching rounds can be one of the best things for a debater. You learn what it takes to be in the final rounds, and if you approach it with the right attitude, it can motivate you for the next tournament.

2. Use All Speech Time

Never be so confident that you think you can "give away" time in any of your speeches. Your judge expects you to speak the full time, so it is not an insult to use all of your time. You will never know for sure how a judge is going to vote until you see the ballot. Who knows, you may stumble onto that last argument that could win you the round.

If you have trouble finding enough things to say in a speech, it is probably due to a lack of research time. The more you research a topic, the more you will know about the topic, and the more you will have to say. Do not get frustrated in a rebuttal and assume that you have already lost the round. Many rounds are awarded to the debater who stays in the game and keeps swinging. You might throw that one lucky punch that could win the round. Stay in the round, use all of your speech time, and never believe you have won or lost the round until you get your ballots back.

3. Create Mobile Cases

If you have developed a strong case, do not be surprised when your competition starts to block out your case (prepare their arguments to your case structure prior to the beginning of the round). The structure of your case will soon become common knowledge as debaters trade flows and exchange information. Don't write more than one case for a topic. Generally this will mean sacrificing quality in any one of your cases. If, however, there is a way that you can easily switch contentions or subpoints without destroying the fluency of the case, you can defuse much of your opponent's advantage. If switching points and subpoints around does affect your persuasiveness, do not make the switch. Remember, a little elusiveness goes a long way.

4. Save Your Flowsheets

You can learn a great deal from what your opponents have to say. As you proceed through a tournament, save and label the flowsheets from each of your rounds. Label all flows with your opponent's school name and number, his or her name (if you know it), and which position he or she defended (affirmative or negative). Later in the tournament you may face this same opponent again. There is a chance that you might even face this same opponent with the same case at a different tournament. You will be prepared to face this individual, because you already have a copy of his or her case. This can also be helpful if you face other debaters from the same school as previous opponents. Many schools share the same debate cases, and if you face one of their debaters, you have the case for their whole team. This only works, however, if you save your flowsheets and label them with the appropriate information about your opponent. Over the course of a tournament, you will have so many flowsheets that it will be impossible to know whose is whose if you do not label each of them.

If you know you will be debating the same topic at another tournament, you should not only save flows, but also make notes about your opponents' evidence sources that were particularly hard to beat. You should also note arguments that were tough to beat, and adapt your responses to these arguments into your case if applicable.

5. Become A "Renaissance Man or Woman"

Debate is like the most elementary communication: the more you know about diverse areas of human activity, the more you will be able to relate to a diverse number of topics. Knowledge is understanding, and from understanding comes reason and logic. Your ability to present persuasive arguments concerning social dilemmas (resolutions) will increase as you develop the ability to understand the people who are involved in the controversy. Learn to love many different facets of life, not just debate. Literature, history, science, philosophy, athletics, sociology, etc. all reflect the human experience. All delve into solving human problems. Through your increased understanding you will be able to see the possible answers to resolutions that you must debate. Expanding yourself exposes you to many different people with many different opinions. Good debaters are made from great research. Great debaters are made from truly understanding great research.

6. Read Your Ballots Carefully

After a tournament, pay close attention to your ballots. Your ballots help you approach them with the right attitude. In Lincoln-Douglas, it is easy to take what is said on a ballot as a personal attack. You should realize, however, that your debate judges have better things to do than spend their weekends insulting high school students. Ninety-nine percent of what you take as a personal attack on a ballot is probably not meant to be an attack. Instead, the judge is simply trying to tell you how to improve. Note the areas in which you can improve. Start a binder full of your old ballots. Never throw them away! As you get a set of ballots, make sure the judge's name and school (if applicable), and the tournament name is on the ballot, and then put the ballot in your binder. The next time you go to that same tournament or area, review your ballots to study what the prevailing philosophy of the judges was. You can make your adaptations for that tournament based upon that information.

You should also make a set of two notebooks in which to record your progress. The first notebook ought to detail areas where you can improve as well as areas in which you are currently strong. After each tournament, make an entry in that book describing how you excelled and how you can improve. The second notebook ought to detail preferences certain judges have for debate styles (see Chapter 22). Make a page for each judge, and record preferences. You can gain this information from your ballots, coach, and friends you might have at other schools.

7. When Alone, Talk to Yourself

Fluent communication is the basis for persuasive speech. It really doesn't matter that no one is listening, as long as you practice the process of converting your thoughts into fluent speech. Debate with yourself. Picture yourself at the final round of nationals, and practice what you might say. Go ahead and dream a little.

8. Be Conscious of the Room Structure

If your judge is in the room before you arrive, do not risk insulting him or her by rearranging the room. If you arrive at the room prior to your judge, make any rearrangements in the room structure you feel are necessary. You should position your desk so that you can peripherally see both your judge and your opponent at the same time. This allows you to see your opponent while he or she speaks, and see which of your opponent's arguments the judge is recording and/or agreeing with.

If the podium is movable, you should place it closer to your opponent's side of the room. In this way, when you speak you can look down on your opponent and your opponent literally will be forced to look up at you. This will make you look more authoritative to your judge and will often intimidate your opponent. When your opponent speaks, you will be out of the judge's line of view (any potential distractions that could weigh against you will not be noticed by the judge). During the cross-examination period, debaters tend to stand in the middle of the room. With the podium placed towards your opponent's side of the room, you will be free to stand to the side of the podium (in the middle of the room) while your opponent will be forced to stand behind it.

9. Be Polite and Professional

In and out of the round you should carry yourself in a polite and professional manner. You should be courteous to adversaries you may not like, and should especially show respect to each debate coach and judge. If you have a problem with a judge or opponent, keep it to yourself. You never know who is within hearing distance at a debate tournament. A judge about whom you make bad comments may be the judge of your next round.

Show courtesy to your opponent. This includes shaking hands with your opponent after the round, and thanking both the timekeeper and the judge as you exit. Once again, do not let emotion control your better judgement. Even in discussions with your coach, you should reserve comments about other debaters and judges for the bus ride home.

10. Only Debate In the Round

It is not wise to debate after the round is over, nor is it wise to debate in the hall or anywhere other than the round. When you are in the round, pull out all the stops to give the debate topic every argument you have. Once you leave the round, however, do not discuss the issues in the round. While this discussion seems innocent, you never know which of your future opponents will be picking up on the arguments you give away through "hallway" discussions. A sharp opponent can gain an advantage by anticipating your response to different arguments merely by knowing what you said prior to the round. Do not give away ground before the round begins! Besides, even if you win the discussion, there are no medals for hall debates.

Also do not tip your judge off as to how he or she should vote. As you leave the round, do not make comments on how you performed.

Saying, "I won that round easy," is not only arrogant, but also insulting to your judge. This is enough to entice some judges to vote against you on that reason alone (especially in tight debates). On the other hand, saying, "I lost that round big! I really got clobbered," is also not a good idea. This sends the message to the judge that you expect to lose the round, and thus he or she will not feel bad about voting against you. You just spent 45 minutes trying to persuade the judge you are the better debater. Why dispel those efforts now?

If someone asks you, simply say you feel confident in your performance, and you will have to wait and see how the ballots come back. If you must talk about a round, go to the bus or some other place away from the tournament to do so. Even then, only discuss rounds with your coach or with a trusted teammate. Back-stabbing is common in high competition tournaments. It is not worth the risk of discussing other debaters, coaches, or cases with people you do not fully trust.

11. Concentrate on The Reason You Are at the Tournament

Be polite and friendly to your peers, but remember your purpose at the tournament. You come to tournaments to put your debate skill on the line against the competition's skill to see how you measure up. Hopefully, you have come to the tournament to win—not to win the tournament, but to win experience and knowledge. Stay focused on the reason you have put in the time and effort in practice and research. A focused novice can always "knock off" the distracted veteran debater.

While you want to gain a reputation in the tournaments, you do not want to gain a bad one. A somewhat mysterious identity is not all bad. Avoid the "extra-curricular" activities that inevitably accompany tournaments. Dancing in the common area, "hanging out" around loud and obnoxious groups, and trying to "find dates" while at a tournament are all sufficient distractions to throw you off course. You should go to a tournament to win in debate, not find a date to your prom.

12. Increase Your Vocabulary

As you have seen in the sections on rebuttals, the success of the Lincoln-Douglas debater depends upon his or her ability to convert thoughts into meaningful language, and to do so efficiently. The larger your vocabulary, the better your chances of finding the right word to convey a complex thought to your judge. Furthermore, if you can say what you mean in one sentence instead of three, you will have three times the amount of time to convey other information. Choose ten new words a week, and see how many times you can use those words in day-to-day sentences. Your debate coach and other teachers can assist you with what words will benefit you the most in debate rounds. It is imperative, however, that you practice using the words in normal contexts so that you are comfortable with their use. Vocabulary and word efficiency can be the tickets to greatness in Lincoln-Douglas debate.

Glossary of Terms

ad absurdum argument – An argument that is absurd or ridiculous

ad hominem argument – An argument that attacks the person and not his or her ideas

adaptability – Being able to change arguments or style to be suitable to new or special situations

aesthetics – The branch of philosophy that concerns itself with the value of beauty

affirmative – The debater arguing in favor of the resolution and the affirmative value

affirmative constructive – The first speech for the affirmative debater

ambiguity – Not clear, vague

analogy – Explaining a concept or principle by drawing upon a familiar example as a comparison

anarchism – The political theory advocating no social government

anecdotes – Stories, vignettes

a priori – Knowledge derived by reason, deduction

arbitrary – Random, selected by chance; no preference being given to one side or another

argument – A reason given in support of a position

artificial reality – Arguments common to cross-examination debate that create situations that are often unrealistic but require a judge to accept them as real for debate purposes

attacks – Clash against an opponent's argument

auditory – Related to the sense of hearing

biased definitions – Definitions that are unfairly prejudicial

big three issues – The three main issues to address in the first rebuttals

block – Arguments and evidence organized to refute a particular argument

blocking out a case – Having a set of arguments against a particular case or case type prepared ahead of the round

brainstorming – A discussion technique which attempts to uncover possible issues and case areas through random listing of ideas or known facts on a topic

card – A piece of evidence or a quotation

case – The reasons for supporting a particular value

case opening – The beginning of a case

case spike – An argument planted to be used to answer an opponent's case attacks

cause and effect claims – A claim that an event or action (cause) actually produces a certain outcome (effect).

clarification – The process of making something clear or more understandable

cognitive – The act of knowing or being aware of a condition

comparisons – Contrasting two different things

composure – Ability to stay calm and collected

consequences – The results of an action or a set of conditions

constructive – The first speech given by each debater in a debate round; the negative constructive includes the first negative rebuttal

contention – A major assertion about the truth of some issue or question

continuum – A continuous scale on which one element is distinct as a result of its reference to another on the scale

cost benefit analysis – The decision-making standard by which the costs of an action are weighed against the consequences

criteria – The standards by which a decision is made

cross apply – Applying arguments made on one issue to another

cross-examination – Asking a series of questions to clarify or discredit arguments made in a speech

cross-examination period – The three minutes allocated after each of the constructive speeches for the opponent to ask questions

cross-examination traps – A question or series of questions to which the person answering must agree or provide information in response but that are used against the person answering when the opponent uses the responses in a speech

debate type – Where a person's delivery and argumentation style fits in relationship to the oratorical and debate theories

deduction – The process of reasoning in which a conclusion is claimed to follow a series of premises; the elimination of possibilities to find a conclusion

deliberation – The act of weighing arguments and evidence carefully

delivery – The verbal and nonverbal aspects of oral communication

democracy- –A governmental philosophy by which the opinion of each member of a society is employed in making social decisions

deontological theory – Actions are right or wrong for reasons other than their consequences; the means are more important than the ends achieved.

dialectic – The critical thinking process whereby an idea is formulated, analyzed, and reformulated

dialectic mind-set – The ability to think of two sides of an issue at one time

dialectic resolutions – Resolutions in which two sides are built into the wording

dice – To cut a piece of evidence in such a way that its meaning is potentially altered; to define the words of a phrase separately rather than to define the phrase as a whole

discourse – Discussion

dream case – Your idealized or perfect case

drop – (as in, "to drop an argument") To fail to address an object of discussion

empirical – Based on observation or experience

esoteric – Ideas that are understood by a small group of people

ethics – The branch of philosophy concerned with making the correct, just, or moral choice

evidence – The information used to support arguments made in a debate

extemporaneous speaking – A forensic event in which students have 30 minutes to prepare a speech on a current event topic

extend – To take an argument given in a previous speech and add depth to its analysis as a result of the opponent's attacks

extension – An argument that is extended

extrinsic – Not characteristic of originating within; not inherent to

eye contact – Looking at the judge or members of the audience during an oral presentation

fallacy – A defect in argument logic that renders the argument invalid

fallacy busting – Discovering fallacies and revealing them to a judge

flipped analogy – An analogy you present that an opponent later uses against you

filtering – Selecting the most important arguments

first negative rebuttal – The time allocated in the first negative constructive to refutation of the affirmative case

flow – The process of taking notes in a debate which shows the relationship of one debater's arguments to another's and to the debaters own arguments made in earlier speeches

flowsheet – The actual notes taken in a round

fluency – Smooth, polished, effortless speaking

forecast – An overview of what arguments and organization will be used in a speech

futurism – A philosophy which holds that a person's only responsibility is to create a society/human race that is superior to the one that exists at present

game plan – The plan of action that will be followed in order to win the judge's ballot

handbook research – Evidence prepared by someone other than the debater which is sold in a book form to be cut and pasted onto cards or used as briefs

heterogeneous – Consisting of a number of different things

hierarchy – The arrangement of a group of ideas or things based upon some preference of arrangement, such as a value's worth

homogeneous – Consisting of the same thing; pure or similar in constituency

horizontal method – Flowing arguments horizontally

hypothesis – A statement or assumption of belief that is put up to be verified by testing

ideologies – Political or social beliefs of a person or society

inclusive – All encompassing

indict – To find fault with

induction – The process of arriving at a conclusion by inferring upon the whole the knowledge of a small part of the whole

inherency – A stock issue in policy debate which requires an affirmative to show that a problem is an essential part of the present system and cannot be solved without a change in the system

inherent – Existing as an essential characteristic; intrinsic

innate freedoms – The belief that individuals are born with freedoms or rights

interim – The section of a constructive speech that connects the opening and the case points

intricacies – Many complex details about an object or idea

intrinsic – Within, characteristic of being inherent to an object or idea

intrinsic good – That which is desirable for its own sake

judge adaptation – The ability to adjust delivery and arguments so that they are suitable to a judge's tastes, attitudes, and motivations

jurisprudence – The philosophy of law and justice

lay judge – An inexperienced judge

Lincoln-Douglas debate – Two-person debate involving a value proposition

Lincoln-Douglas Senate debates – The series of debates held between Abraham Lincoln and Stephen Douglas during their campaign for the United States Senate; slavery was the all-pervading issue

Lincoln-Douglas spectrum – This refers to the range of debate styles from the oratorical, persuasive style at one end to the structured debate style at the other

litmus test – A test that will be determinative

logic – A form of reasoning

misused argument – An argument misanalyzed or misapplied

mobile cards – Cards that can be used on a variety of cases

morality – The condition of being in accordance with a moral or ethical law or standard

National Forensic League (NFL) – A national organization for high school students that promotes participation in forensic activities

nebulous – Having an indistinct meaning; unclear or foggy

negative – The side in the debate disagreeing with the topic

negative case – The arguments and evidence that support the negative value

negative constructive – The first speech of the negative debater; this includes advancing the negative value and attacks upon the affirmative case

negative behaviors – Actions such as rocking, weaving, etc. that detract from a debater's presentation

negative debater – The debater arguing against the resolution and in favor of the negative value

opponent adaptation – Changing arguments and style to adapt to an opponent's style

optimism – The attitude of hope toward the future

oratorical theory – The style of debate that is persuasive, logical, and less structured

paradigm – A model used to demonstrate or prove something

personal overview – Opening a speech with a personal story

persuasion – The ability to convince someone

pertain – To relate to or to have reference to something

phenomenon – A reality as it appears to us; a state of existence of some event

philosophical – Based on philosophy

politics – The playing of favorites to advance certain schools or individuals over others

pragmatic – Practical, realistic

prep time periods – The time allotted for preparation between debate speeches

preparation time – The maximum time allowed between speeches for preparation

presumption – Belief based upon prior knowledge or evidence; in debate, the assumption that something is acceptable unless proven otherwise

preview – A forecast of what is to come

prima facie – A case which is adequate to prove its position prior to refutation

proposition – A topic for consideration, debate, or discussion

rapport – Making a connection

realism – The belief that material objects exist as real outside of our sensory experience

rebuttal – The second speech given by each debater in a debate round

rebuttal circle – The four-step approach to addressing the opponent's case points

red herring argument – An argument intended to divert attention from the real issues

refutation – Evidence and argumentation which deny the validity of an opponent's position

resolution – The subject for debate

resolution style – The form Lincoln-Douglas topics take which presents a dilemma and resolves it

road mapping – Giving the judge indications as to what part of the debate the debater is going to next; aids in flowing

second affirmative rebuttal – The last speech for the affirmative debater

second negative rebuttal – The last speech for the negative debater

significance – A qualitative or quantitative measure of being important or meaningful

signposting – Highlighting and previewing arguments in such a way to aid in flowing

slug – A name or label for an idea

social contract – The agreement by which the individual unites with a society and agrees to sacrifice some individual rights (agreement to be governed) in order to enjoy the benefits of society

socialism – A socioeconomic philosophy by which each individual member of society works for what he or she needs

solvency – The ability to solve a need or gain an advantage

spectrum – A group of characteristics arranged in some type of order

spontaneity – Fresh, unplanned

static- Not moving or changing; stationary

status quo – The present condition of events

stock issues analysis – A method of examining the debate topic to reveal areas of harm, significance, inherency, etc; used primarily in cross-examination debate

symbols – Abbreviations or representations used to aid in flowing

synthesis – The combining of two or more objects or ideas into one whole

thesis – A proposition that is supported by an argument or arguments; a theme

topicality – The concept that the case must be concerned with the subject for debate

tone of voice – The sound and inflection of a debater's voice

transitions – The part of the speech that moves one part to another

type I research – Focuses on the actual resolution

type II research – Supports the merits of the value regardless of the resolution

utilitarianism – The ethical standard that dictates that the choice that provides the greatest good for the greatest number is the correct choice

value – That which is valuable to a person, group, or society; an ideal, object, or action that is seen as worthy

value comparisons – Comparing and contrasting two different values

value determination – The process of determining which of two or more values is more important

value hierarchy – The placement of values in a manner which indicates that in given circumstances some values are given more importance than are others

value testing – Ways of determining which of two values is more important

vertical method – Flowing arguments vertically

warrant – The justification for an action; a call to do something because it is justified

Appendix A
Lincoln-Douglas Topics

Resolved: When they are in conflict, the right to a free press is a higher priority than the right to a fair trial.

Resolved: A victim's deliberate use of deadly force is justified as a response to physical abuse.

Resolved: Human genetic engineering is morally justified.

Resolved: That individual obedience to law plays a greater role in maintaining ethical public service than does individual obedience to conscience.

Resolved: That government limits on the individual's right to bear arms in the United States are justified.

Resolved: That the protection of society's health interests through broad-based mandatory testing for AIDS ought to be more important than personal privacy rights.

Resolved: That development of natural resources ought to be valued above protection of the environment.

Resolved: That communities in the United States ought to have the right to suppress pornography.

Resolved: That the United States ought to value global concerns above its own national concerns.

Resolved: That all United States citizens ought to perform a period of national service.

Resolved: That competition is superior to cooperation as a means of achieving excellence.

Resolved: That the advantages of genetic engineering outweigh the disadvantages.

Resolved: That the rights of non-smokers have been protected at the expense of smokers' rights.

Resolved: That the right to strike should not be denied public employees.

Resolved: That national security is more important than government honesty.

Resolved: That it is morally unjustifiable to require an individual to join a labor organization as a condition of employment.

Resolved: That developing a sense of personal responsibility is of greater educational value than developing self-esteem.

Resolved: That the United States government ought to provide for the medical care of all its citizens.

Resolved: That the pursuit of scientific knowledge ought to be limited by a concern for societal good.

Resolved: That liberty is preferable to life.

Resolved: That the protection of public safety justifies random, mandatory drug testing throughout society.

Appendix B
Topic Analysis on Some Common Topics

The following section is a summary of some of the more popular arguments on common topics. Each of the arguments is designed to give an example of the thinking you should employ in evaluating ethical decisions. Some of the arguments are much more plausible than others, but the realistic and powerful arguments come about as a result of allowing the unrealistic arguments to be put on paper.

The following arguments are also designed to give you a look at some of the issues you might face. This framework is only designed to stimulate thought, not to make cases for you. Since there's no explanation of each argument, you will be forced to explore each. Remember that the purpose of Lincoln-Douglas debate was to create an event that "trained" future professionals to think in creative and original ways in solving ethical decisions. What most Lincoln-Douglas debaters need is not evidence, but original thought on resolution dilemmas.

While it is probably not the concern of most debaters to begin working on society's ethical problems, universally it is the concern of all debaters to succeed in their event. Both cross-examination and Lincoln-Douglas debate reward their participants for original thought by giving them ballots. Creatively thinking up a new policy on the resolution will win rounds for a cross-examination team. Creatively exploring and understanding a question of ethics is rewarded in Lincoln-Douglas with numbers in the "win column." Creativeness wins rounds, not cutting and pasting pre-written cases from here or other handbooks. And the creative solutions you come up with now may contribute to society later.

DEVELOPMENT OF NATURAL RESOURCES (DNR) SHOULD TAKE PRIORITY OVER PROTECTING THE ENVIRONMENT (PTE).

Affirmative

- DNR Increases the Quality of Life
        Increases Luxuries
        Reduces Human Suffering (Medicine)
        Prevents War (Deterrence; Patriot Missiles)
        Increases Jobs = More occupational security
        Increases interpersonal contact (the world village)
        Destroys political barriers by shared technology

• DNR Increases Progress
   Progress perpetuates life
   Progress replenishes natural resources (solar, nuclear energy)
   Provides for new growth
   Gives new freedoms to humans

•DNR Is Not Necessarily Bad
   New resource development stops harms (pollution control
      devices)
   Provides for space development – new resources and environ-
      ment
   Accidents overrated
   Protects against more disasters than it causes (earthquakes,
      weather)

Negative

•PTE Increases Progress
   Reduces human suffering – pollution reduced
   Resources saved for future years
   PTE allows researchers to devote time to solving (not creating)
      problems

•Excessive DNR is Destructive
   Society overdevelops upper classes; minorities stuck with the
      pollution
   Economic competition destroys all natural resources
   DNR leads to war – war technology is used by smaller countries

•Protecting Environment Increases Quality of Life
   Aesthetic value is important
   Environment important to human life (new bacteria, sunlight,
      insects)
   Leisure value of environment is important
   Nature critical to religion
   Current DNR is not necessary for sustaining life

•Majority Uses Technology – Lower and Minority Classes Receive the
   Harms (racism)

EUTHANASIA (E) SHOULD BE ALLOWED FOR ALL INDIVIDUALS

Affirmative

•E is Foundation of Individual Rights

Social Contract guarantees right to live and right to die
Control over one's body is the premise of individuality
There should be a freedom to die, like there is a freedom to live
God delivered the individual life, did not deliver society that life

•E Limitation is Unfair Restriction of the Individual by Society
     Society's morals make an individual suffer in pain
     Individual choice is unfairly limited by social concern

•E is the foundation of Q of Life
     Q of Life > Life itself
     Life is living, not lying on a hospital bed with a respirator
     Individual should not be made to live as a vegetable
     Family's lives should not be destroyed by pain and financial
          stress

•E is Foundation of the Family as a Value

Negative

•Society Is Justified In Maintaining Life
     Society was responsible for maintaining that life up to that point
     Life is precious, and taking life should be prevented (E = suicide)
     Society supports life = society regulates the taking of life

•Value From E Are Overrated
     Individual does not make the choice; family does- thus no indi-
          vidual rights
     Q of L cannot be judged by a third party. Life is important
     No one should play God in determining when life should end

•Values of the Collective Good are Important
     E destroys "hope" for life in society
     Reduces medical institutions obligation to heal when E is an
          option

CAPITAL PUNISHMENT (CP) IS A JUSTIFIED RESPONSE TO MUR-DER.

Affirmative

•The Taking of A Life Is Too Sacred To Be Dismissed
     Society is justified to make restitution with an equal punish-
          ment
     Breaking of the social contract relieves society of its obligation
          for life

•Value of the Collective Good
> Provides deterrence against future acts
> Assures collective consciousness- prevents anomy
> Maintains social order
> Prison costs of detention cause criminals to go free
> Ensures Social solidarity

Negative

•Shows Shades of Racism
> Minorities receive the blunt of death penalty sentences
> Does not consider social influences
> No one should play God in directing death

•CP Does Not Ensure Life
> Does not deter future murders
> Killing for killing is not logical
> The killing of the murderer creates as much stress on society

•Society is Out of Line
> Social Contract does not override human contract with God
> Innocent individual cannot be revived- justice cannot be restored if there's a mistake

RIGHT OF FREE PRESS SUPERSEDES THE RIGHT TO FAIR TRIAL.

Affirmative

•Free Press is the Cornerstone of Individual Rights
> Cornerstone of individual expression
> Other values fall without free press
> Provides for social cohesion by showing punishment of violators

•Free Press is the Foundation of Freedom
> Freedom from "mind control" via tyranny
> Individual accused gains freedom via public pronouncement of innocence
> Brings in evidence and witnesses that could help the defendant

•Fair Trial Not Compromised Due to Free Press
> Change of venue clause reduces publicity
> Publicity has not been proved to increase guilty verdicts
> Free press in courtroom ensures justice system plays fair (not tyrannical)
> Free press educates society on court procedures (legal system)
> Ensures fairness for all individuals in court (all races, sexes, etc.)
> Press regulates itself – no significant harms to the process

Negative

•Freedom Of Press Can Still Be Maintained
        Reports after the trial still give all benefits of free press

•Right To Fair Trial Is a Preeminent Value
        Fair trial is foundation of the whole judicial system
        Fair trial is foundation of democracy
        Society and individuals support fair trial over free press

•Free Press Hurts Individual Rights
        Causes prejudiced jurors via trial publicity
        Influences juror decision by trial presence in the courtroom
        Causes reputation damage to innocent individuals
        Intimidates witnesses who might come forward to help the de-
                fendant
        Official's actions (judges, D.A.s) go with press opinions for voter
                support
        Pretrial information is one sided and not limited by regulation
                for fairness
        Forces no bail detention = greater chance of guilty verdict
        Press distracts defendant and lawyer during presentation of the
                defense

•Press in the Courtroom is Harmful to Society
        Press fosters politics over justice
        Press is not responsible to a higher authority for review- public
                misinformation
        Press is business, must sell papers/ads; popular desire depicts
                individual guilt

•Free Press Outside of Courtroom is Important

RIGHT TO CENSOR SHOULD BE GREATER THAN THE RIGHT OF EXPRESSION.

Affirmative

•Censorship Ensures Individual Thought
        Weeds out obscenity= censorship can save the corruption of
                children
        Weeds out misinformation
        Saves individual Integrity via Limiting Personal Attacks
        Pornography is maintained via no censorship
        Ensures "pure knowledge"

•Free Press Important, but Value of Collective Good is Greater
   Free press guaranteed by collective good
   Collective good is the source of censorship
   Censorship can protect national security- prevents leaking of
      information
   Censorship prevents social conflicts
   Censorship can prevent individual and racial slander
   Protects the value of the Aesthetics

•Censorship Enhances Other Values
   C enhances the family as a value
   C enhances aesthetics as a value
   C enhances knowledge as a value
   C enhances freedom as a value
   C enhances truth as a value
   C enhances collective good as a value
   C enhances progress as a value

Negative

•Censorship Limits Values
   Limits right of free expression
   Limits creativity
   Limits individualism
   Limits the quality of life

•Censorship Destroys Values
   Destroys the social contract
   Destroys individualism
   Destroys trust in the political institution

•Censorship Prevents Progress
   Prevents racial understanding; racism results
   Prevents free and creative thought; social problems are not
      solved
   Elite majorities can control minority expression and issues via
      censorship

•Free Expression is an Inherent Right
   Social contract (collective good) cannot limit inherent human
      rights

DRUG TESTING SHOULD BE ALLOWED IN THE WORK-PLACE.

Affirmative

•Rights of the Collective Good Predominate Over Those of the Individual

Safety is a preeminent value

Social contract mandates the limitation of individual excesses

•DT Actually Helps Individual Rights

Gives each individual safety and piece of mind

Can locate individual that needs help with a drug problem

•DT Enhances Values

Enhances Q of L via piece of mind, and less accidents

Enhances life by preventing accidents

Social safety is enhanced by quality products

Negative

• DT Source of Individual Rights Violation

Tests are often inaccurate = reputation damage

Employer cannot control lives of workers

Positive tested workers are not a threat to work-place

Company, not society, owns the individual (industrial age
     oppression)

Limits freedom of individual

•DT Destroys Justice as a Value

Individual is guilty until proven innocent = this destroys justice

Can be a source of manufactured discrimination

Invasion of privacy (body) is the last refuge of individual rights

Social contract does not include social violation of individual's
     body

Only lower classes (industrial jobs) are subjected to this inva-
     sion (no equality)

•DT Causes Harms

Worry over DT causes an increase in accidents

Life and Q of L are thus diminished

Individual sabotage products in rebellion to DT= decrease in
     social safety

THE RIGHT TO CHOOSE SHOULD BE PARAMOUNT IN ABORTION ISSUES.

Affirmative

•The Right To Choose Is the Premise of Individual Rights

Choice gives individual control of her body

Gives same liberty to woman as given to man

Question of life is religious, not political; the state should not
     regulate

Right to privacy over one's body is not a social issue
Male dominated legal and medical professions control women

•Improves Life and Quality of Life
Gives child a good Q of L
Gives individuals of all social classes individual rights
Abortion would continue anyway- only with little medical care
Progress of individual and society (less welfare) is increased via
abortion
Enhances free expression of one's self
Unwanted children are often targets of abuse or neglect

•Right to Choose is the Foundation of the Value of Equality
Women must be granted equal opportunity, not enslaved to
their biological circumstances
Unwanted pregnancies cannot be fully blamed on the woman;
women should not have to bear the full responsibility by
birthing the child
An unwanted child can threaten a woman's life due to reduction
in economic level

Negative

•Abortion Lessens Life's Importance
Termination of Life destroys social value of sanctity of life
Life of child is not the parent's, it is the child's. Society must
defend the child
Parent does not have the right to play God
Who judge's Q of L? Child should make the choice to live
Abortion becomes a method of contraception

•Value of the Collective Good Ensures Other Values
Destroys self-actualization of mother
Destroys freedom
Life is too precious to be wasted in any circumstance

•RTL is the Premise of the Family as a Value
Protecting the unborn child is the foundation of protecting the
family

THE BENEFITS OF GENETIC ENGINEERING (GE) OUTWEIGH THE HARMS.

Affirmative

•GE Enhances Life

GE can prevent genetic diseases
Allows medicine to better understand diseases = more cures
Allows for the artificial production of therapeutic drugs
Potential elimination of oncological genes (genes causing cancer)

•GE Enhances Quality of Life
GE upholds Nietzsche's criteria of making a better tomorrow
Less retardation and birth defects via GE

•GE Enhances the Value of Progress
Gives the tech. to grow more food with same areas of land
Could develop strains of grain that would grow in 3rd world
deserts
Some bacteria can be altered to absorb oil spills and/or pollu-
tion
Gives humankind control over life, creates a new responsibility =
progress
GE spawns research in other scientific areas

•Harms of GE are Overrated
Regulation would prevent misuse of GE
The possibility of truly creating a "superior race" is almost
impossible
Spills of GE strains are small enough to be insignificant

•GE is Justified by the Values of the "Common Good"
Society deserves to reduce genetic defects amongst the popula-
tion (costs!)
Society has an obligation to improve the quality of its members

Negative

•GE Destroys Q of Life
Scientists impose standards of "life's quality" on the whole of
society
The question of Q of L is relative to the individual, and thus
cannot be assisted by a privately controlled definition of
what constitutes a "good life"

•GE Destroys the Individual
The individual will lose uniqueness via genetic replications
Self-actualization is lost due to "sameness"
The individual's right to be as created by God is forfeited to
social interests

•GE is Dangerous to the Society

Genetic "mishaps" could create a foreign virus or bacterial strain

Genetic mutations in plants, bacteria, and animals could harm the environment

Since private companies own GE, there is not social regulation

Marx's theory of exploitation is demonstrated by the rich controlling the poor via controlling their genes

The values of religion to society are lost as religion is replaced by GE (god?)

VIOLENT REVOLUTION (VR) IS A JUST RESPONSE TO OPPRESSION.

Affirmative

•VR is the Only Alternative to True Oppression

Revolution is the only mechanism by which lower classes can challenge society

The "normal channels of society" are created by the oppressors, and this is their mechanism of maintaining oppression. Social channels cannot be followed

The threat of violence is the only power the underclass has; it has no other bargaining chips

•VR Increases Q of Life

No one deserves to live under the restrictions of oppression

Social and economic reforms follow revolution

A greater number of people enjoy "life" following a revolution (the elites are ousted)

•VR Increase the Fundamental Values of the Individual

Freedom and liberty come from breaking the bondage of oppression

Self-actualization comes from establishing a society in which the individual is a part

•VR is Justified When Put in Response to Oppression

Oppression causes death

Oppression destroys social stability

Oppression can create horrors that are worse than death

•The Social Contract does not Include Oppression

The individual is bound to a standard of "no violence" by the social contract

When society forgoes its responsibility to the individual, this contract is resolved

Humankind has an obligation to find truth and justice no matter what the struggle

•VR Can Help the Value of the Common Good

> VR can create a more stable society by ending internal conflicts against oppression
>
> A greater consensus of social values can be realized via revolution

•VR Enhances Social Equality

> All men and women are reduced to their ability to fight for their ideals
>
> VR re-establishes social, economic, and political equality

•VR Enhances the Value of Justice

> Justice is given to those who oppress
>
> Reestablished society fulfills justice

Negative

•VR Destroys the Value of Life

> Death results from violence
>
> Life is absolute; any loss of life is not justified
>
> Life is destroyed as social support mechanisms (food, medicine, protection) are disrupted

•VR Destroys the Value of Q of Life

> Social conditions following a VR are worse than before
>
> Famine, disease, and homelessness often follow VR

•VR is Harmful to the Common Good

> Governments that arise from VR are often worse that their oppressors
>
> VR rarely works, and thus the common people are hurt the most from a failed revolution

•VR is Harmful to the Individual

> The loss of life, property, and security are damaging
>
> The individual is intimidated by the use of violence- he feels compelled to participate in a non-ethical action

•VR Destroys the Foundation of Society

> All communication patterns are forgone for violence
>
> Revolution is often instigated by an exterior third party
>
> Small fractions of society participate in VR; there is not an increase in individual representation in the government following a VR

THE RIGHT TO PRIVACY (RTP) SHOULD TAKE PRECEDENCE OVER THE PROTECTION OF SOCIETY.

Affirmative

•RTP is Fundamental to all Individual Rights
>To invade the individual's privacy is to control his or her mind
>Individual must see self as individual
>The right of the press, free expression, speech, and religion are all based on the right to be autonomous from govern mental control

•RTP is Guaranteed Via the Social Contract
>Society guarantees protection of privacy in return for individual loyalty
>Invasion of privacy has implications in alienating individual from society

•Invasion of Privacy in the name of Social Protection is Contradictory
>The greatest threat to a society is from within (revolution)
>Invasion of privacy creates individual alienation= despondency and revolution
>The harms from social tyranny far outweigh the benefits gained from invading privacy in the name of national security
>The respect for privacy is the foundation of interpersonal rela- tionships within the social order

•RTP is Essential to True Individual Self-Actualization
>The individual must have a private life to actualize him or herself as an individual
>Fear of governmental oppression on privacy leads to social conformity

•The Q of Life is Destroyed by a Lack of Privacy Protection
>Orwell's 1984 comes to life in this scenario. Fear dominates the individual
>The quality of society is destroyed by allowing a few elite mem- bers to control the lives of the masses

•Privacy is Fundamental to the Value of Justice
>Justice assumes that the individual's rights are not compro- mised by the state
>A contradictory social statement on privacy would unravel the justice system's premise of individual primacy

•The Need for National Protection is Overstated
> The need for social protection is a "cover-up" line used to justify the invasion and oppression of individual rights

Negative

•The Rights of the State Outweigh the Rights of the Individual
> The protection of the many must outweigh the privacy of the individual
> The state has an obligation to protect its members, take the necessary measures to do so – even in the face of the minority's privacy

•Society has Supported the Precedence of Society Over the Individual Before
> War time situations where individual privacy was compromised was accepted and supported
> The collective good supports the value of national security over the RTP

•The Harms from Invading Privacy are Over Exaggerated
> The individual is not destroyed by momentary invasions
> Totalitarianism does not necessarily result from privacy compromises

•The Protection of Society Upholds the Value of Life
> The lives of millions rest upon the protection of the national security
> The infringement of privacy does not cause death

•The RTP is Used as a Cloak to Hide the Breaking of Social Rules
> The individual is not granted the RTP to hide from social responsibilities

•The RTP Is Not an Inherent Right
> Joining society predicates that the individual must relinquish the absolute right to privacy

LIBERTY SHOULD TAKE PRECEDENCE OVER EQUALITY

Affirmative

•Liberty is the Foundation of Individual Rights
> Freedom of expression derives from liberty
> Freedom from social control allows from full appreciation of what it is to be an individual
> Creative thought and discourse only arise from a feeling of being free of social restrictions
> Freedom of religion is dependent upon the individual's ability to be free of social restrictions

•Knowledge Is Dependent Upon Liberty
> Only with an unrestrained search can humankind truly find truth and knowledge
> Humankind is called to fulfill the value of knowledge

•Liberty is the Foundation of Social Order
> The social order is enhanced by the individual liberty that predominates
> Individuals are happy, and the social order is secure

•The Individual has a Moral Obligation to Find Liberty
> "Human contracts" require that the individual seek out liberty, truth, and justice

•Liberty is the Foundation of Equality
> Until all of mankind is truly liberated from social oppression, there can be no equality

Negative

•Equality Is the Foundation of the Social Order
> Equal treatment under the law establishes equal responsibility
> Without the premise that all individuals are alike, social institutions will falter – i.e., the justice, political and social institutions

•Equality Underlies Freedom and Liberty
> Only when all of humankind is protected from oppression from other individuals, can the individual be "truly" liberated
> Equal regard for each individual well being must surpass the individual liberty if every individual is to be afforded the value of liberty
> The greatest misjustices in human history have occurred when one segment of society was given liberties the other segment was not given (i.e., Nazi Germany, slavery, etc.)
> Unless liberty is guaranteed to all individuals equally, it is a mechanism of oppression, despite the benefits one segment of society might enjoy

•Society Has an Obligation to See to It that Every Individual is Treated Equally
> The nature of the social contract requires society to protect equally its members

•Equality Is the Foundation of Individual Rights
> Preference to some individuals over others destroys the concept of inherent individual worth

Index

A

additional value enhancement
    method for comparison, 22
ad absurdum argument, 72, 74, 219
ad hominem argument, 138,139, 141,
    219
Adler, Mortimer, 46, 92, 96
aesthetics, 15, 219
affirmative, 4-5, 17, 19, 84-91, 92-94, 98,
    99-100, 100-110
    defined, 4, 219
    case, 84-91, 92-94, 100-110
analogy, 5, 22, 55, 58, 61-62, 67-68, 118,
    120, 160, 202, 207-212
    defined, 61, 208, 219
    flipped, 58, 62, 222
argumentation, 42, 55, 86-87, 127-129,
    138-145, 156-157, 159-160, 188-
    189, 219
    fallacies, 139-141

artificial reality, 52, 53, 219
    defined, 53, 219

B

ballots, 71, 215, 216
Bicentennial Youth Debates, 9
Big Three Issues, 121, 122-123, 124, 131-
    132
    defined, 220
    affirmative, 122-123, 124
    negative, 131-132
Black's Law Dictionary, 46, 75, 95
brainstorming, 42, 81, 87-88, 220

C

Campbell, James S., 95
case, 2, 4, 42, 43, 58-110, 115-116, 135-
    136
    affirmative, 84-91, 100-107
        sample, 92-94
    components, 84-91
    contentions, 43
    defined, 4, 82, 220
    definitions, 70-71, 72-80
    interims, 64-71
    negative, 5, 76, 84-91, 98-104
        sample, 94-96
    openings, 58-63, 65, 102, 220
    preview, 69-70
    spike, 81, 87, 220

Constitution (U. S.), 35-36, 76, 139
constructive, 2, 4, 70, 82, 97-110, 113-
    114
    defined, 4, 98, 220
    affirmative, 100-107
    negative, 5, 98-104
contentions, 42-43, 69, 220
contextual method for value comparison,
    22
continuum, 16, 221
cost benefit analysis, 27, 28, 29-31, 34,
    101, 104-105, 110, 132
    defined, 30, 221
criteria, 16, 24-25, 27-39, 85, 101-102,
    109-110, 122, 123, 124, 125,
    132, 134
    defined, 24, 221
    varieties, 30-33
cross application, 108, 112, 116-117, 123,
    127, 133, 135, 221
cross-examination, 4, 69, 99, 105, 107-
    108, 110, 154-161, 221
    period, 2, 4, 143, 155, 157-158, 161,
    209, 221
    skills, 156-161
    traps, 154, 160, 221
cross-examination team debate, 4, 9, 49,
    54

D

debate styles, 52, 55, 56, 180-186, 189,
    195
debate theory, 8, 52-56, 181-185
Declaration of Independence (U.S.), 9
definitions, 70-71, 72-80, 97, 102-103,
    122, 124, 125, 135, 220
    affirmative, 79-80
    defined, 73
    dicing, 78-79
    negative, 76-77
    rules, 73-75
    sources, 75-76
    standards, 77-80, 109
delivery, 49-50, 56, 147-153, 159, 182-
    183, 184-185, 188, 199, 200, 221
deontological theory, 27, 28, 32-33, 34,
    221
dialectic, 19, 221
    mind-set, 81, 90, 221
    resolutions, 16, 19, 221
dicing, 72, 78-79, 222
Dos Passos, John, 92
Douglas, Stephen, 8, 19
dropped arguments, 130, 136-137, 222